Town on a Hill
People and Place

Volume 1

Debrah Anne Nixon

Notes to the Reader

This book is a tribute to the people of Eshowe in KwaZulu-Natal, South Africa; many of whom have contributed invaluable anecdotes and statistics, enriching my casual journey through history.

Terminology sways between that of old (Boers, Europeans, Natives, coloureds) and that of new (Afrikaners, whites, blacks/Africans, mixed-race).

Ever aware of the debatable nature of historical events, I cross-referenced where possible, and every effort was made to contact copyright holders of material I have reproduced. If any have been inadvertently overlooked, I determine to make corrections at the earliest opportunity. To those I've made mention of, who resent the slightest intrusion into their lives, I offer my sincere apologies.

Special thanks to my daughter, Keri Schultz who helped with the book cover design, her in-laws, Denise and Alwyn Schultz for the many hours of professional tutorage, and to Richard Yardley who helped with research and improved quality of photographs. Also thanks to the staff at the Eshowe Museum Village, past and present (especially Jenny Hawke and Vivienne Garside), and those who contribute to the facebook page 'Anecdotes of Old Eshowe' from which I gleaned some material. Last but not least, thanks to my long-suffering husband, Mike Nixon.

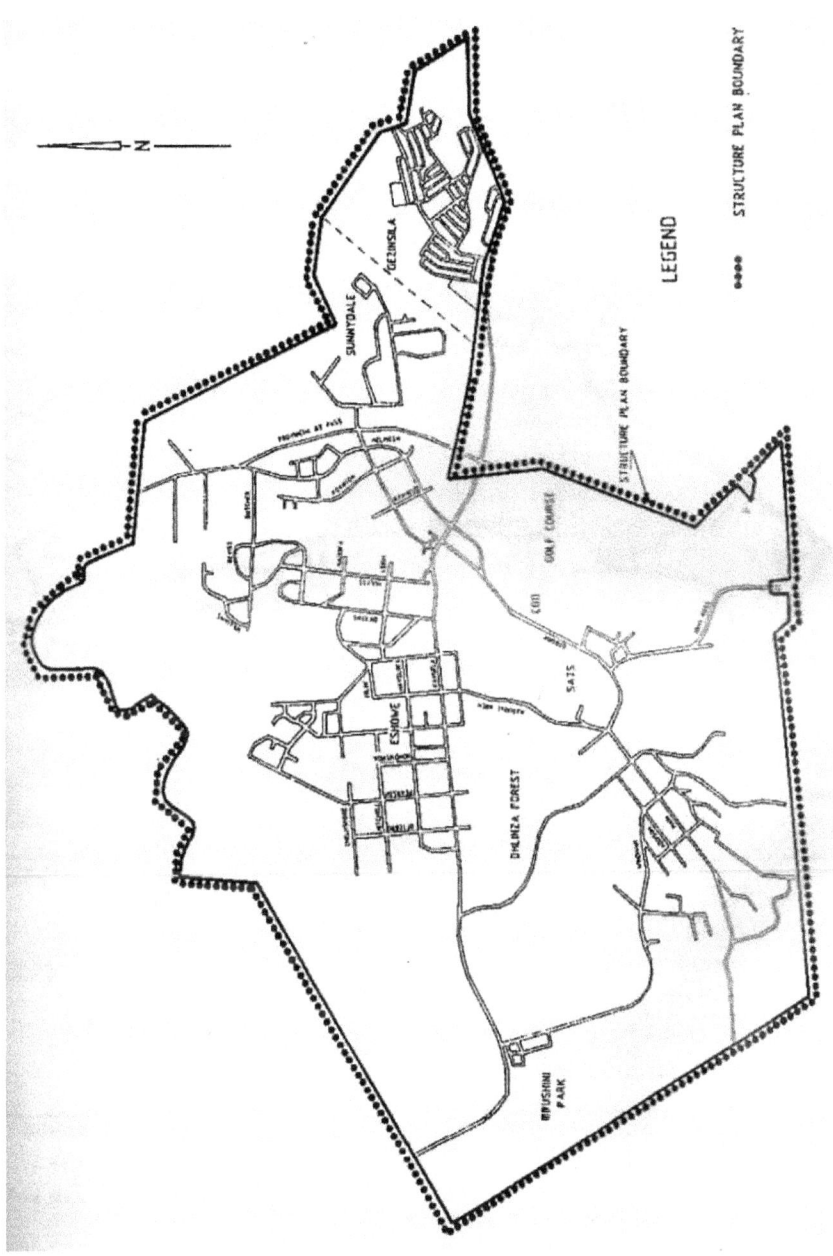

Chapter 1

Although Eshowe, due to its cathedrals, is in fact of city status, I choose to use the term 'town' that better suits the cosiness of Eshowe's close-knitted communities. Situated in the province of KwaZulu-Natal previously Zululand and Natal respectively) in South Africa, Eshowe is a colourful, bustling town conveniently situated between ocean, game reserves, historical battlefields and the modern amenities of big city: eThekweni, formerly Durban.

Zululand was the African province stretching from the Thukela River north to the Pongola River, including all the land from under the Drakensberg Mountains to the sea. It bordered the Transvaal and Natal.

This book's cover design is a Diamond Bozas painting of Mandawe Hill, situated 14 kilometres out of Eshowe, where the progenitor of the amaZulu, Malandela first settled. Malandela was born in 1597, some five hundred years after his forbears arrived from the north, appropriating for themselves the land called 'Nguniland', later 'Zululand'.

Malandela and his wife, Nozinja who was renowned for her herd of pure white cattle, had two sons, Qwabe and Zulu. Their sons adopted the family name 'Zulu', and eventually settled in Eshowe.

Shaka Zulu was born in 1781. As a great warrior he was brought to the throne after a series of inter-tribal wars. He founded the Zulu tribe – The People of the Skies ('iZulu' is the word for 'skies' in the isiZulu language). They are by far the most part, a nation of friendly gaiety and good humour. Today, the amaZulu are the largest population of ethnic groups in South Africa. They make up to ten - eleven million people.

When Shaka's mother, Nandi tried to hide her illegitimate pregnancy by Prince Senzangakhona, she complained that she was suffering from a tummy bug (itshaka'). At his birth her son was named after that perceived illness.

Forty-eight years later, in September 1828, Shaka was murdered by his half-brothers, Mhlangana and Dingaan. The latter would succeed him as king.

During Shaka's lifetime of numerous loves and wars he ensured that his own offspring were aborted, leaving no one to threaten his seat of power. He also altered certain traditions like putting an end to circumcision and introducing the compulsory piercing of ears.

When his mother, Nandi, died in 1827, Shaka filled a donga with murdered pregnant women so that his people would feel the pain of his own loss.

Dingaan's nephew, (his half-brother Mpande's son) Cethswayo was king of the Zulu kingdom from 1873 to 1879, and its commander-in-chief during the Anglo-Zulu War of 1879. 'Den of Thieves' is what he named his royal homestead in the area then called 'Eziqwaqeni', which is today called 'Eshowe'. A mission station was soon established when Cethswayo granted his permission to Norwegian missionary Reverend Ommund Oftebro, uncle-to-be of Dr Christian Oftebro who was the first ever European medical man to settle in the Eshowe district.

Reverend Ommund Oftebro

(Dr Balfe would be the very first civilian doctor to arrive in Eshowe to service British troops in 1887).

Reverend Ommund Oftebro died in 1893, after 44 years of missionary service trying to replace the power of the Zulu's beliefs with a newfound faith in Christ. During his time, until the Anglo-Zulu War, that first mission station, KwaMondi ('Mondi came from the isiZulu pronunciation of 'Ommund'), had been the only settlement at Eshowe. It was comprised of a church built with plastered sun-dried clay bricks which sported a bell tower and clock. There was a school classroom, storeroom, workshop and a large house with a thatched roof and veranda. Zulu women used a mixture of ox blood and fat to polish the rock- hard dried mud floors to a shine. The gardens included fruit tree orchards and a stream providing clean fresh water. Later, during the Anglo-Zulu War of 1879, that mission station was used by the British forces who were besieged there by the amaZulu for ten weeks.

The position of Eshowe being on a plateau earned it the status of Capital of Zululand in 1887, when the province was annexed by the British. But since the Consummation of Union in 1910, the city called 'Pietermaritzburg' carries that status.

Flash-forward to 1994 when Zululand became a part of South Africa, merging with Natal, the province south of the Thukela River, to become the province called 'KwaZulu-Natal'*.

The effect of ex-president, Jacob Zuma, on the region in recent years also has Eshowe bustling with dignitaries. This is because Eshowe is only 52 kilometres from

---

*This is where Eshowe falls under the Umlalazi Local Municipality, which is part of the larger King Cethswayo District Municipality that also embraces 14 tribal authorities.

Zuma's enormous thatched home, Nxamalala at Nkandla.

It is argued that 'Eshowe' (pronounced 'Esh-ow-wee' in English) is a name derived from the *Xysmalobium* (milkweed) shrub called 'Showe' in isiZulu. This is possible since so many nearby towns are named after plants*.

Another popular belief is that, although Eshowe's name is indeed derived from the local ethnic language, its meaning better describes the sound of the wind blowing through the trees of the local coastal scarp, Dlinza Forest Nature Reserve, that covers an area of 250 hectares around which Eshowe is built.

'Dlinza' means 'Sacred Grave', named in those days, before King Shaka even, when elephants were hunted and killed in the forest. Of course that meaning too is debatable. There are those who argue that the word 'Dlinza' means: 'To contemplate something with foreboding'.

The main road through the Dlinza forest is called 'Natural Arch Drive' after the curved branch of a huge Albizia under which ox-wagons and motor cars passed. Inevitably, during a storm, in 1949, that decayed branch came crumbling down.

In 1951 the Dlinza forest was handed over to management by the Natal Parks Board who fenced in the whole area and took on stronger measures to curb poaching**.

*'Hluhluwe' is a monkey rope species; 'Umfolozi' is from the bark of a wild fig tree; 'Mdhloti' was a shrub formerly used as tobacco; 'Tongati' is derived from the Zulu name for the Umthongati tree (*Gardeni amaena*); 'Empangeni' is of the Mpange tree (*Olinacymosa*) and 'Entumeni' from the Ntuma shrub (*Solanum aculeosatrum*).

Within the actual forest there is the shorter Impunzi hiking trail and the longer Unkonka trail. These hikes are most rewarding in the early mornings when birds are most active. In fact, Dlinza is one of the most important forests in Southern Africa from the aspect of biodiversity.

Bishop's Seat is an enchanting clearing in the heart of the forest where plays, concerts, picnics and weddings are held. It is named after Bishop Carter who, in 1891, moved his Anglican headquarters to Eshowe where he took to taking walks through the Dlinza forest. He had a favourite spot where he would sit and meditate on his sermons. He cleared a larger open space around that seating to hold an annual picnic for the town's children.

I

**Today, Dlinza Forest is run by a dedicated board of directors that includes chairperson Jane Chennells, farmer Louis Gunter, actress Ida Gartrell and retired First National Bank manager, Willie Axford.

Coastal Farmers'
CO-OPERATIVE LIMITED

ESHOWE
17 RYNHOLD STREET

NOW OPEN TO THE PUBLIC!
for all Farming Requisites
and many more
other commodities

BEST PRICES IN TOWN!

I arrived at Eshowe in 1996, heavily pregnant with my third daughter, Jodie. My husband at the time, Pat Brenchley, drove our Isuzu bakkie up a long driveway past the magnificent gardens of The Chase Guest House, a traditional sugar cane farm homestead. There we were to spend a week with hosts, Jane Chennells (née Addison) and Jonathan Chennells, known affectionately as 'Janey and Jono'.

Our stay with them was a fitting introduction to the farming community where Pat would serve as an extension officer, providing the link between local farmers and the researchers at the South African Sugar Cane Research Institute, formerly the South African Sugar Association Experiment Station. From 1996 Pat Brenchley was to offer advice on improving sugar cane varieties, protecting crops from pests and disease, and improving a crop's sucrose performance.

Sugar cane is a species of tall perennial grass of the genus *saccharium*. Plants are two to six metres tall with thick, jointed, fibrous stalks that are rich in sucrose that accumulates in the stalks' internodes. It is a desirable cultivar in any country with a warm climate and a rainfall of over a thousand millilitres per annum. The cultivated species are said to have originated in New Guinea. In 1848 one such specie was brought to Natal from Mauritius, proving a worthwhile crop by Edmund Morewood on his north coast farm, Compensation. According to travel author, TV Bulpin, the success of cane cultivation had a similar effect on Natal as the discovery of gold in the inland areas of South Africa.

The residue of crushed cane provides fuel for the sugar mill. Called 'bagasse' it also makes excellent paper. Once the juice is purified with the addition of lime, and heated to boiling point, impurities settle as a sediment that makes an effective fertiliser. The juice then goes through an evaporation process turning it into sugar crystals that are separated to leave a thick liquid called 'molas ses' which serves as an excellent feed for livestock. It is also used to brew rum and other delicious alcohols.

Almost a century before Pat Brenchley and I arrived in 1996, the sugar industry was finally extended to the Eshowe district when the 32-kilometre-long railway extension, from the small village, Gingindlovu, to Eshowe was completed.

Expansion of sugar cane plantations in Eshowe was slow.

At first all the sugar cane grown was sent to the Hulett mill at Amatikulu near Gingindlovu. That mill had crushed its very first cane in 1908.

Eventually, the Natal Estates Mill, at Mount

*It is interesting to note that, from 1859 to 1870, the famous Dick King ran his own sugar mill on his land at Isipingo – Along with his Zulu companion, Ngongeni, in 1842, Dick King was rewarded with a piece of land by the then government for their ten-day, 950-kilometre, horse-ride to Grahamstown, to get help for the Boer-beseiged British garrison at Port Natal (now the Old Fort, Durban).

Edgecombe, near Durban, entered into contracts with growers to the north of Eshowe, while other growers supplied cane to the Gledhow mill near Stanger, about 80 kilometres south of Eshowe. The lack of a local mill was the main problem for the Eshowe sugar cane farmers. Consequently, transportation costs stunted expansion.

But then, in the 1920s, Englishman Sir Charles Smith of the CG Smith group of companies became interested in building a sugar mill at Eshowe. You can read more about the interesting Charles Smith in Bulpin's 'Discovering Southern Africa'.

Production of cane in the Eshowe area during the 1920s was small, but the initiatives of Sir Charles Smith for a sugar mill led the local farmers to establish a co-operative so as to be able to supply a new local mill.

Accordingly, a group called the 'Eshowe Co-operative Sugar & Timber Co Ltd' was established.

By 1925, only 612 hectares in the district were planted to sugar cane. For the 1925/26 season only 6 300 tons of cane were sent off to the mills. This was in part due to the effects of East-Coast Fever (tick fever) on transport oxen, and the fact that no railway served the best growing areas north-west of Eshowe.

In 1926 the area under sugar cane expanded as a result of the Eshowe Town Board leasing out blocks of land for the growing of sugar cane.

In 1927 CG Smith Co began building a railway extension from Eshowe, north-west to Entumeni, running for approximately 11 kilometres. It was officially opened on 14th May 1928.

Although the initial estimate of costs to build the railway extension had been £17 thousand, it ended up costing the co-operative company almost £30 thousand. They also had to pay the Eshowe Town Board £8 hundred for a right of way to link up with the Eshowe

Station. This rail link was achieved specifically for the transportation of cane, but the co-operative company struggled with maintenance costs and repayment of their loan.

Efforts were made to get the government to take over the line, but all to no avail. So, in 1941, the co-operative company liquidated their debt on the railway line.

In 1944 the Eshowe farmers again agitated for a sugar mill – either a co-operative venture or put up by the government, but, once again, to no avail.

By the 1980's the district had the most successful entrepreneur in Tongaat Hulett, whose company operates three mills in South Africa today.

Tongaat Hulett also developed large areas to grow sugar cane in the rural trust lands. The expansion of this agricultural sector is of much benefit to our rural communities. In 2004 the annual turnover of agriculture was 700 thousand tons of cane grown by small-scale growers alone.

Excluding mill employees, fifteen thousand people were employed on cane farmlands in and around Eshowe.

Today, the entire area supplying Amatikulu Mill is estimated at R134 billion.

II

When Pat Brenchley and I arrived at The Chase, in 1996, I was immediately impressed with the Chennells' passion and pride for their town.

Jono has been involved in raising funds to build over three thousand rural Zulu classrooms, while over the past 30 years I have witnessed Janey, with the whirlwind energy that she is known for, working passionately beyond the call of duty in her quest to promote tourism in Eshowe.

The boardwalk by Mary Swindell

The Dlinza Forest Aerial Boardwalk is just one of Janey's ambitious projects seen to fruition. It was her brainchild triggered by a David Attenborough documentary featuring canopies of the Amazon Jungle on trapeze walkways between treetops. The Dlinza Forest Aerial Boardwalk extends across 127 metres of decking high above the forest's floor. It leads to an even higher 20 metre tower offering breath-taking panoramic views of forest mahoganys, ironwoods and other botanical giants. Tree-orchids are among some of the 180 local wildflower species. Birders come from all corners of the earth in search of the elusive Narina Trogon, Spotted Ground Thrush and Delegorgue's Pigeon, among others.

Birding guide, Jotham Maduna, makes himself available over weekends and holidays to show off our birdlife to perfection. He previously worked with Pat Brenchley on a farm in Mpumalanga. Following our relocation to Eshowe, Pat recommended Jotham's suitable appointment to manage the Entumeni Pest and Disease Team. During my marriage to Pat Brenchley, Jotham's wife, Alice helped to run my household. Their three sons, Bonginkosi, Gladwell and Seun are

Seun and Jotham Maduna

especially gifted on the sports field. Seun Maduna went on to win a scholarship to Glenwood High School in Durban and was signed up to play rugby for the Lion's junior team on a two-year contract in Johannesburg. There he was part of the Under-19 Currie Cup team that won the Junior Currie Cup in 2017, and the Under-21 team that won in 2018. On completion of his contract he was called back to play yet another year at the age of 21. Having spent five years away from home he moved back to KwaZulu-Natal in 2021, and started playing for the College Rovers. He made the squad for the Sharks Currie Cup team in 2022.

Jotham's and Alice's eldest son, Bonginkosi was due to start school when they arrived in Eshowe. He was enrolled into John Wesley School, a ministry of the Eshowe Methodist Church that was built in 1901, and then added onto in the 1950s. It is situated on the northern traffic circle in Osborn Road.

In 1994 the Eshowe Methodist Church opened the doors of Noah's Ark Pre-School, consisting of one volunteer teacher and three children. Within three months 35 children were accommodated in two classes.

In 1996 the pre-school reached its capacity of 80 children, four teachers and a secretary. Classes moved out of church rooms and into its own building (still on

the church property) which was generously sponsored by SA Breweries. Parents urged the school to expand since other schools in Eshowe were overwhelmed by the number of Grade 1 applicants each year. The decision was made to 'grow' a class one year at a time.

Presently the school has a venue for each class from pre-school to Grade 7. The present enrolment is 210 learners with a staff complement of 15. They have a dedicated venue for their library. Their extra-mural program includes swimming, cricket, soccer, netball, athletics and cross-country. They offer cultural activities such as chess, drama, choir and a Wildlife Club. They are, however, challenged in that they have no sports grounds and presently have to transport learners to the Eshowe Sports' Club, two-and-a-half kilometres away, for practices and matches.

John Wesley School is the only school in Eshowe to work for and obtain 'International Eco-School' status. They wish to continue promoting a love and respect for the environment through this program.

Doug Sumner was principal of John Wesley School from 1998 to 2004. He was relieved by principal Loreen McDonald (married to Dr Kevin McDonald), who served for 15 years until Mr Alan Stuart took over.

III

By no means a devil-may-care type, my ex-husband, Pat Brenchley was always one to prize achievement over fun. But, boy oh boy, did we have fun with his achievements in contributing to nature conservation. A keen amateur ornithologist, Pat found much delight and pleasure in the rich and prolific birdlife of Zululand. During our several years of marriage he lived and breathed 'birding', serving as chairman of Birdlife South Africa and, with the help of an invested committee, he also established the Zululand Birding Route. The route starts between towns Mtunzini and Richards Bay, moving inland through estuarine swamp forest and up to coastal forest in the foothills of Eshowe. There are numerous forested areas with self-guided hiking trails. The signature locality of the birding route is in fact the mystical Ongoye Forest, situated 50 kilometres from Eshowe, and known for the rare Woodward's Barbet which is the logo of the Zululand Birding Route.

Each month at Bird Club meetings held at the Eshowe Scout Hall, we would enjoy guest speakers presenting stunning slide shows followed with a social braai. Regular locals were brothers, Derek and Vernon Coley, whose interest in birding began while collecting eggs during childhood. The Coleys are hard-working traders, yet no matter how late they had worked that week, there was never a hint of exertion about them – just enthusiasm and pleasant company. Since 1986, Derek and Vernon along with their respective wives, Wendy and Lyn, have owned a large grocery outlet in Eshowe called 'Coley's Supermarket'. They operate together there with their sister, Lynette Raftopoulos (née Coley) and her husband, Jimmy.

One could say that trading is in the Coleys' blood; Derek, Vernon and Lynette are third generation traders.

Their paternal grandfather, George Cecil Coley (1886 - 1971) arrived in South Africa from England in 1913. In 1919 he married Sarah Louise Pask. They began trading at Blood River near Dundee (about three hours north-west of Eshowe) under the name of 'GC Coley & Sons'.

This store is still operational today and run by Colleen and John Malan, the offspring of George's eldest son, George Lawrence and Sarah Coley had another

The market outside Coley's Supermarket

two sons: Arthur Rodney, and Derek John who struck out in business on his own. After exploring opportunities in Southern Rhodesia he returned to South Africa where he settled alongside Hluhluwe Game Reserve at a trading post called 'Makhowe'. It was there that he earned the isiZulu nickname 'Mgalomude' meaning 'long arms' – he was a tall man and seldom used a step ladder. He married Waltraut Gevers from Blood River. Their son, our Derek Coley was born in Nongoma during the time that they were trading at Makhowe. When Derek was a toddler they relocated to Maxuma Trading Store which was situated between Babanango and Fort Louis. John and Waltraut produced another two children at Maxuma: Lynette and Vernon. John lost his first wife, Waltraut to a tragic accident. He remarried Vera Roeloff who bore him a son, Steven. Vera tragically lost her life in a motor vehicle accident.

    John married for a third time. His new wife, divorcee Moyra Frisby (née Owen) had two young children, Emma and Giles, whom John adopted. The Coley family, now totaling eight members, called Maxuma their home. It was a typical rural general dealer trading store selling a range of basic foodstuffs and household goods, hardware, cookware, haberdashery, blankets, shoes and clothing. Animal hides and bones were also brought in for sale. Derek recalls how the hides were stacked, bundled and tied before being shipped off on trucks returning to the railway stations, mainly in Vryheid. Maxuma, north-west of Eshowe between Babanango and Fort Louis, had its own postal code: 3015. Post was brought in on the railway bus to Fort Louis and then collected and delivered by donkey cart to the 'Post Office'. It was operated from within Maxuma Store by 'Uncle' Albert Howard. The post bag contained both ordinary mail and registered letters containing money and postal orders from sons and husbands working on mines up north. Post was sorted for 'post days' when community members would arrive and patiently wait for their names to be called out. As the 1950s, 60s and 70s passed by, John acquired land surrounding the trading post to grow crops and run cattle. Another ode to the past is the travelling salesmen*

---

*Salesmen represented the likes of Tom Oosthuizen for WG Brown and Co, Unilever, Boardman Brothers, Bata; Trevor Cuff for GS, Vickers and John Cross for Mills Distributors.

Salesmen were often characters in their own right and some became family friends. It was no coincidence that some arrived at lunch time when the store was, as tradition dictated those days, closed. Some would take a nap under the trees while others were invited up to the house for lunch. Some were assured a bed and a meal for the night, with the only payment being the pleasure of their company. Living remotely during a time when the radio was the only outside means of news, sales reps were the welcome bush telegraph relating goings-on in the surrounding districts.

In the late 1970s television arrived, although it was little more than a snowy intermittent picture transmitted by a homemade repeater.

Newspapers were a luxury. Sunday papers were obtained by driving up to the main Dundee/Babanango Road at the turn-off from the main tar road (which was also the turn off to Nkandla Village) much further on beyond Fort Louis, where the newspaper delivery van (driven by a most under-appreciated hard working group of people) would hand over a copy of the paper. A newspaper would be read in its entirety including the comics. It was considered a treat, then recycled to wrap goods in the store or stoke a wood-stove.

In 1978 John and Waltraut's daughter, Lynette Coley, a qualified nursing sister by then, married James (Jimmy) Raftopoulos who was studying accounting.

Through a travelling salesman, John Cross, news came to John Coley that a trading store on the farm, Fort Yolland (owned by Mr Aubrey Fry in the Entumeni district and just over an hour's drive from Eshowe – longer by lorry or in the common Entumeni mist), was coming up for sale. The farm, Fort Yolland, was at that stage run by fellow birding enthusiast, Hugh Chittenden, thus beginning a lifelong friendship between the

Chittenden and Coley families.

And so it came about that Lynette and her husband, Jimmy moved to Fort Yolland where they lived in a charming thatched cottage. In the store they were ably assisted by their father, John, and the then Barclays Bank manager, Des Shuttleworth. Later they were assisted by localite Theo Van Rooyen, who, like Des, was most encouraging and supportive. He ran Fort Yolland Store until 1988.

Under Derek and Jimmy, they had traded under the Lucky 7 banner and later the 'bigger brother' Four Square banner of the Metro Cash & Carry group. During those days most stock, ordered through the 'travellers', as reps were referred to, were sent by rail to the Eshowe Railway Station. Because Derek later lived in town (Eshowe) he would visit the local wholesalers like Metro Cash & Carry. He also called past the railway station, with its large platform, huge sliding doors and helpful friendly staff, to collect stock which included bales of blankets, clothing, shoes, hardware and boxes of cooking oil. Derek conducted these rounds in a yellow 4-ton Toyota Dyna that, by the end of its days, certainly earned its keep. It was eventually upgraded to a 4-ton Toyota Hino truck that enabled a more efficient means of collecting stock. It became a familiar sight around Eshowe as it had the name 'Coley's Comet' emblazoned on it, as a joke by a supplier who did not realise that it wouldn't wash off.

Wendy Butler met Derek Coley on a visit to Eshowe to watch the Bozas Rugby Cup match. She was a student at Edgewood Teachers' Training College at the time. She subsequently taught in Durban on the Bluff at Glenardle Primary. Coincidently, Wendy's own Class 1 teacher from Gingindlovu was the class 1 teacher there.

Wendy's parents, John Butler and Ethelwyn Butler (née Willows) originated from the Eastern Cape. My in-laws, Ken and Shirley Nixon became firm friends of theirs. As a child, Wendy had been school mates with my husband, Mike Nixon and his brother, Nigel at Gingindlovu Primary School where my father-in-law, Ken Nixon was principal. Ken had previously been teaching in Northern Rhodesia, so John Butler, in jest, nicknamed him 'Kaunda' in reference to president Kenneth Kaunda of subsequent Zambia.

Derek and Wendy married in 1980. Wendy got a transfer to Eshowe Junior School where she taught until joining the family's trading business.

In late 1985, Mr Clive Vivier, who owned Sibuyile Store in Eshowe before John Burger took it over, approached Jimmy and Derek to offer his SaveMor shop up for sale. His shop was, at the time, being run by Barney Flett (more about him in Volume 2). It occupied premises in the shopping centre that was at the time called 'Viv's Centre' (now Four Square).

The Coley family considered their options. Although they realised the viable opportunity, they knew they would be unable to run the new shop as well as Fort Yolland. They approached Derek and Lynette's brother, Vernon Coley, who was at that stage working at Metro in Pietermaritzburg. Vernon was newly married to Lyn Black who hailed from farming stock in the Natal Midlands. Lyn, as she has come to be known (because having two Lynette's was confusing), like Wendy, was also a qualified teacher.

Thus it came about that two teachers and one-time farmer and Metro employee (Vernon Coley), took over the day-to-day running of the supermarket which took on the name of 'Coley's Supermarket' trading as 'Coley's Four Square' – the logic of the name being that the family name was known in trading circles and could give the business a helping leg-up. It was later called 'Square Deal' and now 'Saverite', but is still commonly known as 'Coley's Supermarket'.

Mention must be made that the Metro Cash & Carry buying group already had a shop under the banner 'Four Square' being 'Jabulani Store' opposite the Eshowe Provincial Hospital adjacent to Dr Clark's old consultation rooms. This store was run by Peter and Geraldine Wright who generously allowed the Coley/Raftopoulos family to also use the 'Four Square' franchise.

As Coley's Supermarket at Four Square in Eshowe became busier, Derek often left Fort Yolland on a Saturday morning to assist. At Fort Yolland fond memories of delivering goods for customers to the bus stops and homesteads on the Nkandla district road, Sibudeni Clinic, Mphapala and Mbongolwana umVuzana, et al remain. The lorries, initially driven by Derek who was later joined by his younger brother Steven (also known as 'Mkhize') and an employee, Joe Khumalo, were often met by donkeys and sledges to haul the heavy maize meal and other goods back to homesteads. It was not a foreign concept to deliver goods to the existing bus rank with its Washesha buses and taxi vans. A routine and goods ticket system was set in place, and daily deliveries were made in the rusty old orange 3-ton lorry, fondly known as 'Skorrie' – short for Iskhorokoro meaning 'rattle trap'. When the driver, Mr Gumede, died suddenly, either Wendy or Lyn would drive the delivery lorry to the bus rank, accompanied by a strong male staff member to handle heavier stock. They never at any stage felt unsafe or threatened, even sitting in the back of the lorry on top of the stock, sometimes accompanied by their children.

To their credit, none of the children cringed openly, as children often do if set apart from their peers, when collected from school in Skorrie or other lorries which the town shop inherited from Fort Yolland.

Eventually road transport took over delivery of stock, particularly after tropical Cyclone Domoina damaged the railways in 1984.

All of the Coley and Raftopoulos children were born during those earlier days of running the shop: Jane, Teri, Brent, Cassandra and Cameron. They would often visit the store, playing happily in the aisles on their push bikes and scooters, carefully watched over and often balethed (carried on the back) by indulgent staff.

Both shops, Fort Yolland and Coley's Four Square, ran concurrently for two years until the Browning family bought the Fort Yolland complex. During those two years, the Fort Yolland side of the family were also involved in the success of Coley's Four Square with Lynette and Jimmy burning the midnight oil. Together they handled much of the administration. In 1988 they relocated from Fort Yolland to town and joined in the day to day running of Coley's Four Square Supermarket. Derek and Wendy, already living in Eshowe, also joined the active management thereof. The name of Four Square stuck to the point that the whole shopping centre is now known as 'Four Square Centre'. A neighbouring bottle store also adopted the name.

In 1993 drama struck when a whole wing burnt down. This included the Coleys' storeroom, a butchery, CNA, Pep Stores and John and Julie Upfolds' sewing and fabric shop. As it turned out, with the insurance payout, hard work and determination, the business recovered. It continues to succeed since January 1986 when manager, Vernon Coley, arrived with the eagerness of a well-prepared scholar, and called 'Umfaan' (young boy) by the customers. Nowadays all the owner/managers are fondly called 'Umkhulu' (old man) and their wives 'Gogo' (grandmother).

IV

An Eshowe Bird Club member of interest was Hamish McLaggan, married to Rose whom my present husband, geographer Mike Nixon fondly nicknamed 'Mrs McDragon' when she served as Eshowe High School's secretary during Mike Nixon's years of teaching there*.

Hamish and Rose McLaggan owned one of the last authentic trading stores in Eshowe called 'Dominoes', which was where the Bird Club was initially founded by men only: Hamish McLaggan, Derek and Vernon Coley, Hugh Chittenden, renowned wildlife photographer Nico Myburgh, and Hamish's close friend, farmer Barry Emberton. After the club moved from the store to the Scout Hall, Barry added much entertainment to meetings by calling out humourous remarks from the back of the hall.

Hugh Chittenden has since received an honorary doctorate for his scientific contribution to ornithology. He also put Eshowe on the map by producing the most recent edition of the Roberts Bird Guide. Born and bred Eshowe-ite, Guy Upfold (son of John and Julie), compiled the illustrative plates. Guy Upfold's other claim to fame is that he took a stray bullet in his own yard during the July 2021 lootings in Eshowe. In July 2021 the 'July 2021 Riots' erupted in South Africa. This was triggered by the imprisonment of former president,

---

*Other prominent members of the Bird Club were entomologist Dennis Eckard, surgeon Mike Damp, Eshowe Provincial Hospital superintendent, Dr Kevin McDonald, Natal Parks Board game ranger, Glen Holland and legendary wildlife raconteur, Nico Myburgh.

Jacob Zuma, for Contempt of Court related to his failure to appear before a commission investigating corruption. These riots badly affected Eshowe Eshowe when buildings were damaged and looted, trucks were burnt and roads were barricaded. Many businesses never recovered and jobs were lost forever. Nationally the unrest caused a 2.4% depreciation of the rand.

V

Bird Club members included a number of educationists, one of whom was Alwyn Schultz whose eldest son, Carl is married to my second daughter, Keri. Prior to lecturing at the Eshowe College of Education (also known as the 'Teachers' Training College'), Alwyn taught alongside his wife, Denise Schultz (née Turney) at Eshowe Junior School. This was when Doug Sumner was principal there after Ken Nixon left. Mike Nixon, at that time, was graduating from Natal University in Durban with a BA in geography and psychology followed with a Higher Diploma in Education.

For decades, Alwyn Schultz made himself available to the community for snake identification and conservation. He maintains that snakes in your garden are an indicator of a healthy eco-system. However, poisonous snakes often need to be relocated due to potential dangers.

Mike Nixon, whom after teaching at Eshowe High School for 19 years, transferred to become Alwyn's colleague at the Eshowe College of Education. He also became Alwyn Shultz's right-hand man in his serpentine capture and release efforts. Others to help on occasion (teenagers at the time) were Gareth Coleman, John Gaisford and Gareth Lagerwall – all boys who attended Eshowe High School with my daughters, Lara and Keri van Schalkwyk.

Alwyn Schultz is regarded as somewhat of an expert on herpetology, but humbly refers to himself as an 'amateur enthusiast'. His interest started as a child when he was astonished by the excitement roused when a snake was sighted, and horrified when it was usually beaten to death. He was further intrigued when those who killed the snake could not accurately identify the species. Nine times out of ten it was said to be a Mamba. In short, Alwyn's interest was a reaction to the kill-one-kill-all mentality: 'The only good snake is a dead snake.' An example of tarring the reputation of an entire species is the relatively harmless Night adder (common in Eshowe), being mistaken as a deadly Puff adder (uncommon in Eshowe). When cornered, the normally passive Night adder will inflate its body and hiss just like the Puff adder that lived on Eshowe businessman, Fergus Upfold's, stoep. Alwyn called it 'Boomerang' because whenever Fergus caught and released it into the neighbouring forest, it would come back again.

We know that dogs are able to find their way home, such as the Great Dane that Gavin and Betty Wiseman gave to the Stort family, over ten kilometres away, and that had been transported in a closed vehicle.

Reptiles have been known to do the same. Localite, Jenny Hawke's grandmother, Una Adams had a frog make itself at home in one of her fern pots. It repeatedly returned when put out into the garden. Her husband, Charlie Adams was an Eshowe-ite businessman as well as the official auctioneer for all the Zulu's stock sales in Zululand. When he next took a trip to carry out cattle auctions, he painted a white cross on the frog's back and promptly dumped it in Entumeni, some 20 kilometres out of Eshowe. Believe it or not, three weeks later, the frog was back at its favourite spot.

Other common but harmless snakes found in Eshowe are the Natal Green and the Variegated bush snake. Although harmless, the Variegated bush snake can produce a performance which is terrifying to the uninitiated. Just as the Night adder imitates the Puff adder, so the Variegated bush snake, when enticed, will mimic a Boomslang by raising its head, inflating its neck and waving its head. They are inclined to follow geckos into the house, sometimes dislodging ornaments in their travels. My friend, Judy Martens, once summoned Alwyn to retrieve a skinny 75- centimetre-long Variegated bush snake from inside her bathroom scale.

Sometimes the Boomslang reported is actually a Boomslang such as the one, measuring well over a metre, found among potted foliage in Eshowe's Amble Inn's bathroom. A Boomslang, although venomous, is placid by nature and unless provoked it is unlikely to bite. Alwyn and Mike were once summoned to capture a Boomslang high up in a bush. Mike pulled the top branch down to afford Alwyn access with the callipers, but the snake saw its gap and, in a flash, slithered down the branch, down Mike's stretched out arm, around his torso and over his feet. Alwyn and Mike were so taken by surprise they were paralysed into watching the snake disappear into nearby bushes.

When one is told that a Boomslang has much bigger eyes than a Variegated bush snake, one imagines the likes of Alien ET. But, unless comparing one directly against the other, and observing the bright emerald green colour of a juvenile Boomslang's eyes, they can easily be mutually mistaken. My step-son, Travis Nixon, realised he had pulled a Boomslang, and not a Variegated bush snake, out from the bushes when the snake opened his mouth to reveal back fangs.

One time when Alwyn and Mike were helping neighbours poison invader plants in their garden, Mike sprang back gripping a snake by the tail and yelling,

'Olive House Snake!'

Astonished onlookers yelled the usual, 'Mamba!'

It was a magnificent female Olive house snake measuring a full metre in length and as thick as Mike's wrist. No amount of persuasion would allow the neighbours to accept the snake into their garden. In the meantime, rats had begun a nightly dance in the Schultz's ceiling, and Alwyn was hesitant to use poison lest owls be affected when eating the rats' contaminated corpses. Although slow-moving, the Olive house snake soon marked a decline in the Schultzs' vermin infestation. Alwyn introduced a male to keep his heroine company and was delighted, some time later, to discover young ones coiled up among the pot plants.

Owing to its notoriety, the Black mamba always deserves mention: while out fishing Alwyn came across two Black mambas peeking their heads out from between a mass of boulders. At the water's edge, and shielding himself with his hardy canvas fishing bag, Alwyn proceeded to pass by at the distance of about three metres. The snakes drew back at his appearance, then they slowly inched forward again with the obvious intention of simply watching him pass by. Alwyn agrees, tongue in cheek, that he might've paled beyond visibility, because Black mambas are extremely nervous and would normally move off when approached. However, preferring the ground to trees, they are known to become resident in one's outbuildings and take to habits such as basking each day in the same sunny spot, where it feels safe.

Together Alwyn and Mike have relocated more than one Black mamba, after which they would raise their beer glasses on high to toast their success and cheer their lives' motto: 'If it's not fun don't do it!'

Then there was the very last time they rescued a Black mamba: when they got to the site they saw the snake lying under a sideboard on the veranda. Alwyn lifted the sideboard while Mike secured the snake behind its head with the callipers. At first they thought it was a Brown house snake, but as they extracted it they saw it was much bigger than expected. Alwyn, as often, was barefooted that day. It was with nervous trepidation that he identified the snake as a Black Mamba. He told Mike to 'Not Let Go.'

Mike held it out at arm's length, its tail nearly touching the ground, while Alwyn called Gareth Coleman and asked him to please bring an industrial dustbin. The pillow case in this instance would not do.

Mike's arms were shaking with the strain of the snake's weight by the time Gareth arrived. Later, it was transported to Fitzsimons Snake Park in Durban. After that particular incident I asked Mike to please refrain from playing with deadly snakes. Apart from him being the love of my life, I was the veteran of two previous failed marriages and did not have the stamina to pursue yet another.

Nowadays, when slithering strangers find their way into neighbouring gardens Eshowe-ites are encouraged to contact Eshowe Snakes and Reptiles – a team led by founding member, Gareth Coleman whose American-born wife, Amy Panikowski manages administration on top of her involvement in rescue and relocation. Amy asks that we please don't try to kill any snake because if we are close enough to kill a snake, we are close enough to possibly be bitten. Two of Amy's teammates, Mzwandile Gazu and Apollo Mthethwa, are instrumental in educating the isiZulu speaking communities, dispelling popular misinformation about snakes and reptiles.

Chapter 2

Melmoth Osborn

Just weeks before our Jodie was born, Pat and I moved from The Chase into our new home in Mangosuthu Buthelezi Drive that was then called 'Melmoth Road', named after Melmoth Osborn*.

In 1880 Melmoth Osborn was appointed as British Resident based in Eshowe, relieving WD Wheelwright who was the very first judicial officer in Eshowe, from 1879 to 1880. In 1887, when, as I have mentioned, Eshowe was established as Capital of Zululand, Melmoth Osborn became the resident commissioner and magistrate. He was joined in 1889 by resident commissioner Colonel F Cardew.

Melmoth Osborn implemented a new set of rules, including a hut tax of 14 shillings per hut per year from 1st June 1888. This was met with a force of arms by amaZulu in the Ndwandwe district resulting in the loss of a dozen white lives. Osborne retired to Pietermaritzburg in 1893, after being relieved by Sir M Clarke who served as civil commissioner and chief magistrate until 1897, which is when Charles JR

*Melmoth Osborn started his career as an isiZulu interpreter in 1854, with the colonial office in Natal. In 1858 became clerk to the magistrate, transferring to Pietermaritzburg in 1858, and on to Ladysmith in 1860. In 1865 he was magistrate of Newcastle.

Saunders took over.

In 1899 Melmoth Osborne was knighted as commander of St Michael and St George and died just a few months later. His uniform is on display at the Fort Museum in Eshowe.

Melmoth Road was renamed 'Mangosuthu Buthelezi Drive', at the suggestion of Alderman Stan Larkan, after the Zulu tribal leader who founded the one-million-strong Inkatha Freedom Party.

The actual 'inKatha' was a magical coil of entwined grass encrusted with parts of royalty such as their nails and hair, and then wrapped in snake skin. Closely guarded, it was passed on from one king to the next as a means of power believed to be preserved by the Zulu soul itself. During times of conflict and battle, kings would sit on the coil that measured about half a metre in diametre. Sadly, when the British beat the amaZulu at the Battle of Ulundi, flames consumed that centuries-old talisman, the inKatha.

I

In Mangosuthu Buthelezi Drive, in 1996, Pat and I awaited the birth of our new baby girl, as well as the arrival of my two daughters from my first marriage to Zimbabwean, Ray van Schalkwyk: twelve-year-old Lara and ten-year-old Keri, whom we'd left in boarding to complete their school term in Mpumalanga.

During a lapse in my induced labour at Eshowe Provincial Hospital, Dr Eric Brits and I looked out the window to admire the night skies. Scorpio was out and, although it was the month of May, I found Scorpio's presence fitting in that there I was, a Scorpio born in November, about to receive one of my most wonderful gifts ever. Weighing in at a whopping four kilograms Jodie Brenchley was finally delivered, by emergency caesarean section, by Dr Eric Brits and the very

Front section of Eshowe Provincial Hospital

popular Dr Giovanni Baldassini who was another local doctor in private practice at the time.

II

Eshowe Provincial Hospital is a red brick building situated just one kilometre from the town's main shopping mall, the Atrium. The hospital maintains four hundred beds spread over 26 wards that are attended by over six hundred staff members.

Staff members have included medical technologist, Suzie Raymond who ran the laboratory until she retired. Judy Martens, also a medical technologist, took over as manager after a decade of working there. This position requires five-and-a-half years of studies and internship to finally qualify with the Society of Medical Technologists. Judy Martens retired in 2018 after a total of 28 years, having been ably assisted by Judy Steenberg (née Percival). Incidentally, Judy Steenberg's great-grandfather, Robert Rogers was the earliest person present to witness the delivery of the 'Ultimatum' back in December 1878. That historic ultimatum was delivered to the king's emissaries under a fig tree (known today as the Ultimatum Tree) on the south side of the lower Thukela drift, just a mile away from Fort Pearson that was built by the British in 1878, when they were preparing to invade Zululand.

It was difficult for the Zulu king to agree to the terms of the ultimatum, that served to enforce British demands, ordering that he disband his army. So he did not respond.

Thus began the Anglo-Zulu War when, in January 1879, British troops crossed the Thukela at the lower drift from Fort Pearson to Fort Tenedos, through land belonging to Alfred Adams (more about him later), following the old wagon track to encamp at St Andrews Mission Station. Robert Rogers was yet to also witness the first shot fired into Zululand from Fort Pearson at the beginning of the Anglo-Zulu War. And he was present when John Dunn (also more of him later), answered to the strong call of European blood by siding with the British, as a soldier and special advisor, and crossed the Thukela with all his tribe and cattle. King Cethswayo considered this an act of treason by a long-standing trusted friend.

Judy Martens, medical technologist, was to become my next door neighbour and friend after I married my third husband, Mike Nixon in 2007. I know Judy to be a strong independent person who, alone, raised three well-adjusted and successful children. It transpired that they are related to Eshowe's surgeon, Mike Damp whose mother was a Martens from the Kranskop area.

Keith Jones was principal pharmacist at Eshowe Provincial Hospital before Michael Balwanth from whom Dion Dirksen took over. Dion has been working in the pharmacy for over 30 years, since August 1993. During the 1990s, Mary Swindell and Vanessa Russell were physiotherapists at the hospital. The former is a very talented artist and I am proud to have prints of her work grace my walls. The latter was to marry Charles Cadman, a farmer and friend of Pat Brenchley's.

Some radiographers of the past included June Holden, Anne Blaylock and Lois Freese.

Angela Bird, who was married to local tour guide, Henry Bird (more about him in Volume 2) ran the blood bank for many years, assisted at one stage by Estelle Goodall who later worked for Dr Eric Brits. I was yet to relieve her duties in his front office. The particular office chair that we sat in is jokingly cautioned against since both Estelle and I ended up with bipolar diagnoses, that she and I like to joke about.

Eric Brits' consultation rooms were, in the beginning, the practice of legendary doctors, Hilton Horsley and Jan-Hendrik Venter. They were then joined by Dr Derek Topliss.

Eric had previously served his housemanship at Grey's Hospital in Petermaritzburg where he met his wife-to-be, Liesel Webb. Liesel was in training as a nursing sister at the time.

From Grey's Hospital, Eric moved on to serve his military duties at various missionary hospitals throughout Zululand. During that time, he met Dr Jon Larson who, impressed with Eric's work ethic, encouraged him to work in Eshowe.

Following Eric's national service, both he and Liesel applied for posts at Eshowe Hospital. Eric left the hospital after a year when he was invited to join the partnership of Drs Derek Topliss and Jan-Hendrik Venter, because Dr Horsley had left.

It was during that era (from 1991 onwards) that the hospital took on their first junior doctors doing internship. They are six persons per annum from Pretoria, Bloemfontein and Wits Universities. Some years later the internship programme was replaced by community service doctors who continue to do duties.

At around the time of the 1994 elections the partners, at what is now Eric's practice, emigrated. Not long after, lady-doctors Marlene Herbert and Ardi Armstrong assisted Eric Brits. Sue Rautenbach (then wife of farmer Aubrey Rautenbach), Glenda Carpenter (Brian Carpenter's mother), Linda Meyer, Jan Tudor-Owen and I managed the office and reception.

Richard and Jan Tudor-Owen were truly wonderful in taking Pat and me under their wing when we first arrived in Eshowe. Jan kindly arranged my membership with her Book Club*.

When Eshowe Provincial Hospital, situated diagonally opposite Eric Brit's rooms, first opened its doors back in 1956, Dr Mike Adhams was the medical superintendent. Later, in the 1980s, there were medical superintendents: Dr Terry Dennehy and Dr Scheurmans. Dr Isabel Johnson was the first female medical superintendent. She was followed by Dr John Nel. When he retired, Mr Roger Blaylock took over in an acting capacity until the appointment of Dr Kevin McDonald in April 1993. Kevin McDonald had previously, years back from 1985 to 1989, spent four years in the stone building at Nqutu, serving as medical superintendent. There, at the Charlie J, he shared in the joys, hopes and frustrations of the other staff who were mostly young doctors from overseas.

---

*Book Club members included Helen Braatvedt (married to Ron Braatvedt of Washesha Bus Services), Toni Williams (married to farmer Dave Williams), Liesel Brits (wife of Dr Eric Brits), Penny Damp (wife of Dr Mike Damp), Mary van Tooren, Estelle Goodall, Tanya Dahl and Renée Lee (wife of farmer Hugh Lee) who remains one of my closest friends.

South African medical students came from Wits university.

Debating the management of patients and solving troubling clinical problems, they shouldered a significant part of the clinical load. Kevin learned much and grew a great deal during his four years there. Kevin is also a talented painter and photographer. I am delighted to own a print of one of his fantastic watercolours of a raptor.

Serving as secretary to the respective medical superintendents at Eshowe Provincial Hospital was Felicia Lawrence. Felicia worked for the hospital for 25 years and thereafter for Dr Eric Brits for 20 years.

Since the 1980s, the hospital has had an influx of Polish doctors who included husband and wife teams: Drs Grabinska, Hordynski, Janowski Kolokowski and Dr Janowska.

III

In 2002 Mrs Ellen Mkize (pictured above) became the first African female chief executive officer of Eshowe Provincial hospital. A fellow Anglican, she generously opened her home to the ladies' bible study group each week for years. Softly-spoken and kindly Ellen Mkize (née Ndelu), was born in Pietermaritzburg in 1942. Her father worked as an interpreter for a doctor, and her mother as a domestic worker. Her father died early in his life, leaving Ellen's mother alone to raise their family. When Ellen left high school she immediately began training at the nearby Edendale Hospital in Pietermaritzburg. Four years later she qualified as a professional nurse. In 1966 Ellen began working as a nursing sister at Eshowe Provincial Hospital. Revealing her innate social conscience, she describes the staff there as a family unit with whom she worked happily, sharing concern and commitment to the proper treatment of patients. Hard workers were praised and each year awards were ceremoniously presented. She remembers Dr Donald Clark being selected as the hospital's 'best person' on more than a few occasions.

In her gradual shift from social reformer to national guardian, so to speak, Ellen nursed in every ward and section of the hospital including medical, surgical, paediatric, neonatal and theatre.

As the first black African female to ever hold the position, she was promoted to serve as nursing manager (matron) from 1972 to 1997. Thereafter she served as chief executive officer until 2007, when she retired after more than four decades of service.

In 1993 Ellen bought the house in between the Guest House Bed and Breakfast and Zanele Lushaba's house which is diagonally opposite the George Hotel at Tally's Corner. For years she had walked past that house en route to the nurse's hostel in Mansell Terrace, never dreaming that she would one day own it.

Friends of Mike's and mine, educators Brian and Hilary Cawood lived in that house during the early 1980s.

In 1984, at the age of 42, Ellen married Lawrence Mkize, an Eshowe-ite businessman. There was a large age difference and Ellen was widowed after 25 years.

Ellen and Lawrence had been keen on politics.
They attended many meetings and speeches on helping the poor, by opening career paths freely to the natural talents of every class and race of person, and implementing minimum wages. Ellen represented the ANC on the Eshowe Transitional Local Council, from 1995 to 1996, when Andy Craig was mayor.

Ellen had two daughters. Lungile, the youngest, sadly passed away from cancer.

Ellen's eldest daughter, Lindiwe shared her mother's interest in healthcare and became a doctor.

Other Eshowe-ite nursing sisters whose children became doctors are Liesel Brits, Trevlyn Palframan and Liz Hanbury-King.

Lindiwe Ndelu matriculated from Inanda Seminary, a girls' high school north of Durban. She spent a gap year teaching maths and English at Mlokothwa High School in Nongoma.

Ellen was concerned that medicine would take too long for Lindiwe to study – she wanted Lindiwe qualified as soon as possible so as to become readily self-reliant if and when necessary. So Lindiwe got a BSc degree at the University of Zululand, majoring in botany and geology. She then obtained her Higher Diploma of Education at the University of Natal (Durban). Then she spent a year teaching at the same school from whence she matriculated.

Finally, being able to pursue her interest in medicine, Lindiwe qualified, in 1994, from the Medical University of South Africa in Pretoria. She did her internship at Thembisa Hospital.

Tiring of the monotony of similar problem cases, year after year, Lindiwe felt that she had served her national service to the community there, so off she went to work for the National Department of Health. She started off as director of the Medical Bureau of Occupational Diseases in Johannesburg.

After Lindiwe acquired her post-graduate qualification in occupational health, she took up the position of director of occupational diseases for the National Department of Health. A decade later she moved over to the Department of Mineral Resources and Energy.

Since 2011, she is chief director for that department. She loves the practice of occupational health, and acting as a conduit through which ideas are translated into effective policies and guidelines for all the mines in South Africa.

IV

I was to befriend more than one nursing sister who previously carried out shifts at Eshowe Provincial Hospital.

They include Mary van Tooren (wife of Eshowe High School's principal from 1985 to 1991, Colin van Tooren, under whom Mike Nixon served as deputy), Liz Hanbury-King (wife of farmer Jeff and fellow Convent class-mum) and Sue Rautenbach (a fellow Convent class-mum with whom I would work alongside at Dr Eric Brits' consultation rooms and paint with in Diamond Bozas' art classes).

Caryle Kippen (née Illing) worked in the maternity and general wards at the hospital for a few years before becoming manageress of the Borough Clinic, now called 'Eshowe Gateway Clinic'. There she weighed and vaccinated the town's infants for 33 years. Late one night a certain hell-raiser (who shall remain nameless), rocked up at Caryle's ward, inebriated, sprawled out in a wheelchair and loudly proclaiming that he had a broken arm. After the trouble-maker woke all the patients

These naughty faces belong to siblings Caryle and Tony Illing

in the ward, Caryle determined that he was not going to get any sleep either. She set his arm, which was actually not broken, at a most inconvenient angle.

Caryle and her brother, Tony Illing, were born in Ladysmith where their parents owned a farm on the Winterton road. Their great-grandfather was missionary, Reverend WA Illing, who was born in Germany in 1827. He was a talented musician and played in one of the principal bands in Berlin. They were often called upon to play before the Kaiser

While in Germany he joined the Berlin Missionary Society. There he was ordained and shipped off to South Africa where he worked in the Cape for a few years before transferring to the Orange Free State.

While there, he met and married Isabella, daughter of Maritz, the voortreker ('voortreker' literally translates to 'path finder') after whom Pietermaritzburg is named.

They joined the Church of England for which Reverend Illing became a priest ministering to blacks and whites living in Utrecht. In 1860 Reverend and Mrs Illing moved to Ladysmith where they started St John's Mission, an English congregation composed chiefly of liberated slaves. Under Reverend Illing's tuition and guidance, some of those liberated slaves became landowners.

Reverend Illing then started another mission – St Philips at Inkunzi, 25 miles from Ladysmith, where he frequently ministered.

His school at St Johns was much admired by school inspectors of the day. Students were well turned-out. In fact, several of his black students could converse in French and Hebrew.

During the Zulu War, no regiment of soldiers ever left Ladysmith en route to Zululand without a send-off from Reverend Illing and his Zulu choir. Reverend Illing himself, continued to play the violin, harmonium, cornet and clarinet. Also, he could speak, read and write fluently in nine different languages including English, Hebrew, Greek, Latin, Dutch, German, French, isiZulu and Xhosa.

His son, August Illing was born in May 1871. When he was seven-years-old, he and his brother, Willie, got the idea to earn some money by selling eggs to the 58th Regiment. They got some ten dozen eggs together from their own and their neighbours' layers. They took these eggs to the military camp that was stationed on the hill behind Ladysmith because there was a natural spring there for drinking purposes. Here I quote August's words: *'We were received very well by the soldiers and made much of. Our English was very indifferent and we had a bit of trouble to make ourselves understood. However, we brought back wealth in silver amounting to about 5/6. This we repeated each day after school and we started buying eggs and selling at a profit. About a month after this the soldiers, addressing both Willie and myself as 'Johnny', asked us whether we could bring them any milk. We told them that we had no cows with young calves, and had no milk ourselves. But next day, when in the morning before school we let out the goat kids to suckle, we started thinking, why not milk the goats for the Johnnies? When we took up the eggs we mentioned to the soldiers that we could let them have goat's milk. They at once offered us, I think, 6d a bottle. This we accepted, and that evening took every kid from the mother – about 100. And next morning before daylight started to milk them and got about 2 gallons of milk, and each day the quantity of milk increased. We had to hire labour to help us milk the goats and carry the milk up to the camp. The goat kids, after sucking the mothers dry in the morning were put into a barn or kraal and kept there while the goats went out to graze. We had to go after school to get them back so as to suckle the kids before bedtime. We got very tired of walking all that distance, so we picked the biggest kapaters and broke them in. We always rode them back, driving the goats in front – wonderful how fond our steeds became of us. After a month or two we felt we were becoming quite rich, and this kept on for about six months. Then the regiment was ordered to the Zulu War. We were very sorry to lose them as we had got so fond of them, and they would do anything for us. I remember distinctly a soldier very much upset and very sorry having to leave Ladysmith, gave me as a memento a small black cloth bag with needles and cotton and buttons, asking me to keep this as a keepsake. The morning this regiment left, we all went from home to the junction of the road coming from the government boys school to Egerton Road. My father and his choir always gave the soldiers a send-off by having his choir sing to the soldiers as they marched past to the field of battle. Often the officers stopped the march past, so the men could listen to the songs and the music. You often saw these men, tears running down their cheeks, many of them, with permission, leaving their ranks to say goodbye to us (this was when the Soldier Smith handed me his sewing bag). The route followed by the regiment then went via Newcastle Road leading to Dundee, to Isandlwana in Zululand, from where we got the very disturbing news about two months later, that the amaZulu had crossed the Buffalo River and were on the road to Natal, making direct for Ladysmith, after having wiped out the soldiers at Isandlwana and Rorke's Drift'.*

V

Nine of Reverend Illings' grandchildren were born in Ladysmith. One was George Herman Illing who married Ruth Catherine Traford – these were Caryle and Tony's parents.

In 1980 Caryle Illing and her Austrian boyfriend at the time came out to Eshowe for a drive in the country. They stayed with Ro Bennett who persuaded Caryle to talk Tony into selling up in Ladysmith and buying a farm in Eshowe.

Tony bought a farm outside Eshowe, so beautiful that artists have painted those breath-taking vistas and landscapes.

In the meantime, Caryle, wanting to experience the world, went nursing in England while Tony moved to Eshowe with their mother, which is why Caryle settled in Eshowe after her return from England. She bought a lovely Victorian house, at 11 Leigh Avenue, that had been built in the early 1900s by farmer Bryan Hulett's father, Herbert Liege Hulett.

At the time, Herbert Liege Hulett was regarded as the most influential businessman in the whole of Natal: In 1857, at the age of 19, he arrived in Durban from England on board the 'Lady Selbourne', with only £5 to his name. His subsequent wealth was built mainly by tea and sugar cultivation and milling. He opened his first sugar mill at Tinley Manor in 1901. He subsequently built two sugar mills in Zululand. By 1912 his farm was producing more than one million kilograms of tea. He was knighted in 1903, becoming 'Sir Liege Hulett'. His magnificent home and farm was called 'Kearsney' after the Kearsney Abbey in the Kentish village near his ancestral home. It is now a private school for boys, mostly under the jurisdiction of the Wesleyan Methodist Church. Sir Liege Hulett died, in 1928, at the age of 91.

Local pianist, Jean White, also lived at 11 Leigh

Avenue with her husband, attorney David White until the house was bought by Dr Hogan and his wife, Rosie.

When looking to buy property, Caryle Illing took one look at this house – the first one she viewed – and instantly fell in love with it. For many years, while Caryle was married to agriculturist, Bruce Kippen, and living with him on a scenic small-holding at Entumeni just out of Eshowe, Caryle's mother lived in that house in Leigh Avenue with her beloved St Bernard, Boot.

By the time I visited Caryle in Leigh Avenue, up the road from Mike and me, she had been living in the house for ten years. During that time, she established the prettiest ram-shackled garden that was totally secluded from the road by dense shrubbery.

Caryle's brother, Tony Illing, married Sue Charleton, a born and bred and extremely pretty Eshowe-ite who attended Eshowe High School with Mike Nixon and his brothers, Neville and Nigel.

Interestingly enough, Mike and I were recently keeping company with Caryle and her good friend, Anita Gardner, only to discover that all three of my companions, Mike, Caryle and Anita, had siblings who were head prefects at their respective schools. What are the chances of that? Due to undiagnosed bipolar my own sojourn at high school had been, unfortunately, one long feud with authority.

A nursing sister to have carried out many shifts at Eshowe Provincial Hospital was Jan Tudor-Owen. She was married to Pat's colleague and excellent artist (I'm proud to own two prints of his magnificent works), Richard Tudor-Owen. Jan worked at the hospital, for over 14 years in total, under Matrons Wendy Dawson, Jenny Hodgon and Christine Mthimkulu respectively. Sister-in-charge was Maureen Smith, whose daughter, Avis worked many hours of night duty together with Jan.

They remain close friends*.

VI

In casualty, Jan worked with, among others, Sisters Margaret Ndlela, Busi Dhlomo and Antonia Dladla. Sister Sheila Mdakane worked in the midwifery department. She went on to become matron and ultimately nursing service manager when, as I have mentioned, Mrs Ellen Mkize was appointed CEO.

Sister Irene Lewis was in charge of the premature nursery that allows babies to reach a discharge weight of two-and-a-half kilograms. She, too, went on to become a matron until her retirement. The establishment of that neonatal ward as well as the building of a paediatric isolation ward was motivated for by Dr Jennifer Chapman, a specialist paediatrician.

Other specialists included surgeons, Mike Damp and Roger Blaylock, as well as obstetrician and gynaecologist Jon Larsen.

Jon Larsen grew up in Zululand, following which he wrote a fascinating book called 'KwaBaka' which is the story of a rural Zulu community at a mission hospital in Zululand (1930-2006).

Jon, most poignantly, tells how it came about that Anglican Reverend Albert Lee followed Charles Johnson as archdeacon of Zululand. That was before his elevation to the Bishopric (more about that later), and how Mrs Edyth Lee set about establishing a small hospital at their mission station.

*Some other nursing sisters include Ann Hoey, Dee McLaverty (then wife of Pat McLaverty of Zululand Times), Pam Johnson (wife of the Anglican rector Bill Johnson), Mary Apollos, Janet Taylor, Wendy Wilson, Ute Bunge and Lyn Brand.

A portrait of Bishop Albert Lee by Barbara Selley

In 1935 Bishop Albert Lee cajoled the Diocesan medical board into buying a stone building at Nqutu for £650.

Without consulting authorities, he took it upon himself to call it 'Charles Johnson Memorial Hospital' (also known as the 'Charlie J'). Mrs Lee, with the help of Sister Sanna Mbatha (a Zulu nurse who had been trained at St Mary's Mission Hospital near Melmoth) and Matron Wells, moved the pitifully restricted equipment she had set up at the mission station to the new hospital.

Jon Larsen joined the staff of that Charles Johnson Memorial Hospital in 1965. The hospital became famous for the clinical excellence of its services and for its resistance, from the 1960s to 70s, to the assaults of the apartheid government on missionary community life.

Jon Larsen's book puts to rest any romantic notion one might have regarding the lives of early missionary doctors. The deep commitment, compassion and integrity of missionary couples, like the Johnsons and the Barkers, were an inspiration as they faced the daily difficulties and frustrations of their workload.

It was during his time at the Charlie J that Jon Larsen developed a commitment to the delivery of excellent maternity care to rural Zulu women. He then worked at King Edward Hospital in Durban for four years before settling with his wife, Jackie in Eshowe where he worked at Eshowe Provincial Hospital for 23 years (from 1981 to 2004).

In his book, Jon aptly describes the lifestyle of the rural Zulu people. He explains the fascinating tasks of trading store owners who were given a number of other functions by the government as part of their job description. For example, the trader was the local registrar of births and deaths (supplying the coffins as well). He was the postmaster dealing with parcels and letters, and transferring funds to and from distant relatives by postal order, which made him the local banker too. For many years the only telephones in the district could be found at the trading store. As demand grew many stores offered the services of a scribe to write letters for illiterate people.

Stores also had a seamstress or tailor to make up clothes from lengths of fabric sold in the store, and a cobbler like born and bred Eshowe-ite, Paulos Mngumezulu (pictured opposite). For decades, Paulos has been resoling shoes outside Coley's Supermarket. He was born at Eshowe Provincial Hospital 60 years ago. His father's brother was a cobbler who taught Paulos his craft.

Paulos, however, was to spend his youngest adult life working on the gold mines in Johannesburg. He returned to ownership of the shoe-repair business after his uncle died.

Larger stores housed a hammer-mill to process customers' mealies free-of-charge. Beans are a common part of the Zulu diet, one favourite brand in particular is given a Zulu name that means 'thunderous buttocks'.

Often in tribal dress, men wore a square of oxhide just covering their buttocks and an array of animal tails or thongs in front. Women's outfits were accessorised with beaded amulets and bracelets, and they plaited their hair into fascinating patterns. Bright white tennis shoes, called tackies, were a popular accessory in the 1960s and 70s, as was a rolled up black umbrella. Today, among fashionable Zulu women, there is a huge market for hair-extensions, braids and wigs.

In 2002 I spent a few months helping out at Daniel da Costa and Fergus Upfold's business in Osborn Road called 'Modern Cosmetics'. It was an extremely lucrative make-up and accessory store catering largely for the younger generation of lady Zululanders.

I had much fun helping our customers select styles to their personal preferences. We were kindred spirits as women finding common ground as cause for hoots of raucous laughter in the midst of broken English/isiZulu conversation.

Chapter 3

Richard Tudor-Owen introduced me to esteemed artist-in-residence, Diamond Bozas – a man who, like his father before him (Alexander Bozas), was hugely loved and respected. I was soon to take up adult art classes with Diamond accompanied by a few fellow Eshowe-ites*. These included dear Waltraud Ahrens who loved doing paintings of trains. She had in fact been in a train accident during her youth that tragically cost her brother's life. Her sister, Agatha Peters served as principal Ken Nixon's deputy at Eshowe Junior School. She subsequently taught with Mike Nixon at Eshowe High School. In 1983, subsequent to Mike serving as Company Second-in-command (captain) in the military, he bought the house we live in. Agatha Peters provided him with boot-loads of plants to get his garden going. I might mention that gardeners in Eshowe are spoilt with at least one full metre of rich top-soil.

Diamond Bozas' father, Alexander was born in Turkey, but ended up in Greece as a refugee. He later lived in Egypt before coming to Cape Town where he worked as a baker. In 1920 he went to Mozambique to attend his good friend, Tony Manosso's wedding. Despina was Tony's wife-to-be's younger sister. Alexander proposed to Despina there and then and they had a double wedding.

Alexander, and Despina who hailed from Izmir in Asia Minor, finally settled in Eshowe, in 1928, with only £36 to their name.

*Other members of my class were Marian Mattinson (née Gunter), Sue Rautenbach, Vanessa Sutherland, Ingalore Wellman, Jean Louw and Edna Grace.

From Mr Karl Vivian Challenor, known to all as 'KV' Challenor, (owner of the Royal Hotel for 17 years since he bought it from W F White in 1920) the Bozas' rented a cottage which got badly damaged by an earthquake that struck Eshowe in 1932.

The cause of that earthquake was a massive tectonic slip along a fault parallel to the Zululand coast about 40 kilometres into the sea. The main shock in Eshowe lasted a full two minutes. The tremors lasted for over an hour.

KV Challenor kindly provided the Bozas' with shelter in the hotel while he repaired the cottage. Alexander Bozas, a trained boxer, was sometimes called in to play 'bouncer' if patrons of the hotel became unruly.

In the meantime, he bought, from an Italian gentleman, a small bakery behind Adams Store in Main Street. With hard work and long hours, he soon needed larger premises. So he relocated to the premises opposite what is now The Holy Childhood Convent School at the northernmost traffic circle in Osborn Road.

Alexander and Despina Bozas had four sons, namely Lambros, Diamond, Achilles (also known as 'Fatti') and Hector. All boys attended Eshowe Public School in Main

Street. The school pool then was a muddy pond with a concrete wall at the deep end. Then, after the 2nd World War, a farmer built the school a tennis court that was immediately very popular, and Diamond proved to be a very good tennis player. He also became the junior lightweight boxing champion of Natal in 1939. He did not particularly enjoy that vicious and bloody rivalry, far preferring to participate in a school play.

Cultural activities in Eshowe received a huge boost, in 1920, when the school obtained a second-hand piano.

There was even a time during Diamond's upbringing that he learned to play a violin that was given to his father to settle an account at the bakery.

Much later in life, Diamond went through a brief acting period. Shirtless and wearing a stuffed bra he was cast as one of the ugly sisters in a local Cinderella production – the cause of much hilarity to this day. He remembered the audience settling in, then silence, then heartfelt applause when he took the stage for that burning performance.

Alexander Bozas was determined that his sons learn to box. He himself was yet to beat up two thugs in Durban at the age of 75. In Eshowe he sponsored cups for boxing, soccer and rugby.

In more recent years, Diamond's nephew (Fatti's son) Alec Bozas was invited out to a luncheon where he was introduced to Lloyd Stewart. Lloyd disappeared only to return with the Bozas Boxing Trophy in hand. He had won the championships three times in a row: in 1954, 55 and 56. So Alexander insisted he keep the cup.

Among lusty cheers and fists pumping the air, the Bozas Rugby Trophy is still played for annually at the Eshowe Sports' Club. Recently, in 2021, Eshowe won the 75th Bozas Cup in their Centenary Year. Spectators cheered until their voices grew hoarse and their throats sore. Alec Bozas offered compliments to local businessman's, Johnny Pinto's committee and the Eshowe Sports' Club for staging such a successful tournament. Indeed, the Eshowe team was to be congratulated for such a special win, playing with moments of pride, elation and love for their fellow small-town teammates.

Diamond Bozas matriculated in 1942. While other boys were getting caned for dipping the girls' pigtails in inkwells, or starting written sentences with the words 'And' or 'So', Diamond was caned twice for chatting in assembly.

And so, after matriculating, Diamond immediately hung up his green and white uniform that remains the same to this day. And he began working among the sweet aromas of freshly baked bread and confectionaries at the family bakery. While working there, Diamond continued to pursue his love for art by painting in his parents' living room at night.

In 1947 he and Sigrid Solberg (an artist and music teacher) presented the first art exhibition ever held in Eshowe. That was in the supper room at the Town Hall. That same year, King George VI, Queen Elizabeth, Princess Elizabeth and Princess Margaret of England visited Eshowe where they met the Zulu king at the time: King Cyprian. The address of welcome was given by Chief Albert Luthuli who was yet to become president-general of the African National Congress, from 1952, until his death in 1967. He won the Nobel Peace Prize in 1960.

Diamond joined those lining the streets, where Shoprite Store and OK is today, to view the royalty. The next day the royal ladies walked around the Cricket Oval chatting with the locals. Diamond was so excited to be close enough to touch the queen's skirts. Head girl of Eshowe High School, Pam Scotney (now Pam Johnson), together with Gayan Haveman and Denise Taylor, presented floral bouquets to the royal ladies.

Tony Wantink and his sister, the fun-loving character, Maisie entertained the royalty with their band called 'Tony's Orchestra'. Maisie never married, but she got engaged six times. She confessed that she did indeed fall in love many times, but at the end of the day no man was good enough for her.

The British royal family visited Eshowe three times in all. They were welcomed by Zulu King Solomon in 1923 and 1925, and again by Zulu King Cyprian and Chief Luthuli in 1947.

In 1925 Prince Edward of Wales had a memorable three-day visit after he and his entourage arrived in the White Train. They were welcomed by town dignitaries and a large crowd. Charlie Adams was both mayor of Eshowe and previously chairman of the Eshowe local board for the second time (the first being from 1918 to 1920). But the official address was made by Sir Charles Saunders, the son of a wealthy sugar farmer who came from Mauritius to Natal in 1854. Like Melmoth Osborn, Saunders started out as a clerk of the court and isiZulu interpreter. That was in 1876. By 1886 he was assistant administrator of native law. In 1897 he was appointed civil commissioner and chief magistrate of Zululand. He was knighted in 1907, after which he continued living in Eshowe for some years while faithfully serving St Michael's Anglican Church, as well as the Country Club as its first president. He retired to Melmoth and died in 1935.

Back to Prince Edward's visit in 1925: forty thousand amaZulu (followers of 80 different chiefs) in full tribal dress converged on Eshowe from every corner of

Zululand. They were accommodated in large tents on the golf course. And they presented a most picturesque spectacle as they gathered to greet the son of then 'Great White King' himself.

Paramount Chief Solomon arrived in full military dress eliciting a huge spontaneous 'Bayete!' from the crowd. He was matched by the Prince of Wales who arrived in an impressive military uniform topped with a plumed helmet which much pleased the amaZulu, whose own kings had worn blue crane feathers in their headgear.

Later that day, a magnificent Zulu war dance was staged, in Prince Edward's honour, by the huge gathering of warriors, many wearing warriors' plumes and cow tail arm and leg decorations. They drummed assegaais (spears) against their shields and chanted war cries. Perspiration outlined their magnificent muscles.

Among various presentations and tea parties there was a parade of Boy Scouts, Guides, Brownies and school children. The prince presented a medal to Cub Vinnicombe who had recently rescued his little brother from drowning in a swimming pool.

Because there was still no Town Hall in Eshowe, the Grand Royal Ball was held in a large marquee on the Royal Hotel's bowling green where a portable dance floor was erected.

Despite their formal dress, mayor Charles Adams and His Royal Highness were anything but reserved. Together they ended up in an impromptu dance on the huge Norwood dining table.

I

Diamond Bozas, during the early days, was prevented from following his dream to study art in London until the family bakery made enough money to sustain his absence and his studies. Finally, in 1955, after he had worked in the bakery for 11 whole years (from 1943 to

1954) he was able to do the course at Heatherley's in England, followed by three years of study at the Chelsea School of Art. There, at the end of each year, they held unforgettable fancy dress parties. Bagpipes played and girls did Scottish dances. Hundreds of colourful balloons fell from a net on the ceiling.

After Diamond's marriage to Tasia in Greece, their spare time in London was spent attending concerts and theatre productions. Diamond's hair stood on end when he heard Maria Callas sing in the sleepwalking scene from Macbeth at the Royal Festival Hall. Together, Tasia and Diamond haunted the National, the Tate and the West End galleries. On their return to South Africa, Diamond and Tasia would have three children: Alex is a guitarist for the Capetonian band called 'Benguela'. Arthur (also a musician) manages the family property and runs a successful carpentry workshop from the old orchid shed. Despina (Diamond's mother's namesake) is a preschool teacher.

Diamond and Tasia had met during Diamond's first visit to Greece when he got off the flight to find her accompanying his father, Alexander to meet him at the airport. She could not speak English and Diamond's Greek was not good, but in photos taken at the time they were always smiling or laughing at each other.

They married in the Greek Orthodox Church in Pangratia. After a honeymoon on the Island of Rhodes, they returned to London where Diamond resumed his studies at Chelsea. There he qualified with a National Diploma in Design, specialising in painting.

Diamond and Tasia came from London to Eshowe, in 1960, because Diamond's mother, Despina was ill.

Diamond had to pass up an invitation to exhibit at the Paul Kington Gallery in London. This invite was a huge compliment. To his dying day he wondered what course his professional life would've taken had they remained in London. He had been so successful at the Royal Academy exhibitions.

In South Africa, Tasia was amazed by the rolling green seas of sugar cane and the Umsini trees that were flowering her favourite flaming colour.

Diamond resumed work at the family bakery, starting each day at 4 am, to supervise the loading and dispatch of bread. He opened for trade at 7 am.

Diamond's brother, Hector, was a master baker. Their brother, Achilles (Fatti), was a chartered accountant who undertook the main bookkeeping aspect of the bakery while pursuing politics. He was the first mayor of Empangeni, chairman of Gingindlovu Health Committee and, later on, custodian of St Lucia Health Committee. He also became a member of the Provincial Council and went on to become a senator.

Flash-back to the 1960s to the bakery in Eshowe: with a staff count of over 100. Diamond's wife, Tasia offered to help out in front of shop where she managed very well despite her lack of fluency in English.

Finally, when the bakery (the business that his father had held so dear) was sold to SASKO, in 1975, Diamond could once again concentrate on painting, albeit on a part- time basis while he developed a plant nursery on the five- acre family property.

Diamond brought camellias, azaleas and magnolias from Johannesburg. He introduced conifers and proteas and built a shed for orchids.

Then he decided that he wanted to be a painter, not a nurseryman. After adding the studio extension to the house he took up creating his own masterpieces, and giving lessons to the likes of aspiring wanna-bes like myself.

During her high school years my daughter, Lara

attended Diamond's evening classes. Years later, my son, Colin attended classes during the school holidays.

Other than the arts of painting and horticulture, Diamond's experiences were hugely invested in flower arranging. He liked to use indigenous materials such as grasses, dried leaves, twigs, vines, strelitzia and even birds' nests. He exhibited in France, England, Belgium, Tasmania, Australia and Zimbabwe. In 1996 he participated in the ten-day International Flower Arrangement Festival held in St Petersburg in Russia. The Russians had never seen thorn twigs before.

While there, the South African participants were shown original art by the likes of Picasso, Monet and Matisse. They saw a ballet production of Romeo and Juliet at the Marinsky theatre: the music of Prokofiev was superb and the dancing, effortless. Another highlight of their stay was a visit to the Hermitage Museum.

Later, in 1999, Diamond participated in the World Flower Show in Durban.

Then, finally, came the time when Diamond decided to devote his time fully to painting. To date he had served on so many committees, including the Zululand Society of Arts that existed into the 1990s. Members held several exhibitions in Eshowe*.

One member was Wendy Ferguson (wife of businessman Stan Ferguson and mother of spear fisherman, Rory Ferguson). Wendy Ferguson's parents, town engineer Maurice and Bonnie Salberg (the first female councillor in Eshowe) were instrumental in proclaiming the Nongqayi Fort as a museum in about

*Other members of the Zululand Society of Arts Committee included Shirley Murray, Pat Clark (wife of Dr Don Clark), Merle Hulett (wife of Bryan Hulett), Sue Weidermann and Barbara Robinson.

1951. During that time Bonnie took it upon herself, with the help of municipal labourers, to plant up the streets of Eshowe with trees. Most of those trees still stand today – jacarandas in Kangela Street, bauhinias and azaleas in Hulett Street, yellow woods all the way up Clarke Avenue where Mike and I live, and more.

In fact, in 1990, Eshowe won the national Arbor Town Award that is aimed at recognising municipalities that go the extra mile to preserve and green up their areas of jurisdiction. As I've mentioned, Diamond's art studio was an attachment to his and Tasia's rambling home set at the edge of town bordering the Nyezane stream. During weekly classes students would all share our mutual love of art, music, cuisine and literature, while listening to Diamond's much loved collection of classical music floating, rising and falling to the strokes of our paintbrushes. Diamond would point us in the right direction when we were stuck, and celebrate, with us, our serendipitous 'happy accidents'.

Diamond and Ingelora Wellman would tell us about their monthly Music Club meetings where members shared a meal and introduced a classical program chosen by the alternating host*.

Tasia would interrupt our painting lessons with a tray

---

*Other members of the Music Club included Denise Schultz and Richard and Jane Aitken. Richard, a noted academic, was a great asset to the club in that he was particularly knowledgeable. Also pianists: the extremely talented Jean White, the beautiful and gracious blonde Renée Lagerwall who was Mike Nixon's colleague at the Department of Education – both serving as senior education specialists, and Irene Strachan (née Language). Always pleasant and super-efficient, Irene was exceptionally sharp. She had been awarded Dux of Eshowe High School in 1959. Her father, CW Language was Eshowe's town clerk from 1953 to 1955.

Ingelora Wellman, Diamond Bozas and Edna Grace in the studio

of tea and delicious melt-in-your-mouth Greek confectionaries baked in her kitchen.

Edna Grace would have us in stitches when threatening to ravish Diamond each time he came up with something profound or funny, which was often, slapping his lap and wiping tears from his olive green eyes. Diamond's own painting themes included his magnificent garden, the verdant hills of Zululand, various still life subjects and portraiture. He liked to define peace in his paintings that were of a style somewhat influenced by his great admiration, like my own, for the works of Paul Cezanne.

In 2013 Diamond was thrilled to be offered, by Brendan Bell, director of the Tatham Art Gallery in Pietermaritzburg, a retrospective exhibition in honour of his 90th birthday. This caused much excitement throughout KwaZulu-Natal. Art lovers knew the Tatham to be respected as an institution conforming to the highest standards of display. Diamond's work would no doubt be one of the highest calibre by an artist par excellence and connoisseur of 'all things beautiful'. The exhibition was extremely successful and ended up having an extended run. A beautiful coffee table book

was produced, from which I gleaned much of this written material.

This is Diamond's painting of the view we enjoyed through his studio's window. Included is his cherished collection of famous Nesta Nala Zulu pots, which he bought before he found out they were hers.

Diamond Bozas was also instrumental in saving the Vukani Museum – a collection of traditional Zulu artefacts where I would work for a few years after my marriage to Mike Nixon. The Vukani Association had originally been set up, in 1972, as a co-operative with Swedish missionary, Kjell Lofroth who actually owned the initial collection. Due to his wife's ill health, Lofroth returned to Sweden before his dream of the museum was finally realised in 2001.

The circular building housing the collection at the Museum Village was designed by architect Paul Mikula, husband of famous potter Maggie Mikula (née Suttie). Maggie was the only sibling of the previous curator of the Zululand Historical Museum at Eshowe, Jenny Hawke.

I absolutely loved spending my days among those fine examples of Zulu basketry, beadwork, tapestries, pottery and wood carvings that remain somewhat shrouded in African myth and mystery. Pottery is usually done by Zulu women, and wood-carving by men.

The museum has an extensive collection of both historical and contemporary cultural artefacts that, since Vivienne Garside's curatorship, grew substantially –

benefactor, college lecturer Rob Wissing's generous contributions notwithstanding.

Lining the circular wall is a fine collection of basketry, recognition of which has helped to revive a dying craft In fact, several of the artists whose work is exhibited there have received international acclaim: tapestry weaver Alina Ndebele (Madiba owned some of her works), basket weavers Reuben Ndwandwe, and Angeline Masuku who was the winner of the 2007 First National Bank Vita Award (Willem Boshoff owns one of her works), and potter Nesta Nala (Diamond Bozas sometimes used her pots as still life subject matter). The pottery of the talented Magwaza family is also to be truly appreciated.

Vivienne Garside instilled in us, her staff, the highest of museological standards. Zama Mbatha is currently the curator, but Vivienne Garside has continued to serve on the board since her retirement. Other assistants were Edna Grace, who also painted with me at Diamond Bozas' studio, and Jess Wilson who also led the Boy Scout movement in Eshowe for many years.

The Museum Village offers educational programs for schools, a research room housing the history of Zululand, and guided tours to visitors. There is also a picnic facility in the Ian Garland Arboretum. Up until COVID*, between the Vukani Museum and the Norwegian Mission Museum Chapel, was a fabulous craft and curio shop. And if you were wanting a meal or a snack, there was the charming and fully licenced Adam's Outpost Restaurant. The building is a 19th century wood-and-iron settlers house called 'Norwood', previously the home of the Adams family (more about them later). The house was dismantled by Lawrence Dunn and relocated to the Museum Village. It was originally on a 13-acre property close to the centre of town.

The Museum Board 2022: Vivienne Garside, Bruce Hopwood, Mavis Mdluli, Ida Gartrell, Vukani curator Zama Mbatha, Fort Museum curator Hannes Diemont, accountant Nola Ladwig. Nonceba Lushaba was absent

Left: assistant curator Elizabeth Mazibuko has worked for the Fort Museum for over 30years.
Right: Thembi Mthabela of the Phumani Paper-Making Project

*In March 2020, COVID-19 pandemic struck. A 'lockdown' forced the closure of many businesses, leaving thousands unemployed. Ironically, this authoritative decision led to long queues outside relief grant distribution centres, placing crowds of people in close proximity which is what the lockdown was supposed to prevent in the first place.

Behind the restaurant there is the Phumani Paper-Making Project led by Thembi Mthabela. They make sheets of paper and beautiful gift boxes out of sugar cane leaf fibre and recycled paper. Produce is sold on site where the paper maché, once mixed, is spread out thinly on gauzed screens to be dried out in a huge oven. The project was begun by Kim Barney in about 2013. Other stockists of these lovely paper products include the Vukani Museum at the Museum Village, the Craft Shop in Empangeni and Mtunzini Tourism.

Behind the craft shop is an enormous butterfly dome measuring 20 metres wide by ten metres high. Since butterflies only thrive in warm, sunny weather, the butterfly dome is open only on sunny days. Among leaf-littered garden paths one finds 80 different species of butterflies including the Dusky- Veined Acrae, Blue-Spotted Charaxes and various Swallowtails. Guides and all property maintenance falls under the supervision of Argentinean zoologist and biologist Américo Bonkewitz. Américo pursued his MSc in Biology at the Universidad Nacional del Sur in Bahía Blanca, Argentina. Following that, he obtained his doctorate in Zoology from the University of KwaZulu-Natal (Pietermaritzburg). Back during the late 1990s Américo ventured into butterfly farming, focusing on breeding the Emperor Swallowtail. In 2007 he conducted numerous butterfly surveys in KwaZulu-Natal resulting in his involvement with the African Conservation Trust in 2010. This project, that was funded by the National Lottery Distribution Fund, included the installation of four large butterfly domes, one of which is that in Eshowe's Museum Village.

Since April 2012 more than three thousand visitors have toured Eshowe's dome, in addition to hundreds of bus tours from schools. The dome is a fantastic venue where a biodiversity programme has been established to

train communities to look after local indigenous forests. Visitors have the unique experience of working on their laptops or reading a book while surrounded by butterflies at the tables. Free Wi-Fi is accessible and self-service coffee and tea is on the house. Attracted to the fragrance of perfumes and perspiration, butterflies will often settle on visitors.

In 2018 Américo established and developed an initiative called 'Inquisitive Minds', an environmental educational program aimed at fostering a passion for nature among children. On the property adjoining the butterfly dome is a delightful playground and a two-hundred-metre path through the surrounding forest. There is a cave that is a two-metre underground chamber transformed into a child's laboratory. Decorated in a Halloween theme it invites intrigue and adventure. Adjoining the cave are two braai areas. There is ample parking and the entire venue space can be booked for parties.

The main focus of the Museum Village is the Zululand Historical Museum housed at the three-turreted picturesque 'Beau Geste' type white fort (pictured above).

Captain CE Fairlie with the Nongqayi in 1902

The fourth turret wasn't completed because authorities ran out of money.

II

The fort was declared a National Monument in 1939, fifty-six years after it was built by the British in 1883, to house the barefooted Zulu Native Policemen called 'Nongqayi' – a Bantu word meaning 'Bald heads' owing to the shiny helmets they sometimes wore. Their uniform, designed by Colonel Stabb Officer Commanding, consisted of navy blue knickerbockers and blue jerseys. They wore a felt slouch hat for field service, and dark blue putties although they went barefooted. In summer they wore a white version of this uniform. For ceremonial drill they wore a jaunty pill-box hat. Their marching to their own bugle band, with a measured tread and swinging gait, could be bettered by very few British regiments.

Armed with rifles and bayonets, and a number of them mounted, it was the Nongqayi's task to protect and enforce British administration following the Anglo-Zulu War of 1879, during which over nineteen hundred British and almost seven thousand amaZulu were killed.

Led by Colonel Addison, the 90-men-strong Nongqayi trained in this fort. They then fought with bravery at the Battle of Ceza and Hlophekhulu in 1888. They fought again during King Dinuzulu's uprising. King Dinuzulu succeeded his father, King Cethswayo, as king of the Zulu nation after King Cethswayo died in Eshowe the following year, in 1884.

At the museum there is a plaque honouring the Nongqayi for taking part in the 2nd Anglo-Boer War, from 1899 to 1902, during which time their force was increased to two hundred men, doing guard duties and scouting, under the command of Captain Fairlie.

The Nongqayi of Eshowe were disbanded in 1904, said to have been as an economy measure, but possibly an action assumed as part of the disarming of the amaZulu by the white government. The fort then stood empty for several years until 1915. It then served, for many years, as a depot for the Natal Roads Department. Finally, in 1939, it was declared a national monument. In 1965 it was turned into the 'Zululand Historical Museum' (also known as the 'Fort Museum' or 'Fort Nongqayi'). It is home to various treasures, including a forlorn manikin of a British soldier in his hot red jacket and white helmet. Red coats remained the Royal Army's dress uniform up until they were phased out due to the high price of red dye. A dark khaki uniform was phased in from 1902.

Focusing largely on Zululand history and culture, the Fort Museum houses many collections. And it shows the military history of conflicts including the Anglo-Zulu War, and the Bambatha Rebellion of 1906 that was the last time, until the 1960s, that Africans resorted to armed insurrection in South Africa.

A large focus of the museum, besides its reference to the Tsetse Fly Campaign, is the cross-cultural influences of the past two centuries, including Zulu ethnology. There is the mobile wooden chair made my missionaries in the 1850s, for the ailing obese King Mpande (Cethswayo's father) who had great difficulty in walking. Bishop Hans Schreuder was the first Norwegian missionary in Zululand to gain a reputation as a doctor among Zulu converts*. The missionaries, in those days, received a fair bit of medical training before their arrival in Africa.

III

John Dunn did not ask to be a chief. Immediately after the Anglo-Zulu War the British decided to cut Zululand up into 13 independencies called 'kinglets', offering John Dunn chieftainship of an area to be known thereafter as 'John Dunn's Territory'.

John's autobiography, 'John Dunn Cetywayo and the Three Generals', first published in 1886, is available in the Museum Village's research room. It is a revealing read told by this unique man. John Dunn of Scottish descent was born in 1834 to a couple who immigrated to Durban two years later. They lived on a farm called 'Seaview' until Robert Dunn was trampled to death by an elephant. John Dunn's mother, Anne died three years later.

Seventeen-year-old John took to a life of wandering through Zululand where he was to become a trader, hunter, arms dealer, politician, and, after befriending kings Mpande and Cethswayo, a central figure in the shaping of 19th century Zulu history. His book gives a

*The very first Zulu minister of religion, Reverend Simon Ndlela, was ordained by Norwegian missionaries in 1893.

fascinating account of the rise and fall of the Zulu power – There was no valid reason for the Anglo-Zulu War that, according to John Dunn, would have come sooner or later anyway, due to the Natal Government's dictatorial voice, in an unnecessary tone of authority, towards the Zulu king. However, it must be said that King Cethswayo actually blamed John Dunn for causing the war in the first place, by stealing the king's property and cattle.

Prior to the war, the amaZulu called John Dunn 'Jontoni the white Zulu' due to his language skills and practices of Zulu customs. King Cethswayo was initially so fond of this tall white man that he made him a headman. Together they had control of six thousand subjects. Furthermore, Cethswayo gave John Dunn large regions of land and the daughters of his chiefs to take as wives. This gave John Dunn a position of power, and wealth when he accumulated thousands of cattle. All in all, he married forty-nine women, always paying the necessary lobolo dowry of eleven cattle each.

John Dunn could pass as a Zulu or be completely at ease among the white men at the European gentlemen's clubs. Just prior to the Anglo-Zulu War, at the Smith's Hotel on the banks of the Thukela River, he regularly provided entertainment to the guests who were largely soldiers, war journalists, traders and adventure seekers. He told hunting tales in the lounge and shot crocodiles from the veranda. In the early evenings he summoned half-naked Zulu maidens to dance on the lawn.

On 11th December 1878, an awning was set out just below Smith's Hotel. Governor of the Cape (also Commander-in-chief of the British forces) Sir Bartle Frere's Declaration of War was read there to King Cethswayo.

British troops, in their quest for war, crossed the Thukela River on 11th January 1879. Military engineers, staying at Smith's Hotel, used a mirror to construct the first heliograph in Zululand. Chelmsford was then able to make contact with Pearson and his soldiers trapped at KwaMondi in Eshowe. They, in turn, responded with their own heliograph signals using a big mirror belonging to one of the officers.

I'd like to point out here that the Anglo-Zulu War was in fact embarked upon without Queen Victoria's or the British government's prior approval.

Unfortunately, John Dunn's autobiography is his only surviving work. Two decades' worth of records that were mostly results of conversations with old Zulu chiefs, regarding the origins of their powers and customs, were destroyed during the Anglo-Zulu War in 1879. This was when Zulus torched John Dunn's home after he moved his wives, children and cattle to the south side of the Thukela River, and sided with the British.

The Dunn Room at the Zululand Historical Museum displays John's fine mahogany and teak furniture which illustrates the life of this man who, although adopting Zulu customs, maintained a love for European trends and fashion.

Together with his forty-nine wives, John Dunn had over one hundred children. Those children were brought up under strict discipline while educated by private tutors or at the mission schools adjacent to John's homesteads. John Dunn had been a friend of that grand old pioneer, Alfred Adams of St Andrews Mission, who provided schooling for most of the Dunn children. Nine of them were baptised at St Andrews and the baptism registrar is signed by Alfred Adams as godfather to each of them.

In the 1920s, Alfred's son, Charlie Adams represented and appealed to the Department of Native Affairs on behalf of the Dunn community, who were experiencing problems in establishing themselves as viable sugar cane farmers. Charlie requested financial assistance, and negotiated the laying of a tram line from Thukela station to the Dunns' farm at Mangete, for the transport of cane to the sugar mill.

Many of John Dunn's descendants still live in Eshowe today. There is a bench at the museum, more recently dedicated to the memory of long-serving trustee of the Zululand Historical Museum, Lawrence Victor Dunn, who was a grandson of John's. Together with his wife, Magdalene Eunice, Lawrence had ten children.

Mike's and my friends, Roger and Anne-Louise Gaisford (big characters in this small town), now own the Dunn family's wood-and-iron house in Mitchell Street around the corner from Mike and me. Lawrence Dunn and his seven siblings were all raised in that house. First records indicate that the house belonged to Theodorus Gerhardus Colenbrander, the post-cart proprietor, in 1903. It then belonged to Mr KV Challenor of the Royal Hotel and was bought from him by Lawrence Dunn's parents, Ned and Nellie Dunn in 1930. After living there for 38 years the Dunn family sold to Norman and Audrey Freeman, in 1968, when the Group Areas Act forced them to move to the newly established suburb called 'Sunnydale'. Lawrence later built another house next door. Those properties still belong to, and are occupied by members of the Dunn family.

Lawrence Dunn's nephew and niece who still live in Eshowe are Etienne Dunn, and Etienne's sister, Denise Dunn who worked for Emdoors timber company for decades. Both of Denise's children attended Eshowe

High School with my daughters Lara and Keri. Denise's daughter, Germaine Dunn, is a senior copywriter and brand manager for an advertising company in Johannesburg. Denise's son, Vaughan Pierce is the legal advisor for Pick 'n Pay at their head office in Cape Town.

From left to right in this photo are Lawrence's and Magdalene's children: For 23 years Roy William Dunn has owned a maintenance business in Eshowe doing tiling, sanding, painting and general renovations. Not only is Roy respected for his quality workmanship, but he is greatly loved for his heartier than hearty laugh. Roy, like me, had five children. His oldest, Miriam, works as a team manager in Durban. His second child, Quaid, wrote a hit song called 'We Are' that South Africans enjoyed listening to on Radio Morning Live. Quaid is now a consultant who assists artists in publishing their music and videos. Jayden was Roy's fourth child. He sadly had a cancerous brain tumor that cost him his life at only 21 years of age. The youngest is Levy who home-schools since COVID.

Next to Roy is Gordon Edward Dunn who was also in the building trade. Next to Gordon is Daryl David Dunn who does dental equipment installations and repairs in Johannesburg.

Gloria Wendy Sing (née Dunn), for decades, worked for the Chennells' at The Chase, mostly doing admin at the farm office.

Calvin Lawrence Dunn has for three decades owned a panel-beating business called 'Eshowe Motor Restorers'. My friend Mali Govender ran his office for

23 years. That business in the industrial area was on Jack Spencer's visiting route (more about Jack later).
Cheryl Anne Lamarque (née Dunn) worked for Standard Bank in Eshowe for over 30 years. She branched out into property dealings and continues to work as an estate agent in Johannesburg. (My own daughter, Keri Schultz also works as an estate agent in Johannesburg).
Barry Dermont Dunn lives on the south coast, felling and harvesting timber for forestry companies, Sappi and Mondi.
Mom, Eunice Dunn (née Reid), was a devoted Anglican. She is remembered for being sweet-natured, loyal and dedicated to home, family and community.
Karl John Dunn served an apprenticeship with Brockwell Engineering in Eshowe. He now maintains large buses in nearby Empangeni.
Ashley Victor Dunn is also a motor mechanic working for NES Diesel.
Lynton Craig Dunn had a plumbing business in Eshowe called 'LC Dunn Plumbing'. His daughter, Sian was head girl of Eshowe High School in my daughter, Lara's matric year. I clearly remember Lara coming home thrilled by that outcome because she had her vote on Sian. Sian has gone on to do very well for herself with Transnet.
Jillian Laura Henri (née Dunn) was absent when this photo was taken in 2006. She works at a call centre in Port Elizabeth

IV

The Gaisfords have lived in Ned Dunn's old house for almost four decades. At a party there one evening Roger Gaisford challenged the then mayor of Eshowe, who shall remain nameless, to cycle around the block stark naked. They were barely halfway when a car came chugging along, headlights blazing. Roger rode straight into the bushes from where he could see the mayor's bottom, bright white on the saddle, his feet peddling furiously and his face turned as far into the shadows as was possible.

Roger Gaisford, historian, Jeep enthusiast and champion speaker and writer of isiZulu, seSotho and seTswana, is a true adventurer at heart. He continues to write articles for off-road vehicle magazines published both in the UK and USA. His and Anne-Louise's son, John walks in his footsteps.

The Gaisfords' house where, previously, Laurence, Peter, Stanley, Joyce, Ethel, Laura, Anne and Stanley Dunn grew up

Traveling extensively in his Jeep, Roger has explored every shoreline starting at the Thukela mouth and bypassing Kozi Bay in order to cross the border, and onward to Inhaca Island, which is the furtherest north one can travel along the coast in Mozambique. He has often explored the Zululand coast and Botswana, and has just recently done another run to Nkandla.

Roger's grandfather had his own business drilling for coal. This enabled Roger, as a child, to explore the veld while learning how to drive and operate all that old machinery. Roger was also a Boy Scout and loved exploring natural habitats.

Later, as a university student, Roger worked as a field assistant to earn extra money. That experience was yet to land him in Eshowe, in 1979, employed by a mining company doing mineral exploration in the surrounding districts of Nkandla and the Thukela River. During the week he lived in tents. Over weekends he stayed in a company house in Eshowe, near the Washesha Bus rank, that served as an office as well as a residence.

From Eshowe, Roger moved to the Northern Cape where he also worked in mineral exploration before going overseas for a while. Then South African De Beers' offered Roger a job in the security office on a ship. Thereafter Roger hitch-hiked up to Johannesburg to find work there. It so happened that the passer-by who stopped to offer Roger a lift was a geologist through whom Roger would end up working first in Botswana, and then, thanks to his isiZulu language skills, back in Eshowe.

In Eshowe Roger has taught at Eshowe High School and temped at the Teachers' Training College. He also got his own touring business off the ground by getting his licence and 'Permission to Occupy' a beautiful place on the Thukela River.

One day, in 1983, Roger was walking down Osborn Road, in Eshowe, when he ran into Gerhard Breedt who asked Roger what he was he was getting up to.

Roger replied, 'As you can see I am taking a walk through town.'

'Let's sit down and have a beer.'

That's when Roger was offered the position as Gerhard's assistant at the Environmental Centre in Eshowe. Roger loved his new position. Every school group that visited the centre had a different itinerary visiting various beaches and forests in Zululand.

After a year, Gerhard once more offered Roger a beer, during the drinking of which Gerhard announced his resignation and appointed Roger as the new headmaster of the Environmental Centre. The Ministry of Education changed the job description and Roger went from being headmaster of that institute to being senior subject advisor and finally deputy director.

Roger recently gave a talk at Eshowe's History Club about the Environmental Centre. He invited all staff whom he could locate to sit at his guests' table. Susan Bateman, who ran the hostel aspect of the centre for decades, was there, as was the cook, Samuel who delighted in that trip down memory lane.

Unfortunately, the centre was reallocated to the educational training of officials, following which, there was an apparent lack of annual servicing of equipment and one of the huge walk-in fridges shorted out, caught fire and burnt the place down.

V

Roger's wife, Anne-Louise Gaisford (née Skelton) lectured at the Eshowe College of Education until its closure in 2001. She then served as administrator for the Anglican Diocese of Zululand for 20 years. Her mother, Barbara Selley owned the first ever bed and breakfast establishment in Eshowe.

Barbara Selley, an incredibly talented artist, was a woman of intelligence and refinement. As a young teacher she had taught art to famous potter Maggie Mikula, and Maggie's sister, Jenny Hawke at St Mary's School when they were growing up in Kloof.

Roger and Anne-Louise's daughter, Lizzie Gaisford is musically gifted. She is joined by her partner the drummer, Strato Copteros, and musician, Dave Starke in the local band called the 'Katembes' who produce music that soon empties your glass and calls you to the dance-floor.

Before devoting his life full time to music, the talented and handsome Dave Starke taught at both Eshowe High School and The Holy Childhood Convent. I strongly suspect that the lady teachers put extra effort into the application of their cosmetics those days.

While on the subject of local musicians, let me tell you about the talented pianist, Jean White. Jean's father, David Alexander Kitchen Carnegie, was born in Northern Rhodesia, later Zambia, where his father, Alfred Carnegie was a mining engineer on the copperbelt. Alfred was the son of missionary doctor, David Carnegie, who was posted at the Moffatt Mission Station in Zambia during the late 19th century.

David Carnegie (Alfred's son and Jean's father) studied medicine at the Charing Cross Hospital in London, where he married Betty Carnegie, (née Carter). They had four children, Jean being the eldest who was born during the 1941 blitz.

Betty was a teacher who had majored in geography at the University of London. David and Betty were amateur actors and performed together in more than one Gilbert & Sullivan operetta. Decades later, during the 1970s, Jean, her sister, Alex, and their brother, John would be active members of the Eshowe Dramatic Society that was started by Vivienne Garside in 1973. They performed mostly in the Eshowe Town Hall.

Jean was only eight months old when her father, Dr David Carnegie was drafted into the Indian army (2nd World War) and stationed in Burma to be in charge of an ambulance train. Although he seldom spoke about his time in the war, it was obviously a traumatic time for him since it required performing surgeries close to the front line.

At the end of the war all troops fighting for the allies were sent home. David was demobilised to Rhodesia, not England. This obliged Betty and Jean to join him there. From Southampton they caught a passenger ship called the 'Carnarvon Castle' to Cape Town, and from there a train to Bulawayo where David met them at the station. Thus Jean consciously met her father for the first time at age five, having been a baby when he left for war.

In Rhodesia, now Zimbabwe, David was a government medical officer in Hartley, now Chegutu, where he built their own home from which he also ran a private practice. Thereafter, they relocated to Kariba, during the building of that great big dam, where David was in charge of the local hospital.

Jean spent her childhood in that medical household that owned a piano and an organ. Her paternal grandmother was a gifted pianist who had taught David to play. Both of Jean's parents had beautiful singing voices and together, during holiday celebrations and travelling in the car, they cheerfully sang along as a family.

Having no television or radio in the house, Jean spent many hours plonking away happily at those ebony and ivory keys. It was only when she started at Queen Elizabeth High School in Salisbury, now Harare, that she took formal piano and cello lessons.

In 1965 David decided to emigrate to South Africa. His brother, Alistair Carnegie, who had studied entomology at Rhodes University, was working at the sugar experiment station at Mount Edgecombe. He saw in the newspaper that Eshowe District Hospital was looking for a doctor.

And so David and Betty Carnegie arrived in Eshowe with the two youngest of their four children, John and Alex who were soon happily ensconced at Eshowe High School. By that time Jean was married and living overseas, and Patricia remained in Rhodesia where she married a farmer who was later ordained as an Anglican priest.

In her third year of studying music in Cape Town, Jean married Belgian-born architect, Ludo van Essche.

Jean and Ludo's first child, Paul was born in 1962. He was two-years-old when they emigrated to Spain. Jean remembers that in Spain the roads were too narrow for cars, so donkeys and donkey carts served as the only means of transport. Between 1964 and 1972, Jean and Ludo continued to travel and work outside of South Africa. Their second child, Cathy, was born in London. Their third child, Alex, was born in Nairobi. Thereafter they spent two years in Denmark followed by a spell in New York. Jean had a fabulous time in New York enjoying all that was culturally on offer. But, in 1972, she and Ludo separated, and that July Jean arrived at her parent's home in Eshowe Provincial Hospital 's staff house, with her three young children, Paul, Cathy and Alex. By then, her father, David Carnegie had been promoted to medical superintendent of Eshowe Provincial Hospital.

Jean soon found herself working as the town librarian and renting a house in Leigh Avenue from Bryan Hulett (As I mentioned, this was the house that Caryle Illing-Kippen bought). Jean's time at the library came to an end due to her staunch stand on equality for women. She refused point-blank to wear the compulsory uniform for women while male counterparts wore civvies.

Jean's mother, Betty Carnegie was very ill at the time. Following open-heart surgery, she died of complications in October 1972. David later married Iris Halse, matron of Eshowe Hospital. He died soon afterwards of a heart attack, in 1976, at the age of 59.

Prior to marrying Iris, David had asked his daughter, Jean to accompany him to the Freemason's annual ladies' night at the Royal Hotel. A fellow Freemason was attorney Wesley Ernest White, known to all as 'Hlope' which means the colour 'white' in isiZulu.

Hlope wanted his eldest son, David White to become a Freemason, so there was David White with his father at the ladies' night as was Jean with her own father, Dr David Carnegie.

A few evenings later, David White roared up that driveway in Leigh Avenue, entered Jean's kitchen and addressed Jean's children who had started attending Eshowe Junior School. 'Does anyone need help with their homework?' he asked.

That was the beginning of the couple known as David and Jean White who, together, in 1978, produced a son of their own, John White, who attended Eshowe schools. Today he lives in Durban. Paul lives in America and Alex lives in Johannesburg. Cathy lives in Eshowe with her husband, Malcolm Munro who arrived from Durban, in 1996, with six months left to complete his articles to be admitted as an attorney. He already had a master's degree in classics.

Malcolm worked for WE White Attorneys, which then belonged to Jean's brother-in-law, Don White. Don is Hlope's second son who is also a fellow artist. He was a good friend to Diamond Bozas and, later, to Anne Colenbrander.

Malcolm Munro subsequently bought the White family's legal practice ('WE White' that is housed in the old Barclay's Bank building on Osborn Road).

It had so happened that Hlope White initially started the legal firm after relocating to Eshowe from Vryheid. He and his wife, Heather White (née Whitehead) had their first son, David in Vryheid. Don and Jonathan were born at the Queen Victoria Hospital in Eshowe.

Hlope and Heather were popular socialites in Eshowe: both of their names appear on the honours' board at the Country Club as do David and Betty Carnegies'.

Hlope hired a room opposite the police station where a block of flats stands today. That building belonged to attorney Syd Brien who lived in the little house that is today the Church of Christ.

Hlope later relocated to rooms in the Star Theatre building. His two elder sons, David and Don, both graduated in law, while his youngest son, Jonathan studied journalism.

Although Jonathon was later to return to university and also graduate in law, he was first employed as the political sub-editor for the Natal Witness in Pietermaritzburg. Politics were rife with unending material those days.

After graduating from the University of Natal (Pietermaritzburg), David and Don joined their father's law firm in Eshowe, called 'WE White'. By then Hlope had served as chairman of Eshowe Town Board from 1952 to 1954, and as mayor from 1960 to 1965. His eldest, David White (Jean's husband and human rights activist), was to walk in his footsteps as mayor of Eshowe, from 1988 to 1989.

Syd Brien's home that is now the Church of Christ

David White was an extraordinary man, fighting relentlessly with government in Pretoria to allow multiracial representation at borough level. He finally got mixed-race and Indian representation, but not African.

David was best of friends with fellow attorney, Bryan Wynne, who had his own practice opposite WE White's offices. Sadly, they both met with tragic, untimely deaths. David, in 1993, at the age of only 49, when he suddenly fell ill and died ten days later. His and Jean's son, John White was a teenager at the time. David had been a wonderful father and step-father.

Bryan Wynne, also a popular man of much integrity, had died shortly before David in a motorcar accident. Jean White and Jan Wynne continue to enjoy a close friendship, travelling extensively together and calling on each other regularly.

Outspoken and animated, Jean White is a breath of fresh air. Always empathetic, she provides respite from life's tribulations. She is great fun with her lively views on family, friends, literature, religion and liberal politics.

Jean is also an excellent cook. Every Tuesday she invites her brother-in-law, Don White to lunch at her cosy and artistic home at Cedar Mews in Main Street.

VI

One of the earliest musicians in Eshowe was Earnest Brunner*.

In 1907 Earnest Brunner served as colonial treasurer under Sir Frederick Moor. He retired in 1916, during which time he served as chairman of Eshowe's local board, and died four years later.

There were other noteworthy Eshowe-ite musicians: the very first band in Eshowe was led by Tony Wantink who was born in Eshowe in 1897. That was the same year that Zululand was formally incorporated into Natal and, in the next few years, was open to white settlement.

Tony Wantink was a self-taught player of the saxophone, clarinet, trombone, piano accordion and penny whistle. He and his sister, Maisie, ran the band called 'Tony's Orchestra'. Besides providing music for dances and hotel openings, they played, free of charge, during the 2nd World War (1939- 1945), for British troops stationed at Eshowe.

For decades, before the age of television, life in Eshowe was not short of entertainment, what with private theatricals, amateur concerts and dances.

Picnics were had at Bishop's Seat or on the shaded banks of the Umlalazi River near Alfred Adam's mill, a little way below the bridge on the road to Melmoth.

Midnight moonlight rides were also popular. Most homes had a stable and carriage-house and harness room, but never a garage. Although Main Street and

---

*Please remember the name of this incredible pioneer who was an early storekeeper in Eshowe, moving on to his committed representation in the Natal Parliament from 1888 until that parliament was superceded by the Union Parliament in 1910. Those were a hectic 12 years during which much business expansion and building development took place in Eshowe.

Tony and Elsie's 50th wedding anniversary celebration in 1978

Gingindlovu Road were hardened with gravel; Kangela Street was usually a mess from the steel tyres of wagon wheels churning up the soil.

Musician Tony Wantink and his brother-in-law started a garage business in Osborn Road where the African Bank stands today. He also built a trading store in Kangela Street that became his little wood-and-iron home complete with an old style pantry allowing for airflow through metal gauzing.

He bought the first Harley Davidson motorcycle to arrive in Eshowe and he proposed to his wife, Elsie on that bike, threatening to ride faster and faster until she said, 'Yes!'

Chapter 4

Arnold Benjamin (Coley) Colenbrander matriculated, in 1930, during the height of the Great Depression. He served more than once as a temporary clerk in the magistrate's office in Melmoth. Getting to know the Zulu people included his attending of various ceremonies such as the customary Ihlamdo ceremony. It is held to wash the rust from the spears which had lain idle during a year of mourning, and to place that late chief's spirit among his ancestors.

Three of Coley's uncles had been magistrates in the Department of Justice causing Coley to repeatedly apply for that same position.

Coley attended his first regimental dance in the Eshowe Town Hall where he was issued with a clean shirt and trousers and a dance partner, in that order, for the occasion.

The Town Hall seats five hundred people, including a gallery to seat another hundred. It has a large stage and dressing room. Everything of consequence happened in the Town Hall: dances, weddings, fêtes, beauty-queen competitions, concerts etc. It has been described as a hybrid between a Norman arch and a Dutch oven. The façade features a bell-less belfry that

symbolises Christianity while the five rocks at the corners of the foundation symbolise the amaZulu's meeting place. The huge arched entrance with moulded motif symbolise the dome-shaped thatched dwellings of the early amaZulu.

I

In 1935 Coley was transferred to Umgeni Court in Pietermaritzburg where promotion was largely dependent on qualifying in law, so he attended lectures at night until completing the final part of the Lower Law Certificate. In 1936 Coley was transferred to Nqutu where he was eventually appointed as assistant magistrate and native commissioner. He continued with his studies, walking in the footsteps of his uncles*.

Coley recorded his memoirs in a book called 'Coley's Odyssey', from which I glean much of this information. The book relates tales including those of close encounters with death after Coley enlisted for the 2nd World War in 1940. He was mobilised with the Umvoti Mounted Rifles which was based in Pietermaritzburg. His wife-to-be, Anne Thorburn was studying at the Teachers' Training College there. Coley described Anne as a well-developed, intelligent and spirited girl who played the double-bass in the Convent Orchestra. She also took the part of the policeman in 'Pirates of Penzance'. Anne was also an extremely talented florist. She, in turn, was entranced with Coley who was to be her romantic hero of war and wilderness.

Along with many fellow soldiers, on 22nd July 1941, Coley boarded His Majesty's troopship 'Dunera' and headed off to suffer the flies, sand storms, daytime

*HJ Colenbrander was a magistrate in the very early days in Zululand when it was under British rule, and Ben Colenbrander was a magistrate in Zululand in the 1890s.

heat, night time cold, and the glare of the big white desert, in Israel. Later, he was to command tanks across Italy during which time he visited Florence to see, among other artworks, Michelangelo's 'David'.

When the war ended, on 30th April 1945, Coley returned home after an absence of five-and-a-half years.

After setting up home and a magnificent garden with Anne, he started studying for the Civil Service Higher Law exam, qualifying at the end of 1952. This legal knowledge was to stand him in good stead, even after his retirement, in 1976, when he continued, until 1989, to act as assessor in the supreme court circuit in Zululand. Anne, in the meantime, competed at the first World Flower Show in Bath, in 1984, and then in Paris, winning an award in 1990. She also served a term of office as president of the Natal panel of floral art judges.

Flash-back to 1952. Coley was offered the official post of administering the four tribes of the Eastern Caprivi in a wild area covering five thousand square miles of reed beds, marshes and untamed bush. There he would serve his tour of duty for four years until 1956. The locals there (largely pastoral people or fishermen) totalled a population of seventeen thousand. Their herds of cattle required that Coley occasionally had cause to hunt out problematic lion and crocodiles. Previously, wounded elephants were also shot when necessary, and their tusks sold for proceeds credited to the local tribal fund. Coley's private collection of trophies were later on display at the historical village at Midmar Dam near Howick in the Natal Midlands.

The 'Residency' at the Caprivi lent itself to gracious entertaining, and at this Anne excelled. There was a swimming pool and Coley and Anne built a tennis court. In fact, the 'Residency' was almost the only place, within hundreds of miles around, with the amenities to entertain. The lawn ran down to boats on the waters of the Zambezi, a hundred miles upstream of the Victoria Falls, and spearfishing was popular among youngsters.

Anne, quite a frontiers woman, became an expert on tiger fishing. She never learned to shoot but was an excellent driver of the Jeep, negotiating deep sand and swerving to avoid crashing into trees, and sometimes dodging lions and elephants.

Back in South Africa, Coley spent a memorable six years guiding the formation of the Territorial Authority and the functioning of the new self-governing state of KwaZulu. While stationed at Nongoma he had many dealings with minister Mangosuthu Buthelezi, Prince Gideon Zulu, and other dignitaries with whom he formed the nucleus of what was yet to be called the 'KwaZulu Administration'.

Coley was well-loved by everyone, black and white. During the 1970s he became particularly friendly with Prince Gideon Zulu with whom he went camping and shooting on the Mkuze flats. Later, in 1992, Coley accompanied the prince to the Zululand Show where the prince had entered several of his pure white royal herd of cattle. He was awarded the 'best on show' cup for his prize Nguni bull.

Coley and Anne lived at the Eshowe 'Residency' for seven years, between 1963 and 1969.

II

Today's Kwikspar used to be the part of Adams Store that sold traditional Zulu items. Today's 'Shoprite' was Adams supermarket and hardware department. Clothing departments were where the other shops adjoin Shoprite today. They stocked babywear, sportswear, school wear, ladies wear and gentlemen's outfitting.

Alfred Adams

Also hats hosiery, gloves, shoes and cosmetics. There was a haberdashery department selling wool and dressmaking materials.

Behind the bakery was a tearoom. Then came the art department complete with sign-writer and window-dresser who painted all the price posters and tickets. The bottle store was the only freestanding bottle store in Eshowe – not an 'off sales' which had to be attached to a hotel.

In 1981 that family business, 'A Adams of Eshowe, Zululand' celebrated its Centenary. Sisters Jenny Hawke and Maggie Mikula, (née Suttie), were the sole owners. Jenny played a major part in buying and selling for the lady's showroom and school-wear departments. By then they had a staff of 160 members.

Maggie Mikula wrote a book to commemorate the store which was founded by her and Jenny's great-grandfather, Alfred Adams in 1881. Maggie's book, 'The Adams' Story', tells about the pioneering lives of the tough, enterprising and daring Alfred Adams and his son, Charlie Adams.

Born in 1841 in Maidstone, Kent, England, Alfred was the son of Aber Adams, a tailor, and his wife Mary Adams (née Baker). Alfred was raised as a 'farm boy' in the Kentish countryside in England.

Blessed with abundant enthusiasm, tempered by both common sense and a keen sense of humour, Alfred joined the University Mission at the age of 19. He served a six-months training period before being sent to Africa.

His party sailed from Plymouth aboard the mail steamer, 'Cambrian', on 6th October 1860. They arrived in Cape Town on 12th November.

Alfred was sent off to central Africa where he bore the title of 'Agriculturist'. His youthfulness earned him the nickname of 'Boy' Adams.

Missionary and adventurer, David Livingstone awaited Alfred's party of 13 people led by Bishop Mackenzie, at the mouth of the Zambezi, in order to send them to the Shire Islands of Nyasaland, now Malawi. Livingstone reported that area as being a fertile region abounding in game, and with a healthy climate. There, Alfred was to encourage the local Africans to grow cotton and coffee, to replace what he thought was the less respectable pastime of that particular tribe – selling off their own people as slaves in exchange for food. Of course spiritual instruction was a given.

Alfred almost immediately came down with malaria, but his constitution was yet to prove the strongest of them all during further ravages of the fever. Passengers succumbing to malaria were buried among the reeds along the banks of the river.

That trip north to Malawi was not easy sailing. They were often halted by sand banks. However, there was much interest in the varied species of plants and birdlife along the shore. Alfred also found the people fascinating: tribal music and dancing was always entertaining, but the physical disfigurements, most curious. Men had a triangular notch filed into their front teeth, women wore big rings in their lips around which their lips grew in the likeness of a snout.

Alfred, himself, was later described thus by fellow hunting companion, Captain Ludlow, in his book 'Zululand and Cetewayo': *'An exceedingly handsome, soldier-like man with expressive features, spoke all the native dialects like a native, and I could not possibly have found a better or more suitable companion'.*

Captain Ludlow's book further relates shared hunting adventures in Zululand. It is a fascinating record of the country and its people at that time.

During Alfred's trip to Malawi, hippo and crocodiles teemed on the banks, providing sport for hunters. But the hippo meat was not much appreciated. I am reminded about the time my first husband's father shot a lone hippo that, for months, made a nuisance of itself at the dam on the family farm, attacking everyone who tried to get near the pump. The biltong was so rock hard we had to use a hammer to fragment it. But it was most tasty on Ouma's home-baked bread and farm butter.

Back to Alfred Adams, in 1860: the missionaries encountered parties of slaves along the river route. They would chase off the drivers, then feed, clothe and free the slaves. They also came across many European hunting parties. It was estimated in those days, that England required more than sixteen thousand elephant tusks for the manufacture of billiard balls and piano keys, and thousands of hippos were shot for their ivory that was used for the manufacture of mathematical instruments and false teeth.

Eventually, the missionaries arrived at Magomero where Alfred Adams proved himself a capable carpenter. Unable to return to their own tribes, many freed slaves remained with the missionaries at Magomero. They were given schooling classes according to their age. Meals were mostly goats' meat with sweet potatoes or porridge.

They drank tea with goats' milk. The numbers in the camp rose to over two hundred.

In 1863, a new bishop arrived to replace Bishop

Mackenzie who had died from malaria. The new bishop found a much depleted party. Of the original 13 missionaries only four remained. Then, ravaged by fever, three returned to England. Alfred Adams was the only one at the station who had been a member of the original party. He returned to England, early in 1864, after the closure of that Zambesi mission, where he had spent three years gaining experience as an industrial teacher.

The Mackenzie Memorial Fund, raised by the late Bishop Mackenzie's sister in England, rose to the occasion when they heard of Reverend Robinson's lonely work at KwaMagwaza, and his need for an assistant. Alfred Adams was the immediate choice.

And so, at the age of 23, Alfred came back from England to Zululand. He boarded a ship in December 1864, docking at Port Natal on 24th February 1865. On that same ship was Selina Wood, who would become Alfred's wife. She was a lovely girl with long golden ringlets and deep-set dark eyes.

Alfred and Selina Adams were stationed at the first Anglican Mission Station at KwaMagwaza where they struck up a lasting friendship with Reverend Robinson. Alfred's first task was to build a long-needed church.

Eventually, in 1869, King Mpande gave his permission for amaZulu to attend church. Previously, death had been the penalty for those who chose Christianity*. At KwaMagwaza, Alfred's chores included building, preaching, schooling and ministering to the needs of the sick. After his five-year contract was up he decided to establish his and Selina's own farm on the north bank of the Thukela River, eight kilometres

*The very first Holy Communion in Zululand, administered by earlier missionaries, took place back in 1837.

 inland from the mouth where Alfred had built their first house on property presented to him by his good friend King Mpande. However, Alfred did continue some involvement with the missionaries that included the building of a house at the new mission station, St Andrews. St Andrews was situated closer to the coast where good crops of maize, pine-apples, bananas and palms grew freely.

Alfred Adams' building efforts required that he sometimes travelled 50 miles, by wagon, to the forests to cut wood and bring it home. Indeed, Alfred Adams was most tenacious (and optimistic) by nature. During the preZulu-War unrest in 1878, he continued making preparations to plant crops at St Andrews. This was despite an uneasy pre-war atmosphere exacerbated by Cethswayo's impis who were impatient to 'wash their spears' in enemy blood, so they could be allowed to marry.

English troops set up on the Thukela, eventually forcing a protesting Alfred, Selina and their young son, Charles (Charlie) to move from St Andrews. Back in 1874 Selina Adams gave birth to Charlie two years before she died from dysentery in 1876.

During the Zulu War in 1879 St Andrews was totally destroyed, as was KwaMagwaza because Cethswayo did not want it occupied by the British. Soon after that war Alfred returned to St Andrews and set about restoring his crops and buildings. Then, from 1881 to 1899, he became

Adams Camp Store

military purveyor for the two thousand plus British soldiers (called 'Tommies' or 'Redcoat Troops') who were stationed at Eshowe in a large tented camp named 'Fort Curtis', after their commanding officer.

During those two decades the soldiers played a large role in the construction of roads and town buildings. Also the digging of the public swimming pool. Much of the labour used to build the very first Anglican Church was also supplied by the Redcoat Garrison.

Alfred was interested in the prospects of trading. After securing the contract as military purveyor, to supply the garrison of troops, he established his own camp store close to Fort Curtis, in the vicinity of where Eshowe Sports' Club and East Toyota stands today, at the northern end of Mangosuthu Buthelezi Drive.

East's Service Station (Pty) Ltd was in fact first established in Osborn Road, in 1943, by Michael East, a returning 2nd World War veteran. In 2004 I did some temporary work in the office of Chris Henstock and Stan Ferguson. They had purchased East's Service Station from Michael East in 1988.

Chris Henstock (born in Swaziland but a resident of Eshowe for 55 Years) was an Eshowe High School graduate, who then, along with my brother-in-law Neville Nixon, Peter Baccus and Andy Craig served articles with Campbell & Craig, later Coopers & Lybrand, now C & H accounting firm.

Chris did his National Service with the SANDF, in 1971, in South West Africa, later Namibia, on the northern border. In 1976 he was appointed financial director of East's Service Station, the BP and Toyota dealer that he and Stan would purchase in 1988.

The old Fort Curtis property near Eshowe Sports' Club was purchased on auction by East's Service Station in 1991. The entire property was then covered with a gum tree plantation, some of these trees being over 60 years old.

Chris appointed Eric Steenberg to cut and clear these trees from the land. And all stumps were removed. Numerous artefacts were found on the property which were duly handed over to the Fort Museum. Then the cleared property was cultivated with maize, and fenced.

A short while after, the property was sold to Dieter Witthoft who developed 'East Toyota'. It stands near to the Fort Curtis site where Alfred Adam's Camp Store had once been situated.

Later, in 1998, Chris Henstock and Stan Ferguson purchased the previously known NMI building (Mercedes, then Nissan franchise). They converted the dealership building to a shopping centre called 'Eshowe Arcade'.

In 2007 Chris paid out Stan Ferguson and was then the sole owner/shareholder of the property and the BP fuel station in town (Osborn Road). In 2016 Chris sold that property and business. He retained the Eshowe Arcade until 2021 and then sold this as well. Presently he is retired in Langebaan in the Western Cape. The Henstock family were close friends of the Gunter family who are sugar cane farmers in the Entumeni district.

III

Alfred Adams became the 'Tommies' advocate, philosopher and friend. His 'Adams Camp Store' was an iron-roofed building with a wooden veranda. The front yard sprouted a number of wattle trees that served as tethering posts for horses. The bulk of supplies included sugar, salt, flour, matches, candles, soap and beer.

The beer was collected from his warehouse on the Point in Durban where barrels were stored after being offloaded from the ships. That warehouse was built of mud and stone to keep the beer cold. Alfred had built up a large fleet of 13 wagons drawn by matched teams of 18 to 22 oxen. Those oxen were outspanned on grazing land behind Camp Store. After loading up the beer, the wagons would collect other supplies along West Street, and over the Berea through to the toll gate that charged 2/6d. It was a long slow haul over rough tracks through bush and grasslands and rivers without bridges. That return trip from Durban to Eshowe took three weeks. Today, by car, it takes less than three hours.

Riding wagons was a regular occupation, those days, as it was the only means of conveying supplies to stores in country districts. Despite their rough lifestyle, transport riders were mostly dashing figures – deeply suntanned and wearing rough flannel shirts, corduroy riding breeches, long riding boots and broad-brimmed hats sporting decorative feathers. Facing daily dangers, they were armed with only a hunting knife and a heavy riding whip.

In 1883 Alfred remarried, but sadly his new wife, Elizabeth Best who had arrived in Durban from England in 1867, died three days later at the age of 45. Over a year later, at the age of 46, Alfred married again. His third wife was Ellen Norwood (also known as 'Aunty Nell'). The Norwoods were a distinguished family from Kent, England.

Alfred purchased a large piece of land in Eshowe where he built the family home called 'Norwood' (after

Aunty Nell). It was a spacious wood-and-iron house surrounded by verandas, and a magnificent garden bordered by tall trees and bush. It was situated just behind the Convent north of the golf course. This was the building which was later relocated by Lawrence Dunn, to the Museum Village, to serve as Adam's Outpost Restaurant.

When Alfred Adams was building Norwood he ordered a fine pair of iron gates from England. There are two stories regarding those gates. Story no 1: The wagon carrying them was overturned in the Thukela River crossing at Bond's Drift. There, the gates lay under the water for six months until they were salvaged and brought to Eshowe to be installed. Story no 2: The wagon carrying the gates overturned and the gates were washed away in the current, making necessary the purchase of yet another set of expensive iron gates.

Alfred and Selina's son, little Charlie Adams had been cared for by his grandmother, Naomi Wood in her wood-and-iron house in Durban's West Street. He attended primary school at New Guelderland and was then sent to the Berea Academy in Musgrave Road. After serving an apprenticeship with Randles Bros, and Hudson General Merchants in Durban, he came to Eshowe to take over his father, Alfred's business.

Charlie Adams, or 'Shali Laduma', as he was known to the amaZulu, was a man with a head for business. He also readily involved himself in many projects in the service of Eshowe's community.

In the meantime, Alfred appointed one of his employees, Norwegian Gabriel Egeland to manage the camp store in Eshowe while he ventured north to expand nomadic trading with the amaZulu. Egeland was later joined at Adam's business by his brother, JJ Egeland, who later became the Norwegian Consul in Durban.

Loaded with two ox-wagons of merchandise, Alfred set off to Nongoma where he hastily outspanned and off-loaded some corrugated iron from the wagons to commence building a shelter against a heavy storm. That shelter developed into a storeroom and, in later years still, into Adams Store and Wayside Inn (subsequently known as the Imperial Hotel). This was where Alfred had, in fact, planned to place his son, Charlie to develop the branch.

Alfred's importing of mealie meal and hauling heavy bottles by wagon to and fro from Durban to Eshowe, for those many officers at the mess, was proving too costly. So Alfred Adams set up a milling plant and mineral water factory on the Yardley's farm, about four kilometres out of Eshowe on the road to Melmoth. His machinery was powered by an improvised waterfall that had been ingenuiusly constructed by mining through solid rock. The marble bottle-stoppers were imported from England and bore the inscription 'A ADAMS ESHOWE'. To flavour the water, Alfred imported, also from England, lemon and ginger syrups that came in large brown stoneware jars.

The mill closed down, in 1920, when it became cheaper to fetch mineral drinks from Durban by rail.

In the meantime, young Charlie fell in love with Una Norwood, a young relative of his stepmother (Alfred's third wife) Aunty Nell's. After their engagement, Una returned to England in 1899, to retrieve her 'bottom drawer'.

They married on her return, in October 1899, on the very day that the first shots were fired in the 2nd Anglo-Boer War.

Charlie and Una Adams' first home in Eshowe was

The old stone and iron mill on the Umlalazi River

a little wood-and-iron cottage situated at the rear of Adams Camp store. They soon became parents of a son named Basil Norwood Adams and a daughter, Gladys Una Adams who were both born in Eshowe. Una had trained at the Slade School of Art in London. Combining her artistic talent with her domestic skills, she created beautiful sketches and embroideries.

The township of Eshowe at that time had only about 50 buildings. The nucleus of the town was the courthouse near the 'Residency', a few houses of other officials, the Queen Victoria Hospital, the Anglican Church, a few government offices, the school, the library and the Masonic Lodge. Slightly northwards, on what was to become known as Tally's Corner, was the Mission Press (later the Zululand Times), and the Provincial Hotel (later the George Hotel). Where the railway bridge is now, was a muddy dip in the road.

At the turn of the 20th century, the military vacated the town, but Adams Camps Store continued a thriving trade with the locals, selling or bartering mostly blankets, salt, beads and tobacco. To this day snuff is a popular product among the amaZulu. They traditionally made their own mixture from home grown tobacco and dried aloe leaves.

Charlie opened a butchery in Osborn road, that was to develop into the large outlet called 'Adams'. Charlie's father, Alfred Adams was, by then, confined to a wheelchair. But even though his mobility had deserted him, he never lost that invincible spirit that always urged him on. For example, in 1906, when the Bambatha Rebellion was breaking out, all the white women and children were evacuated from Eshowe. Men moved into laager for better protection. Charlie's wife, Una, however, remained to look after her father-in-law, Alfred who adamantly refused to budge.

Eventually he was persuaded to move by the commandant and, on 5th July 1906, Una, wearing a hat (as did everyone those days unless they were dancing), hastened him away on a wagon to Gingindlovu to catch the train to Durban. There he suffered a heart attack and died at Lamb's Hotel. His gravestone at St Andrews appropriately reads: 'Rest, for thy day's work is done'. An extract from the Zululand Times read: *'Mr Adams was requisitioned but declined to submit himself to election to the First Natal Parliament. He took a valiant interest in public life and the welfare of everyone, irrespective of colour or creed and was greatly respected and loved by those who had the privilege of knowing his great kindness and benevolence. After a very active and strenuous career, in his declining years, Mr Adams handed over to his son, Charles. He had spent the last years of his life in what he called 'monotonous inactivity'.*

Aunty Nell lived at Norwood with Charlie and Una for a few years before returning to England.

Charlie and Una's children, Basil and Gladys, attended Eshowe Public School. Between school terms the family accompanied Charlie on his many trips to the store and hotel at Nongoma. One time they were held up in Melmoth by heavy rains while the White Umfolozi rose in flood.

After ten days, when the river had subsided somewhat, Basil and Gladys were carried across on the shoulders of the taller amaZulu, while others attempted to push the carriage across, with Una remaining in it.

Charlie had tied the bridles of six horses to each wheel. The water was chest deep and there was the danger of quick-sand but with the help of 23 strong amaZulu pushing and pulling, with Una by this time perched on top of the carriage, they managed to reach the other side. The poor horses came adrift and were washed half a mile down the river tied in pairs. Charlie, stripped to the waist, retrieved them – exhausted but alive.

IV

Prior to his retirement, in 1916, trader and magistrate Earnest Brunner sold up his home, 'Samarang', and his store in Eshowe. Charlie Adams bought the store.

By 1920, Charlie had also acquired Mr A Garrard's store. Mr Garrard retired to grow cotton in the Nkwaleni Valley. His wife, Mrs JG Garrard was awarded the MBE (a British honour awarded by the King or Queen), in 1919, for services rendered during the 1914 to 1918 war.

The main Adams establishment (as opposed to Adams Camp Store) was now concentrated on Osborn Road where, as we have noted, Shoprite and OK stand today. In addition, Charlie owned the store and hotel in Nongoma, as well as other stores as far away as Ulundi.

In 1908 a devastating epidemic of East Coast Fever swept Zululand, resulting in the loss of almost all cattle. This was particularly serious for the amaZulu because their cattle were their monetary system and most important possession. When Alfred Adams started trading the cost of a blanket was one cow. East Coast Fever also took its toll on the trek oxen so mules were used in their place, for carting provisions from Durban, until the railway became effective.

At different times in his career, Charlie was a member of the Eshowe Town Board. He served twice as mayor (from 1918-1920 and from 1925-1927). He was a member of many associations, clubs, societies and sporting bodies, as well as vicar's church warden of St Michaels for many years.

However, Charlie was happiest with a fishing rod in his hands at a quiet waterside spot. Many family holidays were spent on the coast at places such as Compensation Beach, which in those days, was remote and unspoilt.

Charlie loved animals. He had a pet crow that sat perched on his shoulder, and during the era of the Eshowe Race Track, where regular race meetings were held, he kept a fine stable of race horses at Norwood. His racing colours were blue and gold.

Charlie maintained the close friendship which his father, Alfred had established with the Zulu royal house. Dinuzulu's royal kraal was near Nongoma so he obtained supplies from that Adams branch.

Later, during the 1930s, Charlie assisted Dinuzulu's son, Paramount Chief Solomon as his financial advisor and friend. He was a frequent visitor to Solomon's kraal at Malhashini, often with Una and Gladys in tow.

In 1935 Charlie presented a fine collection of historical Zulu items on loan to the Natal Museum in Pietermaritzburg. Called 'The Adams Collection', these items were personal gifts to Alfred and Charlie from members of the Zulu royal family. They comprised of ivory jewelry, snuff boxes, drinking tumblers and walking sticks.

Charlie's fluency in isiZulu and his understanding of Zulu customs resulted in him serving as unofficial

Adams Departmental Store that was later converted into the building that Kwikspar and Shoprite occupy today

adviser, to the government, on the affairs of Zululand. During 1931, he also communicated with the British House of Commons regarding trade between Britain and Zululand. He was frequently called upon to address meetings – sometimes with as many as three thousand amaZulu present.

V

In 1931 a town supply water scheme was put in place. It included a weir crossing over the Umlalazi River which was estimated to supply 35 thousand gallons a day, a purification plant, and a gravity tower holding 40 thousand gallons at a height of 15 metres.

Charlie's son, Basil Adams was the then resident town engineer. Although born and bred in Eshowe, he had trained and qualified as a mechanical engineer in England. He joined Mr M Butt, Eshowe's consulting engineer, and Mr WV Roberts to complete Rutledge Dam which, when finally built, stored seven million gallons with a delivery rate of 100 thousand gallons a day. And so water was turned on in February 1935. The main supply of water before then was from rainwater tanks. Given Eshowe's high summer rainfall figures, that captured water was adequate, providing that residents were not too wasteful with bathwater. The only form of sanitary use was the pit-privy long-drop. A sewage scheme was long in the making due to the expense of implementation due to the scattered nature of the town.

As well as engineering the construction of Rutledge Park Dam, Basil also engineered the water-treatment works that are situated two blocks from Mike's and my home, and he implemented electricity for which, in 1931, two schemes regarding the provision of power to Eshowe were put before the board. One proposed

 hydro-electric power from the Umlalazi River, the other was for the use of crude-oil engines. They went with the latter option and, in February 1933, foundations were laid behind WE White's building which then housed Barclays Bank. Street lights were switched on in May that same year.

Basil Adams was a member of the town board and served several times as chairman. He was elected mayor of Eshowe, from 1946 to 1951, and he hosted the king and queen and two princesses of Wales during their royal visit in 1947 (pictured above).

At the time, Basil's wife, Mrs Lillian Adams was seriously ill so Basil was deprived of her help and support on that day. She was replaced as official hostess by Mrs Riddell, wife of deputy chairman of the board, Mr CWD Riddell, who had been chairman in 1938, and again from 1942 to 1945. The ballroom at the country club on that occasion, in 1947, was tastefully decorated by the Women's Committee. The floor was covered with animal hides borrowed from Captain Potter of the Hluhluwe Game Park.

At the aerodrome, a Zulu war dance was held for the visiting royalty who received a thundering 'Bayete!' The dance was most boisterous with some rushes right up to the royal stand where the royal family appeared to be quite anxious at times.

In the meantime, Basil and Gladys' mother (Charlie's wife), Una Adams was a staunch worker for the Red

Cross. For 23 years she was also the honourable treasurer of the Eshowe Tennis Club. Her home, Norwood, was the centre of hospitality to distinguished guests. On several occasions visitors from Government House and politicians from Britain stayed over at Norwood. Charlie usually arranged to take such visitors hunting or fishing.

In 1942 Charlie died in the Queen Victoria Hospital in Eshowe, at the age of 68. Una died two years later.

Their son, Basil Adams took over his father's business. He and his wife, Lillian had two children: John in 1929, and Ann in 1931. Basil continued the active role which Charlie had played in the rural cattle auction sales up until 1949, when the contract was transferred to the nationalist government which had recently come into power.

Lillian Adams died in 1950. Two years later Basil relinquished his interest in the family business to continue his career in engineering. He left Eshowe for Zambia and then, in 1953, he retired to Kenya.

The Eshowe business, Adams & Son Ltd, was taken over by Basil's sister, Gladys, and her husband, David Suttie who was a retired sugar farmer and former bank inspector then living at Kloof. Young Jenny Suttie, who would one day become Mrs Jenny Hawke, was nine at the time; Maggie Suttie, who would one day become Mrs Maggie Mikula, was eleven. They were attending St Mary's School where my friend, Anne-Louise Gaisford's mother, Barbara Selley taught a rt. Widowed Barbara Selley was 'Mrs Skelton' then, before being romantically whisked away to Eshowe by Zululand farmer Geoff Selley.

Once relocated to Eshowe, the Suttie girls attended the Eshowe Public School where Jenny became classmates with John McHugh (more about him later). They were taught by Mrs Kolbe in the very first prefabricated classroom.

In the same year (1952) Norwood was sold and the old camp store was moved to Adams & Co in town. This was due to that area being rezoned for residential use only.

Gladys did not marry until much later in life. She had adored her father, Charlie Adams, and often accompanied him on fishing expeditions. She completed her high school education in Pietermaritzburg and moved on to study speech and drama in London. She thus gave elocution lessons in Eshowe, as well as assisting as a cashier at Adams. Jenny has, in her home today, the cashier's chair her mum sat on.

Gladys created a magical garden at Norwood by laying out paths among lily ponds, erecting rose trellises and planting myriads of flowers. Her efforts were rewarded by it being judged 'Show Garden of Zululand' for several years running.

As late as the mid-1950s, Adams deliveries were done by horse and cart. A familiar evening sound was the hiss of the rubber tyres on the sandy driveway and the clop-clop of old Whisky's hooves as the tented cart returned to Norwood after a day's rounds.

Jenny and Maggie moved on to live extremely creative lives. Maggie became a renowned potter, and Jenny served, from 1994 to 2008, as curator of the Fort Museum in Eshowe – managing, hosting and arranging re-enactments to arouse strong passions from worlds gone by. Jenny had relieved curator Lynn Oakley, who left suddenly to escape the fear instilled by the Bureau of State Security because she hosted black guests. Gunshots were actually aimed at her house. Jenny, up until then, had been working for the town library since the closure

Jenny Hawke pictured outside Norwood prior to Lawrence Dunn relocating it to serve as Adam's Outpost restaurant at the Museum Village

of Adams Stores. She was told to take her knitting along to the museum while the board found a qualified curator. No one applied so Jenny got the post, and made an excellent job of it too. Leaving at retirement age, she ended what she refers to as 'a very exciting, fulfilling and demanding period in her life'.

I became friends with Jenny, in 1996, when I donated a zebra skin to the museum. Having been brought up in a hunting family it was inevitable that I end up inheriting taxidermy and animal hides. My husband at the time, Pat Brenchley refused to have 'dead animals' in the house. Jenny received my donation with her generous and captivating smile. I was yet to get to know the slender, self-assured and poised Jenny Hawke as a sociable, cultured intellectual with a colourful ethnic sense of style in both home and wardrobe.

Prior to curatorship of the museum, Jenny had thrown herself into all the hype around the local ANC/IFP/3rd Force local violence, with foreign journalists pitching for information, the army arriving in a convoy of two hundred armoured vehicles and six hundred experienced troops billeted at the showgrounds. The commandant visited Jenny at the museum, persuading her to host the four international peace monitors for over six weeks.

Chapter 5

Graham Chennells was mayor of Eshowe from 1984 to 1986. His wife, Meg Chennells (née Braatvedt) was Zululand Show Queen in 1976. Meg's family had a fascinating history. Her great-grandparents, Nils and Elisabeth Braatvedt were Norwegians who sailed from Bergen in 1880, to serve in the Norwegian Mission Society in Natal and Zululand. Their first stop was the Lutheran Mission Station at Mapumulo where they learned to speak, read and write isiZulu.

After Mapumulo, Nils and Elisabeth Braatvedt moved on to establish mission stations at Nkonjeni near Ulundi, then Ekhombe, which is between Nkandla and Kranskop, and finally at Ongoye not far from where the University of Zululand's campus stands today.

The congregation of the Eshowe Lutheran Church was founded much later in 1959. In 1963 Reverend J Muller-Nederbock became their pastor at the church building on the corner of Leigh Avenue and Dickens Street, a few blocks from Mike's and my home.

Nils and Elisabeth Braatvedt had three sons and a daughter. Their sons, Eilert, Hjalmer and John all became magistrates. Their daughter, Marie married Llewellyn Jenkinson, Viv Jenkinson's father.

Eilert and Florrie Braatvedt's children were Douglas, Charles, Harold, Norman and Eve. Harold married Honor Leakey and they had five children: Ron, Sonja, our Meg, Dave and Gray.

Meg's great-uncle, Hjalmer Braatvedt was a native commissioner in Zululand during the 1920s and 30s. The book: 'Roaming Zululand with a Native Commissioner' by HP Braatvedt, published in 1949, is available at

Meg Chennells née Braatvedt was Zululand Show Queen in 1976. On her right is Princess Debbie Radcliffe, on her left is Patricia Bergh and behind Debbie is fourth choice, blonde Kathleen Barratt, next to whom is 1975 Show Queen, Lynette Craig. Next to Lynette is the fifth choice, Correen Reeves

the Museum Village's research room. It is an authentic account of the experiences and activities of one of South Africa's senior magistrates and native commissioners, Hjalmer Braatvedt, the second son of missionaries Nils and Elisabeth Braatvedt.

The book records the experiences of the Braatvedt family during those dangerous days when they sought safety while in flight from Ulundi, during the Dinuzulu Rebellion in 1888. It also documents the opening up of Zululand and hitherto unpublished details and anecdotes connected with the Bambatha Rebellion, as well as the capture of the Nqutu and Ingwavuma Magistracies during the Anglo-Boer War.

Meg Chennells' father's father was author Hjalmer's older brother, Eilert. He and his wife, Florrie retired during the 2nd World War, after which their sons, Doug and Harold joined them in Eshowe.

The charm of Hjalmer Braatvedt's book lies in its obvious sincerity, as it is written by a man who loved the veld and the people who lived on it. Another value of the book lies in the authentic narrative it gives of the customs, hardships and somewhat 'elastic' administration that attempted to meet the needs of any particular set of circumstances those days, sometimes departing from the strict letter of the law to ensure that common sense prevailed.

Of course, in the new South Africa, there is no such official as a native commissioner. Rural communities now fall under their closest municipality.

Traditional Zulu tribal ceremonies such as weddings, burial, and ancestral worship, are written as an appendix to Hjalmer Braatvedt's book. I am particularly fascinated by the spiritual and symbolic value of cattle in Zulu culture. Today, it is not uncommon for our Zulu neighbours in urban suburbs to sacrifice a beast on special occasions. I can see by Hjalmer Braatvedt's accounts that this is so important a tradition it is unlikely to die out.

With regards to the wife's dowry called 'lobolo', messengers are sent from the bride-to-be's family to collect cattle as payment for the bride. Another beast must be handed over at the same time as the lobolo cattle, as a thanks-offering to the bride's mother for having looked after her daughter. If the groom's father is a wealthy man he will also give the bride a beast which is killed and eaten by her followers. The bride's own father invariably kills a beast to serve as an ordinary feast for his daughter before she leaves for marriage.

As I've mentioned, Meg's grandparents retired during

the 2nd World War after which their sons, Doug and Harold joined them to live in Eshowe.

Doug worked for Barclays Bank. Harold was a sales representative for Mr Frolich, a local businessman selling fridges and vacuum cleaners.

Doug and Harold used their combined savings to buy an ex-army truck. They got a bus's body built onto the chassis, and with that vehicle, in 1946, Harold started the bus service called 'Washesha' meaning 'to be quick' (it was also the war cry of the Mandlakaza Zulu tribe). Harold drove that first bus himself, up and down between Eshowe and Empangeni.

Doug and Rene built a house on a five-acre plot near the Eshowe Sports' Club. The very first bus depot was on their property. Rene later sold the property, to Diamond Bozas, when she moved into town. That's where Diamond had his nursery and art studio that I've told you about.

Then the Braatvedts bought a second bus, so Doug resigned from his work at the bank in order to drive that new vehicle.

Their first bus rank in town was in Osborn Road on vacant land opposite the Town Hall. When the Lagerwall brothers bought that property to build the Star Theatre, the rank was running the buses and their father, Harold was farming full time. Routes by then included the entire hinterland of Eshowe.

The Braatvedt family owned Washesha Bus Service for almost half a century before selling to KwaZulu Transport in 1995. By then the fleet had grown to 65 buses with depots in Eshowe, Empangeni and Gingindlovu. One story I heard was that the bus drivers were expected to clean their vehicles after each shift but one driver's bus always arrived at the depot on the given day, in spick and span condition. When asked how he

My daughter, Lara and her husband, Martin Boshoff had some of her wedding photos taken at the depot

did it, he replied that he instructed the passengers to throw all their refuse out of the window to save him the extra work.

Harold Braatvedt, a retired Eshowe-ite farmer by then, died at the age of 84 when the light aircraft he was travelling in crashed while taking up a group of skydivers, including a nine-year-old boy who survived the crash. Harold had been a fighter pilot flying a Curtiss P-40 Kittyhawk powered by an Allison engine during the 2nd World War. He loved flying so much that after the war he bought his own aircraft and got his private pilot's licence.

He was an enthusiastic man who embraced life, and also a generous man who over and above educating his own five children – Ron, Sonja, Meg, Dave and Gray – contributed toward the university education of numerous others. Convent teacher, Alison van Schalkwyk remembers the day Harold took her entire Grade 5 class up for a flip, four at a time. The nuns at the Convent were not at all keen on the idea, but eventually agreed on condition that an indemnity form be completed and signed by each child's parent. When they got to the aerodrome on the given day, Sister Edith asked if all the children were indemnified.

Alison said, 'All but one... now where is little Simpiwe?

Little Simpiwe, who was not about to be left out, was already up in the air with Harold. There were many 'Father, Son and Holy Ghosts' accompanied with fervent prayer until Simpiwe had his little feet safely back on the ground.

To return to Washesha: Eshowe school pupils have fond memories of using the Washesha buses. Mike Nixon recalls that the high school hired up to four buses at a time, to transport sports teams to competitive schools in Zululand and Natal. Mike remembers that it was tradition for the 1st team hockey girls to hold their breath while crossing the Thukela River bridge at Mandeni. The driver would fun-lovingly slow down the speed until the girls were evidently ready to burst. During a 1st rugby team's bus tour, Mike got his hands on a packet of dried mopane worms. Each time one of the boys let off offensive wind, Mike would punish the culprit with one of those chewy bits. Needless to say, the innocent boys quickly pointed out the guilty party, and the air remained uncontaminated for the rest of the trip.

I

In the year 2000, the Norwegian prime minister, his wife, and their ambassadorial delegation of distinguished guests visited Eshowe, generously donating R50 000 to build a mission chapel at the Museum Village, as well as to meet all expenses for events carried out during the prime minister's visit. That visit enabled them to retrace the footsteps of those remarkable early Norwegian missionaries and to meet some of their descendants.

A year later, in 2001, attorney and artist Don White helped me to set up an art exhibition in that Norwegian Mission Chapel, situated at the Museum Village, which displays Norwegian involvement in bringing Christianity to Zululand during the 19th Century*.

Tickets for the exhibition were also printed and sold to raise funds for the opening cocktail party. At those parties (between topping up glasses and sparking conversations with ready smiles) artworks sold generously at the expense of inhibitions shed with the cheese and wine (when patrons took a second look at the paintings with a heightened sense of admiration).

Ten percent of total proceeds were donated to charity causes such as the SPCA and the Zululand Home for the Aged. The tickets and advertising posters were generously sponsored each year by Pat McLaverty of Zululand Times, a printing company founded well over a century ago in 1889. Funded by British troops stationed in Eshowe, it was initially a war publication called 'The Sausage Wrap' which was printed by Mission Press. The printing press, itself, had been established in 1886 by Bishop Douglas MacKenzie of the Anglican Diocese, for 'The Propagation of Christian Knowledge'.

The soldiers took it over as a means of communicating to the inhabitants of Zululand. When the soldiers departed from Eshowe, in 1902, the printing of this publication ceased.

*People worthy of mention regards the organising of those splendid art exhibitions, during in the 1990s and 2000s, are Don White, Richard Tudor-Owen, Michelle Day, Margie Salter, Alice Walker, Elseby Moscou and Marian Mattinson.

Five years later it was resurrected by Thomas Parkins who had originally been sent out from England to run the printers for Mission Press. The printers were turned by the very first internal-combustion engine to make an appearance in Eshowe. The first issue was produced under difficulty with each of the four pages having to be printed separately. Thomas priced the paper, called 'Zululand Times', at only one penny per publication. Subjects included regimental orders and advice on growing crops as well as news of local events.

In 1910 the first drawings appeared in adverts. Only on 12th February 1931 did the first photograph appear. It was an aerial photograph of the fisherman's paradise at Richard's Bay Hotel owned then by KV Challenor, subsequent to him selling the Royal Hotel in Eshowe.

In 1919 Mr George Tallantire took over the publication from Thomas Parkins, at the business premises directly opposite the George Hotel. That sharp bend in Main Street is known to this day as 'Tally's Corner'. George Tallantire had in fact been involved with the printers since 1903, when he worked on the press. He ran the printing business until he died, in 1957, having been joined by CWD Riddell who remained with the paper until his retirement in 1960, after the McLavertys took over in 1959.

II

Pat McLaverty, by the 2000s, was no doubt a pleasure to do business with. He'd had more than one generation of over 30 employees working at the printing factory. On average, each employee had worked there for 14.5 years. In 113 years the company never had a strike or even a one-day stay away.

Enoch Mhlongo was with the firm for 33 years. He started out as a messenger in the Zululand Times stationery shop that was run by Pat's mother, Gwen

The original ZT Stationers and printing press situated at Tally's Corner before relocating to Osborn road

Tally's Corner in 2024

who sold the stationery shop to local businessman, Derek Haines, when the press moved to the industrial area in 1984. Derek Haines ran the stationery business, trading in Osborn Road as ZT Stationers, for 37 years.

Indeed, Pat McLaverty is a genial even-tempered gentleman, but with a no-nonsense streak – a trait quickly learned by someone who swooped into the parking space Pat was waiting for.

Pat hopped out of his car to make his complaint at the perpetrator's window where he was met with the offensive middle finger.

Pat added to his grocery basket, that day, a block of hard margarine. Providence appeared to be in favour of Pat's vigilantism for no sooner had he smeared the intruding vehicle's windscreen with the margarine did it began to pelt down with rain.

Today, Pat and his wife, Sally, operate from their home in Zinkwazi, a picture framing concern called 'Pally's'. Pat has kindly helped me set up my own picture framing business in Eshowe.

III

Now to tell you about the Hardman family: Arthur Hardman was born in Preston, England, in 1913. In 1938, at the age of 25, he moved to South Africa where he worked as a carpenter in Johannesburg, before moving to Eshowe and running his own building company, Black & Hardman Builders, from 1946 to 1950.

He met Muriel Tallantire (also known as 'Tutu'), and married her on 14th December 1946. They had four sons: Michael, husband of Sharon and father of Craig and Claire; Graham, previously married to Angie, now married to Wendy and father of Sarah and Murray; Bruce, husband of Trish and father of Kirsten and Padget; Dave, husband of Bev and father of Robyn, Mandy and Matthew. Dave's wife, Bev was a fellow class-mum, and a slender vision to behold with her long dark hair and exquisitely feminine ankle-length dresses.

Arthur worked in Eshowe, as a building inspector, for the Public Works Department. He supervised the building and approving of new schools, hospitals and government office buildings.

Arthur's wife, Tutu was the granddaughter of James Milne, one of Eshowe's earliest pioneers. After leaving Fette Cairn in Scotland, James Milne spent 80 days at sea in the 300-ton Brig, 'Lady of the Lake'. He landed in Durban in 1860. After building the customs shed at the Point, James Milne joined the Public Works Department in Zululand. He was responsible for the building of many public buildings in Eshowe including the Nongqayi Fort at the Museum Village.

Tutu worked for her father, George Tallantire in his business on Tally's Corner in Main Street. It was then the printing and stationery shop called 'Zululand Times', that, as I've explained, was later sold to the McLavertys.

Tutu talked about a customer who, every week, entered the shop on horseback to purchase his magazines.

Years later, after the McLavertys moved Zululand Times to more central premises in town, opposite Edwards Pharmacy, months passed with nobody showing any interest in renting the shop on Tally's Corner. Then Arthur Hardman had an idea to start a business of his own; a notion so inspired it was incredible that he hadn't thought of it before. And so in 1965, with the encouragement and advice of local businessmen Cecil Bircher, Jim Sutherland and Gary Powell, Arthur Hardman and his partner, Mervyn Smith, started 'Eshowe Mart'. It was the first ever furniture shop in Eshowe.

Arthur continued working for Van Dort's Hardware Store, while, against her wishes, but because of her happy and friendly disposition, Tutu Hardman was appointed manageress of Eshowe Mart.

The first stock included a house full of second-hand furniture bought from a person leaving town. The first week's takings amounted to the grand total of R50. But before long Eshowe Mart was a going concern. Deliveries were made by means of a small trailer towed by a Wolesley 6/90 – after 5 pm when Arthur knocked off from Van Dort's Hardware Store. By the dim light of torches and candles the Hardmans would set up their customers' black woodstoves, pipes and all. Second-hand stock was gradually replaced with brand new furniture.

During that time the business purchased a second-hand Peugeot 303 pick-up for R200. With the help of his sons, Michael and Graham, Arthur removed the box body and fitted a flat one more suitable for furniture deliveries. That vehicle was eventually replaced with a brand new Ford Transit.

Arthur Hardman resigned from Van Dort's to manage the Hire Purchase and Accounts Department that were newly established. Then his business partner, Mervyn Smith decided to sell out his shares in Eshowe Mart to buy a farm. It took a year or so of striving and struggling for the business to get back onto its feet, at which time the Hardmans decided to relocate to Osborn Road where Jwayelani Trading is today.

The move took place on 16th November 1968. Then two gentlemen, Mr Reg Horne and Mr Geoff Oxborrow, joined the business. And there was no looking back. Geoff took over the carpets department.

Mrs Edna Clifford and Lou Nel also joined the staff and, in 1975, the Hardmans bought the premises they had been renting in Osborn Road.

Bruce and Graham Hardman joined their parents as directors of the firm. Bruce took over the carpet- laying and flooring department, expanding later to curtaining and interior decorating services. Of course there's no substitute for experience, so Graham, with his training in electronics, expanded the radio, television and photographic departments. The photo mini-lab's developing and printing service was another 'first' for Eshowe. In 1986, Tutu assisted her and Arthur's eldest son, Michael in

Tutu and Arthur Hardman in 1973

establishing a business at Tally's Corner called 'Tally's' which specialised in the restoration of old furniture and the production of exact copies of antique pieces.

Apart from providing a loving home for her family, Tutu worked in that same shop on Tally's Corner for a total of 60 years.

In her younger days, Tutu was an excellent low-handicap golfer. Her name appears on most of the Country Club's cups including that of the Zululand Ladies' Championship. In fact, the whole family were great Country Club supporters, George Tallantire being one of its earliest life presidents.

Eshowe Mart, in the meantime, had grown a staff-count of 32 members*. And the firm eventually owned six trucks.

In June 1996 the driver of a cement tanker lost control in the middle of town, hitting a minibus and tossing it into the window of Express Foto, destroying all of Mr Hugh Spaight's shop and its contents. The tanker then ploughed into the premises of Eshowe Mart next door, leaving a trail of damaged furniture and electrical appliances in its wake. The accident took place after hours when everyone had gone home, but damages to Eshowe Mart alone were estimated at R1 million – those days! The drivers of both tanker and minibus were critically injured and Daphne Peterson (35) was killed while crossing the road.

IV

Bruce and Trish Hardman moved to Empangeni and started their own successful branch of the Biggie Best

---

*Some staff members were Mrs Edna Clifford, Mrs Gladys Sanders, Mr Stanley Xulu, Mrs Fran Bezuidenhout, Mr Jabulani Xulu, Mrs Elizabeth Moolman and Mrs Natalie Minietti.

Furniture and Interior Décor franchise.

Dave, who ran the TV and appliance repair department at Eshowe Mart, started his own repair business in the centre of town. In the 1990s, he and Bev moved that business to Tally's Corner.

In the 2000s, born and bred Eshowe-ite, Dave Vermaak turned Tally's Corner into a second-hand furniture shop. I purchased a splendid Oregon pine dining table from Dave that Peter Ellis restored for me. It now serves as a workbench in my art studio.

Returning to the 1960s and 70s, during which, the four Hardman boys attended Eshowe Junior School and Eshowe High School. The eldest brother, Michael, remembers certain teachers from the junior school. There was Mrs Cloete, Mrs Spencer who drove a black Morris Minor, and the never-to-be-forgotten Miss Todd who supervised air-raid training and gave hidings with a coat hanger. At Eshowe High School Michael's favourite teacher was Mr du Pisanie (also known as 'Dupe') who wore jeans, a leather jacket and rode a big bike. Dupe's sister, Mrs Renette De Waal, is presently principal of Eshowe Junior School.

Michael Hardman was part of a gang including Daniel Knoesen (also known as Skull*) The main activity of the gang was to meet for a smoke every day at Skull's gypsy-like caravan opposite the high school. Once they built a giant kite that needed a longer tail, so they joined all their school ties together. The nylon broke and away flew their ties, over the aerodrome, never to be seen again. Incidentally, during those days there was a public

---

*Other members of the gang were Trevor Rosewall (Rosie), Peter Bannock (Beep), Andre Pretorius (Cockroach), Nigel Webb (Limey) and Michael himself (George, after his maternal grandfather).

phone booth at the aerodrome.

The gang even had their own car, a 1936 DKW which Skull obtained from Stan Barratt's scrapyard in exchange for a compressor. They painted it purple and added polka dots.

All of these naughty characters moved on to do very well for themselves after school. It goes to show that there is hope for our own little Eshowe-ite delinquents.

In their retirement, the 'Hardman boys' remain active: Michael enjoys rebuilding vintage cars and motorbikes; Graham and Bruce are talented painters, working mostly with watercolour and acrylic paints; Dave is still working but enjoys woodwork and building miniature model workshops in his spare time.

V

The 'Hardman boys' remember, years ago, that when Arthur became too frail to care for himself, they decided that the old age home would be the best place for him, but he was having none of it.

'Just give it a try,' they implored, and duly delivered Arthur, suitcases in tow, to the home where he looked around the premises. In a tone with a definitive suggestion of dismissal, he told the staff that his sons would be taking him home 'immediately'.

'But who will look after you?' they asked.

'Sam will.'

When they got home Sam was in the driveway, waiting for them. He said he knew they'd be back.

As a very young boy, Sam worked as a gardener for Arthur and Tutu Hardman. He was of the same age as Mike Hardman so the boys all played together with him in the garden.

When Sam was older, Tutu trained him up in the kitchen where he became a jolly good chef. The

This photo of Bruce, Dave, Sam, Graham and Mike was taken at a family reunion in 2007

family still refer to one of their mother's recipes as 'Sam's casserole'. Later, when Sam cared for Arthur, he was even tasked to order the oxygen bottles for Arthur's emphysema.

When Arthur died, Sam was not sent on his way without ceremony. With gifts galore, he retired to a rural area outside Eshowe and built himself a lovely home with money bequeathed to him by Arthur. Then he came back to work for Dave and Bev for a while before starting his own business, selling frozen popsicles on sticks. These, he transported on the front of his bicycle in a cooler-box with dry ice, making sales to passer-bys outside Adam's store.

VI

Each year, for decades, commencing in 1953, the Eshowe boy scouts and the MOTHs Service Club respectively convened a soap box (go-cart) derby in Main Street. The starting line was at the top of the hill in front of Bishop's Guesthouse, where electrician Roly Bourne would commentate over a microphone.

Graham Hardman in a 1960's Soapbox Derby

Mike Hardman's son, Craig in the family's final soap-box

The very first champion, in 1953, was none other than Michael Paton of Empangeni, nephew of the famous author, Alan Paton. (Alan, in 1956, would be elected chairman of the non-racial Liberal Party of South Africa, and be briefly arrested during that time).

A fathers' and mothers' race in their children's carts aroused great enthusiasm. Other fun races included a 'Waiters' Race' for the local hotel waiters who were required to walk from the bottom of the hill to what was the Provincial Hotel, trying not to spill the glass of beer on their tray. The first ever winner was Charles Moodley from the Royal Hotel.

In 1957 a bicycle race saw 40 young Zulus cycling furiously at breakneck speed for over two miles on their bicycles. Soap boxes, on the other hand, were released off a wooden ramp to get them going around Tally's Corner, and all the way down the hill to the junior school's gates. There were two sections in which one could participate: The Grand-Prix (with ball-bearings) and the basic disselboom. Some of the original soap box carts had rope-steering and a wooden block controlled with a spring to serve as brakes. The Hardman boys' car was modified slightly over the years but remained as a disselboom cart to the end. They won many prizes. In later years Michael built his son, Craig a new cart for the Grand Prix section. It was a replica of British racing driver Nigel Mansell's Formula 1 Williams race car.

A few families, among many in the community, to participate were the Rosewalls, Barratts and Powells. Also the Balmers (more about them later) whose soap box belonged in the disselboom category. Their first family members to race their soap box were siblings, Terence and Winsome Balmer.

In 1953, during which historic events included the coronation of Queen Elizabeth, as well as Hillary and Tenzing's conquest of Everest, Winsome Balmer wanted to do a practice run before the big day because her soap box had been modified and now had a steering wheel.

Winsome set off down the hill, but when a car came towards her from the opposite direction (even though it was on the other side of the road) she took fright, got into a speed-wobble and veered off course, hitting the car head-on. The soap box went under the car. Winsome connected the front grid and was knocked unconscious. Three days later, sporting a huge black eye, Winsome was on the starting line, ready to win the beautiful wristwatch that she cherished. Terence Balmer also came first in his section and won a bicycle. Tony and Donovan Balmer were yet to also win shiny new bicycles in their years of veering around Tally's Corner, feeling alive with the sun on their back, the wind in their face and the spectators' cheering in their ears.

Harry Rosewall made the very first 'railway sleeper cart' in the 1960s. Then the Pretorius brothers, who lived in Hulett Drive, built one and Roach Pretorius came second in his race. Another was built by Harold and Steve Barratt. Tony Illing also made a railway sleeper cart. It broke records and his children, Louise and Andrew Illing won many prizes with it.

In 1969 Paul Vermaak came first in the BP cart that was later sponsored by Zululand Gas. At around the same time Barry Laing replaced the driver of a cart called 'The Pub', who had taken ill, and won a Golden Delux bicycle.

Scott Wilson's father, Alan built Scott a cart with thick planks and golf trolley wheels. It won the prize for the best looking cart.

Chapter 6

At a field elevation of five hundred metres, Eshowe aerodrome is a small airport situated near Rutledge Park Dam (also known as the 'Bottom Dam'), named after the popular town foreman, Mr Rutledge, who worked hard to create it. Once upon a time white swans were introduced from the royal swanneries in England, as were black swans from Australia.

When the aerodrome was first established the last house in Pearson Road was demolished. That was because the planes got too close to the roof when they took off. A row of gum trees, for the same reason, were removed.

Regular fliers in Eshowe, during my time here since 1996, have included these pilots*: Pat McLaverty of Zululand Times, optometrist Nico Strauss, Dr Mike Damp, Brett Gehrens and Gerald de Beer who is a pharmacist at Edward's Pharmacy and married to fellow pharmacist Linda de Beer (née Chesterton).

In 1949 a Gliding Club was launched. It ended in tragedy when Lawrence East set out to beat his own endurance record. Because, for some unknown reason, his tow-rope was not cast adrift, the glider hurtled down killing Lawrence instantly.

Lawrence had served during the war in the SAAF as a ground engineer. He was very popular in Eshowe and the shock of his death put a prompt end to the Gliding

*Further back in time, pilots included Dr Donald Clark, farmer Dick Herbert, Morris Williams (farmer Dave Williams' father and mayor of Eshowe from 1986 to 1988) and Nate Hulett from Nkwaleni. In the 1950s there were the East brothersof East's Service Station) and Harold Braatvedt who were, all three, pilots in the 2nd World War.

Club. A few years later, however, farmer Dave Williams' father, Morris Williams constructed a glider and hooked it to a cable wound up on a drum at the top of his truck. In order to fly the glider, he had to unravel the cable.

It so happened, on one particular birthday, Timothy McHugh (Dr Tom's eldest son) wanted a ride in an aeroplane, so Micky East took him up for a flip. Come John McHugh's (Dr Tom's middle son's) birthday, he too had a flip in the air with Micky East. When Rory McHugh's (Dr Tom's youngest son's) birthday came around, the McHugh's were driving up Pearson Road towards the aerodrome where, from near the railway line, they saw Morris William's glider take to the sky, promptly pull straight down with nose forward and wings folded, and crash smack into the ridge near the stream. Well, that was the end of that – Rory's flip ended before it had even begun.

Harold and Ron Braatvedt, Roy Cathy, Stan Upfold and Hugh Lee co-owned a plane with Dick Herbert. When I asked if Hugh Lee flew, Renée Lee said, 'With Dick in the cockpit, Hugh was too busy holding on for dear life.'

Then there was the local dentist at that time, Dr Quinn, who tried to fly a Tiger MOTH called a 'biplane' because it had a double set of wings. As he was taking off a gust of wind turned the plane upside down and ditched it in the dip between those notorious ridges.

Accountant Morris Johnson, when doing his first solo flight, took off smoothly enough, but when he tried to land the plane bounced a few times and ended up at the end of the field by the hanger. Severely shaken, he climbed out and never flew again.

Let's not forget John Tomlinson who owned Eshowe Electrical next to Dr Tom McHugh's surgery in Sugar

Building where 'Jus Glass and Aluminium' is now. He lived in a wood-and-iron house behind the store, and was renowned for flying his own aeroplane all the way from England to South Africa. His wife taught those little McHugh boys in Standard 1 at Eshowe Public School.

During the 1960s, Tony Balmer served as a reconnaissance pilot in the SAAF. He recorded some 'close calls' in his lovely memoir called 'This is my Story'. Those hair-raising incidents up in the air resulted in his family insisting that his feet stay firmly on the ground. He was thus prevented from buying into Dick Herbert's aeroplane enterprise and any thoughts of microlighting were promptly nipped in the bud.

I

Tony Balmers' ancestors can be traced back through seven generations to Maria Balmer born in Hesket in Cumberland in 1731. Then there was a George Balmer born in 1761. They both originated from country north-east of England where the 'Balmer' name is derived from the Celtic term for 'town dwellers', although most of the Balmer ancestors have their occupation listed as 'rural farm workers'.

Tony's grandfather, William Balmer was born in the village of Morland in 1862. William's father was James Balmer, born in 1822. James married Eleanor Nicholson in 1846. They had eight children; the first five of which were all girls. William was only three-years-old when his mother, Eleanor died. Almost immediately after, his father, James died in 1881, William set off for South Africa to join the goldfields in the Eastern Transvaal.

It so happens, that when my daughters, Lara and Keri were toddlers, their father, Ray van Schalkwyk was employed as a millwright at New Consort Gold Mine just outside Barberton. The birding there was phenomenal. I worked in the office at the nearby historical Digger's Retreat Hotel that often accommodated bus-tour groups of geologists from all over the world. They came to see those mountains that are among the very oldest formations in the world.

South Africa's Gold Rush began in Barberton in 1883, and had spread to Johannesburg by 1886. Tony Balmer's grandfather, William Balmer saw Johannesburg when it was just tents and bare veld at that time. The Gold Rush at Pilgrims Rest began in 1876, but by 1882 the alluvial gold had begun to run out. William Balmer worked as a bullion courier, carrying gold from Pilgrims' Rest to Barberton, about 135 kilometres away. There is a story of him having to travel nonstop for three days while pursued by bandits. He also befriended Sir Percy Fitzpatrick who wrote 'Jock of the Bushveld', and they often hunted together.

The mining experience that William gained in the Barberton area led him to the open-pit Jagersfontein Diamond Mine, about 110 kilometres south-west of Bloemfontein in the Orange Free State. Established in 1870, it was the biggest hand-excavated hole in the world. William Balmer was involved as a surveyor there from 1887 to 1889.

In the meantime, Cecil John Rhodes was anxious to secure Matabeleland and Mashonaland before the Germans, Portuguese or Boers did so. In June 1890, his pioneer column set off northbound – joined by William Balmer as one of the civilian colonists – to establish three towns in Mashonaland: Fort Victoria, Fort Charter and Fort Salisbury.

William was part of the wagon train heading north from Fort Charter to Fort Salisbury when he contracted black water fever that is a complication of malaria. He spent five days, delirious, in the wagon. At Hartley Hills he was left to die in the care of a local old man. On their return the column expected to see a grave, but instead they were astounded to find William fully recovered.

Serving with various local paramilitary volunteer units, William was involved in both the First Matabele War in 1893/94, and the Matabele and Mashona Uprisings in 1895. He was also a prospector and a surveyor of mineral deposits, roads and railway lines. One of his expeditions was the first to establish that major copper and other mineral deposits exist in central Africa. Being part of this small select expedition, William got to know both Burnham and Fredrick Selous. On his way back to South Africa he saw the railway line to Bulawayo under construction. It was completed in 1897.

Throughout my own childhood in Bulawayo, my father, Errol Clifford Hunt worked for the Rhodesian Railways. We had the most fabulous train trips to the most wonderful places. The children's Christmas parties were not to be outdone, and today my grandchildren play with the teddy bear I received there over 50 years ago.

When William Balmer returned from central Africa, he worked and travelled extensively, on horseback, around the Orange Free State. Let's talk a bit about his involvement in the 2nd Anglo-Boer War that began on 11th October 1899 and continued until 31st May 1902. Lord Roberts was sent from England to South Africa to take command. Fredrick Burnham was given the rank of Major and awarded the DSO for his bravery and contribution to the British. William Balmer was well-known to Fredrick Burnham, through whom, William joined Roberts' staff as an intelligence officer with the rank of Captain. The British occupied Bloemfontein without any resistance on 13th March 1900. Roberts's exhausted army, racked by a typhoid epidemic, was forced to make camp for two months.

The British occupied Winburg and established it as a garrison town and military command centre. William served there as an intelligence officer.

Roberts left Bloemfontein in May 1900. After annexing the Orange Free State, they went on to capture Johannesburg and Pretoria. Roberts, convinced that police work was all that was necessary to win the war, handed over the supreme command to Lord Herbert Kitchener and returned to England.

Having annexed both Boer republics (Transvaal and Orange Free State) the British barely managed to maintain control. A guerrilla war was launched and the Boer Commandos relentlessly raided British communication lines and army bases with swift and efficient surprise attacks.

The British set up barbed wire and armoured trains along the railway lines. When this tactic failed they adopted a 'scorched earth policy' burning Boer farms, killing or confiscating their livestock and eventually forcing the civilians into camps with other displaced Boer families. This led to the formal creation of a concentration camp policy, thus the construction of internment concentration camps in which thousands of Boer women and children, mostly those left homeless and destitute by the scorched earth policy, were interred. These concentration camps were severely mismanaged: food and water was scarce in the camps and starvation and disease caused the deaths of over twenty thousand burghers and prisoners.

Blacks, who had been workers on those scorched Boer farms, were put into British labour gangs, and their families sent to separate concentration camps.

Although no battles were fought in or around the town, a prisoner of war camp was established in Eshowe. Eshowe's burghers were in better shape than those in other concentration camps around Natal, but Sir Charles Saunders did instruct all magistrates to keep expenses in connection with surrendered Boers to their bare needs only. Furthermore, the postmaster at Eshowe was instructed to set aside incoming letters for censorship.

Let me tell you a bit about the Eshowe concentration and surrendered burghers camp before we get back to William Balmer: Great numbers of Boer burghers became despondent about seeing an end to the Anglo-Boer War that, in the end, lasted for three whole years. When the war moved to a guerrilla phase, Eshowe, with its fertile land at Fort Curtis which was a short distance out of Eshowe on the road to Melmoth, provided a safe resort. Within this area, surrendered Boers gathered, but very few remained. Preferring to live with their livestock, they scattered all over Zululand. However, they did have to report each Monday to the police at the magistracy they were residing in. The only people who resided in the Eshowe camp at Fort Curtis, from time to time, were women and children and surrendered burghers with no property. Also those burghers grazing their cattle close to Eshowe's boundary. The Eshowe camp was actually more of an administrative centre for surrendered burghers, controlled by chief magistrate Sir CR Saunders and the local police. Later, in 1902, they were administered by the military.

The total number of people that passed through the Eshowe camp numbered 527. Of these, 91 were concentration camp inmates captured by the British, and 436 who had arrived as surrendered burghers or refugees. Those inhabitants who resided in the Eshowe camp were housed in government-owned bell tents which could accommodate five people each. Those who resided with their cattle and other property in the various Zululand districts lived in their own tents and wagons.

It is said that only four people died in the Eshowe camp, none of whom were captured or concentration camp inmates. Three children were born in the camp, namely Johanna de Lange, Maria Delport and Marthinus de Jager. After the camp was closed some surrendered burghers were allowed to stay and settle around Eshowe*.

After the war, under the Zululand Lands Declamation Commission, sufficient land was demarcated for black locations and the rest put aside for whites. Some Boers lost everything, including their country, when the districts of Vryheid and Utrecht became part of Natal. Those burghers were supplied with household equipment and food, and transported home from Eshowe. Trips took days or weeks by wagon.

Today the only physical trace that can be found of the camp on Fort Curtis' terrain, that served for 50 days as a concentration camp for captured women and children, and for 17 months as a refugee camp for surrendered burghers, is the markers of the War Department.

My first husband's paternal grandmother, Ouma Joey van Schalkwyk spent time as a small child in one of the less fortunate camps. As a result, she refused to speak English. Out in the backyard of her homestead on the family farm near Bulawayo, a friend of mine wished to ask her how many turkeys she owned. Instead of asking 'Hoeveel kalkoene het Ouma?' he mistakingly asked

---

*Surrendered burghers in the Eshowe district included CF Butz, his family and his 100 cattle; HJ Corbett with his family of eight and 135 cattle; CJ and AM Laas with their families and 125 cattle and JL Zietsman with his family of three and 20 cattle. The remainder of over 100 people were allowed to graze their cattle on crown land further north of the Umfolozi River. The influx of the cattle of the surrendered burghers created new strains on grazing and water, and lung sickness took its toll despite best efforts to quarantine affected livestock.

'Hoeveel kaal koeke het Ouma?' (how may 'naked cookies' do you have?)

Anyway, back in 1901, when the scorched earth policy was introduced, William Balmer was able to prevent his family's farms from being burnt. He arranged for his wife, Barbara Aletta Wilhelmina Balmer (née De Bruyn) whom he had married on 14th April 1897, their two children and his parents-in-law, to be accommodated in a safe house. When hostilities finally ceased William took them all back to England for a year to stay with family. They returned to South Africa, in 1903, and resumed farming at Balmoral. The Balmer family continued to grow, and among other children, Tony's father, Stan was born in 1908.

In 1925 the Free State farm was sold and the family bought and moved to the farm, 'Rooipoort', in Babanago, Natal. William died there, in 1935, at the age of 73.

Tony Balmer's mother's (Audrey's) namesake on her maternal side were the Brickhills. Her great-great-grandfather was James Brickhill who was born in 1778. His second son was Thomas George Brickhill, Audrey's grandfather. He was born on 16th June 1849 and at one stage served as Durban's harbour master. He gave that up to join his elder brother, William, in farming at Murchison.

Audrey's grandfather Thomas' own son, named Thomas Frank (1885-1917) was a member of the Natal Mounted Rifles. As a young boy of 16 he took part in the Siege of Ladysmith in the Anglo-Boer War. He was a recipient of the Natal Medal in 1906. Thomas enlisted in the army to fight with the Allied Forces. He and his second wife (known as Aunty Reenie) had one child, Joan, in 1924. Joan Brickhill (Audrey's cousin) became a household name in theatre circles as an actress, singer,

Stan and Audrey Balmer

dancer, director, producer and drama teacher. She was based mostly in Durban, having made her first stage appearance at the age of two. She is known especially for the lavish musicals of the 1960s and 70s which she staged with her husband, Louis Burke. These included 'My Fair Lady', 'Cabaret', 'The Sound of Music' and 'Cinderella'. She was a true legend who was involved in more than 50 large productions.

Thomas Frank Brickhill's sister, Dorothy Brickhill, married William Larkan. They had a son and three daughters including Audrey (Tony's mother). As you know, Audrey Larkan married Tony's father, Stan Balmer who had attended Grey College in Bloemfontein where he shone as an athlete, running one hundred yards in ten seconds. He also held the pole vault and long jump records for many years. Like so many young men at the time, Stan left school after completing Standard 8.

Audrey Larkan, a school teacher, was a remarkable woman. (Incidentally, my own mother was a pre-school teacher named Audrey). After matriculating at Girls' High in Pietermaritzburg, Audrey Larkan attended the University of Natal where she obtained her BA degree and teaching diploma.

After her marriage to Stan Balmer, apart from raising their own children, Audrey took in student boarders and meals were served at the table in a rotating sequence.

Audrey continued to teach following her maternity leave after each of her seven children were born. She loved teaching and taught for her entire life. After qualifying from university, Audrey's first teaching post, in 1938, was in Babanango, Zululand. While she wasn't very happy with her posting being so out of the way, the young farmers there were delighted. Farmer Stan Balmer moved swiftly and secured Audrey's hand in marriage in 1939.

When Stan's father, William became ill, Stan took over the farming of sheep, cattle and wattle. He and Audrey lived in a mud-brick house with a veranda that was regularly smeared with cow dung. Outbuildings included a stable for their horse, Methuselah, and a primitive pit latrine, known as a 'long-drop toilet', that was situated about 25 metres from the house. This made cause for the use of chamber pots during the night. I'm reminded about the time my cousin emptied a bottle of Eno effervescent salts into our grandmother's potty. The naughty little bugger got a jolly good hiding after being dragged out of his bed in the middle of that night.

On a visit to Eshowe to see the king and queen, in 1947, the Balmer family stayed with Bertie and Meyrine White. Stan and Audrey Balmer's eldest daughter, Winsome was four-years-old and recalls being fascinated by their modern toilet which she continually flushed to Aunty Mey's annoyance. She also remembers sitting on her father's shoulders opposite Adams to see the royal family drive past.

There was no electricity on the Balmers' farm, and Stan had to build a furrow to carry water for a distance of 1½ kilometres from the Gologot River. Hot water came from a wood-fire-heated 44-gallon drum that stood behind the bathroom. Beneath the shade of a big conifer tree was their meat safe – a cupboard on legs with double wire-mesh sides that were filled with stones. Water dripped over the stones creating the evaporation that kept contents cool, like a modern fridge.

The school in Babanango where Audrey taught was some four kilometres away from home. Terence often rode to school and back on horseback. A young Zulu boy, leading a donkey that had milk cans attached to the saddle, would accompany him because Stan supplied the school's hostel with milk. However, it was no problem for Terence to ride home alone since the horse knew the way. So it was that Stan and Audrey lived on their farm where Stan raised cattle and sheep and managed a wattle plantation. Stan drove a clapped out 5-ton truck to deliver wattle bark to the tanning factory in Melmoth some 60 kilometres away. The passenger door was firmly stuck closed and on the driver's side there was no door.

The discovery of plastic products as an alternative to leather led to a decreased demand for the wattle bark which was used to cure leather. Hence the farm struggled and, in 1948, Stan moved his family 120 kilometres south-east to the town of Eshowe. There, he bought a butchery in partnership with Bertie White, from Audrey's cousin, Whiskers Larkan. They called it 'Zululand Meat Industries' – ZMI and they moved into the old corrugated iron house behind the shop.

II

And so the Balmers arrived in Eshowe to operate their

own butchery business in the old, conventional way with meat sold to customers in brown paper from behind the counter. The day began at 3 am when meat was taken from the fridges and broken down into various cuts. Usually, by 1 pm, the shop would close for the day. Cattle were bought at auction sales all over Zululand.

Each animal purchased required a permit to move from one area to the next. In rural areas the dipping officer would check that the monthly dipping, which was required by law, had been carried out. Sometimes, if only one animal was bought, it would be shot on the spot and loaded into the back of the bakkie.

In the early days, four Zulu staff members would be given food and water and the task of driving the cattle from wherever they had been purchased, to the abattoir. This trip could take an entire week.

Stan would often take his children along to cattle sales. After a long day at the auction sale yards he would stop in at the Melmoth Hotel for 'refreshments' that took an hour or two to replenish in the pub. After that the trip home would become rather scary, especially when it rained and the road got slippery. On two occasions, while coming down the Melmoth Pass, they slid right into the bank. In fact, Stan had several accidents. Once his car left the road near Kataza, plunging three hundred metres down a steep hill. Luckily, the car collided with a tree which halted its descent. Stan clambered back up to the road and tried to flag down a car for help. However, no car stopped because he was covered in blood and looked suspicious.

Then Stan owned an Austin pickup. He seldom made any use of the handbrake and one day while he was inspecting some cattle for purchase, the pickup, which he had left parked on top of a hill, came storming past him at considerable speed. The hill was steep, the tree crashed into was solid and, believe it or not, the damage to the bakkie was a total write-off.

You would think that Stan had learned his lesson, but a month or two later his newly-bought Austin bakkie suffered a similar fate. This time it rolled down a hill and plunged into a dam. Needless to say, the insurance company refused to provide any future vehicle cover.

The abattoir, which was situated on the road that leads to Sunnydale, was a very crude old-fashioned slaughter house. There were no cold rooms, nor doors for that matter, so as soon as the cattle were slaughtered they would be delivered to the butcheries in town.

Stan Balmer eventually owned all four butcheries in Eshowe: ZMI in the centre of town, Premier Meats situated in the southern part of the town near the courthouse, Cash Butchery near where Pick 'n Pay stands today, and Kangela Butchery which was near the hospital. Butchery licences, issued by the SA meat board, were strictly controlled and difficult to obtain.

Stan's butchery business did so well that, in 1952, he built another one next door, opposite where First National Bank stands today. A bottle store now occupies the building. Soon after, Stan bought from the Leakeys (who might have bought it from Gray Puckle) Audrey's dream house in Dlinza Street where the Puckles' daughter, Win Chennells (Jono's mother) had grown up. Subsequent to the Balmers that residence was owned by the Volbrecht family. It is a five-acre plot with house, cottage, outbuildings and fruit orchards including mango, litchi, pawpaw, bananas and various citrus trees. These were frequently raided by boarders from Eshowe High School nearby.

The Balmers also had an impressive foofie (flying fox) slide that started from a tall gum tree in the Wang's garden next door, and ended in theirs. The seven young

Balmers ran wild in their huge playground that included the Dlinza Forest Nature Reserve that almost entirely surrounded their property. They climbed the trees and swung on monkey ropes like Tarzan. They often came across wildlife that included blue duiker, bushbuck, porcupine, bush baby, mongoose, lynx, bush pig, chameleon and snakes. Also troops of noisy monkeys that regularly raided their garden. One of those monkeys was shot by Audrey's mother, Gran Larkan, and eaten by the Zulu staff.

Because Dlinza forest was a nature reserve, bush rangers complained to Audrey about her children playing in the forest.

Audrey told them, 'If you keep your monkeys out of my garden I'll keep my children out of your forest.'

Audrey ran the Balmer household assisted by a number of domestic workers. Two men, Zulu and Dumisa, cooked for the family for many years. Salamina, a chief's daughter, was a very talented dressmaker. In addition to doing the mending for the family she sewed most of Audrey's and her daughters' dresses on an old Singer treadle machine. In fact, Salamina's clientele consisted of many Eshowe families.

At the butchery, Stan's favourite employee was a Zulu man, Sky, who previously worked on the steam trains that ran between Eshowe and Gingindlovu. Mr Harry Breedt, who lived behind the Town Hall in Eshowe, was the engine driver. In Tony's words: *'Sky's duties were to stoke coal into the furnace and clean the engine. One day when he arrived at work he was disturbed to see that the train had no driver. This was because it was Sunday but Sky thought it was Monday (Harry Breedt did not work on a Sunday). Sky had become so familiar with the workings of the train that he decided to rescue the situation and do his boss a great favour by driving that train, on a Sunday, all the way to Gingindlovu. The*

South African Railways saw things differently and Sky was fired. But their loss was Stan's gain. In the early days, Sky was required to deliver meat to Eshowe Prison, as well as the Queen Victoria Hospital in Mansell Terrace. Sky would set off on foot with the meat in a dish balanced on the top of his head. He performed this task every day, except for Sundays which was when Sky would walk all the way from town to the Balmer's house in Dlinza Street, to deliver the Sunday papers to Stan. By the early 1960s meat orders had become too heavy to carry, so those that weren't delivered by bicycle, were done by bakkie.

Sky would accompany Stan and act like a Garmin when Stan couldn't remember the route saying: 'Turn left, Daddy' or 'We must go right here, Daddy.' Years later, when Sky was tipping out rubbish into a larger bin, he collapsed, falling into the bin itself. Stan mourned his death'.

From 1949, Audrey Balmer taught at Eshowe Public School in Main Street. When Eshowe High School opened, in 1959, she went on to teach there for 28 years. Thereafter she taught part-time at the Teachers' Training College until she suffered a fatal heart attack in 1979. By then she had become an accomplished bowls player*.

III

As I've said, Stan and Audrey Balmer had seven children: Terence was born, in 1940, after a hair-raising drive in the mud and rain down the untarred

---

*The Eshowe Bowling Club was launched, in 1923, with Sir Charles Saunders as the first president. In 1953 the green moved from the front of the Royal Hotel to its present premises in Mangosuthu Buthelezi Drive, which, in days gone by, was the parade ground of the Dublin Fusiliers when they established the garrison.

Melmoth pass. Stan frantically worked the vehicle until it screeched to a sharp stop outside the Queen Victoria Hospital.

Terence was a delightful child who transferred from Eshowe Public School, in 1955, to Weston Agricultural School. There he captained the 1st teams in rugby and cricket as well as the athletics and swimming team. In 1959 he was appointed head boy and then awarded Dux. To this day Terence is the only scholar who has his name on every 'honours board' at Weston.

When he left school, Terence bought a trampoline in hope that it would strengthen his rugby-injured knee. He was also inspired by Trampoline Champion, Ron Munn, who had performed at the Zululand Show in 1960.

Terence Balmer worked in the butchery with his father, Stan. In 1965 he married Sigrid Wang, the family's childhood neighbour and friend. As children, the Balmers had a large lawn for playing soccer, rugby and open-gates. They'd invite friends from down the road, like the Bothas, the Leitch boy, a few little Zulu chaps, and Sigrid Wang who was as sporty as any boy.

Sigrid's history is similar to mine in that she married at 18-years of age, and had three (in my case two) children running around at her 21st. They were little Brett, Kerry and Debbie Balmer.

Three years after Terence was born, Winsome Balmer was born in 1943. Anthony Balmer (Tony) was born in 1945. We will return to him a bit later.

Stan and Audrey's fourth child, Donovan Balmer, was born in Eshowe in 1951. He was especially gifted with water sports and became a top diver in South Africa, but was unable to earn his Springbok colours because other countries would not participate against South Africa on account of apartheid.

As I mentioned, Terence Balmer bought a trampoline

and, of course, having a trampoline in the garden delighted the entire family. However, it was Donovan who excelled at summersaults and other manoeuvres that helped tremendously with his diving. Then he turned his talents towards trampoline skills and became a member of the Springbok squad. One of their test matches, in 1972, against Switzerland, was held in the Eshowe Town Hall – contestants jumped so high they almost touched the hall's high ceiling.

Adrian Balmer was born in 1952. Sharon Balmer was born in 1958. After attending Eshowe schools, she began a teaching career with the Department of Coloured Affairs which was a challenge since the political landscape was volatile at the time. She has also been employed at the South African Jockey and Equestrian Academy as a teacher of isiZulu. In Standard 7 she owned her first horse called 'Rambling Boy' with whom she competed successfully in gymkhanas. She sold him during her matric year in order to buy a motorbike. Sharon keenly participated in motorbike rallies and breakfast runs for many years. Then she purchased a horse and resumed her passion for riding.

Vivienne, the youngest, was born in Eshowe Provincial Hospital in 1959, when Audrey was 43- years-old. When Vivienne was 15 she fell in love with Bryan Tyack who was a fellow scholar at Eshowe High School. They married in 1979 when she was 19. It was a mere two weeks after this that Audrey had a heart attack and died. Viv remembers her childhood as an exceptionally happy time. She says their numerous family beach holidays at places like Sheffield and Salt Rock, with feasts of fish, crayfish and fresh oysters off the rocks, are among her most precious memories. Like other family members Vivienne was very athletic. She also enjoyed ballet, gymnastics, diving and was a member of the Natal

Amateur Trampolining Squad. Like Sharon, she loved horses and rode in a number of Zululand Shows. Viv and Bryan lived in Babanango for four years where Bryan worked with Donovan at BBS (Balmer's Building Supplies) before managing the Eshowe branch.

IV

Anthony (Tony) Balmer, the third of Stan and Audrey's children, started Class 1 at Eshowe Public School in 1951. Today his former play area is occupied by the assembly hall and principal's office. Mrs Peters taught Standard 5. One day she gave the class words to learn for a spelling test. Spelling was not Tony's strong point. He wrote the words on the top of his thigh beneath his shorts. Mrs Peters spotted him peeking beneath his desk and sent him directly to the headmaster for a caning. Audrey Balmer was ready with another hiding when Tony got home.

Together with his siblings, Tony enjoyed a childhood spent in Eshowe*. Life was safe and Stan and Audrey locked neither vehicles nor home when they went out.

Tony was a skinny, agile little chap, thriving in athletics and playing rugby from Standard 4. In Standard 4 Tony also had his first girlfriend, Helen Robinson. They spent their time in class gazing at each other. Over weekends, Tony, the little romantic, would ride out to her house to chat through the fence. It so happens that my own very first kiss occurred between the flowering

---

*Tony's friends were Alan Snow, Thomas Colepepper, Robin MacKenzie, Kevin Pearce, Neville Newborn and Garth Schefferman. Tony loved going through Alan Snow's collection of Popeye, Bugs Bunny and Donald Duck comic books. Alan went on to become a chartered accountant.

granadilla vines on the fence separating our house from my crush next door in Bulawayo. When I ran into him some three decades later it was the first thing he remembered.

Tony Balmer's second girlfriend was Lynnette Williams. Then in Standard 6 he fell madly in love with Karen Evenson, the very beautiful daughter of American missionaries living near the Norwegian Mission eight kilometres outside of Eshowe on the Gezinzela Road – Tony peddled for many kilometres on his bicycle those days. In fact, riding their bikes on every road and path, Tony Balmer and Alan Snow knew Eshowe upside-down and inside-out. Osborn Road was finally tarred, although the parking areas remained gravel for some time. At night the boys would ride to the Star Theatre to watch movies and only get home after 10pm.

Those days the old Standard Bank was demolished and the Old Mutual building built in its place. The Balmer children also witnessed the construction of the Catholic Church and the Convent, the Eshowe Centre, the new First National Bank and the Star Theatre.

'Cinema' or 'bioscope' was held in the Town Hall before the Star Theatre was built. Dress code demanded a jacket and tie. Irene Strachan remembers that even after the big screen relocated from the Town Hall to the Star Theatre, it was still an occasion to dress up. Sporting wide skirts with yards of net petticoats, she battled to squeeze herself into a seat in the peanut gallery.

Movies in Eshowe had very primitive beginnings. It was only twice a year that a travelling entertainer would arrive at the Provincial Hotel with his portable machine in tow. His films were sometimes so scratched that they looked like they'd been filmed through a rainstorm.

During the early 1930s talkies replaced silent movies. In due course films became a weekly feature at the Royal Hotel until the Town Hall was opened in 1926, followed by the Lagerwall brothers building of the Star Theatre. Their opening night, on 12th July 1952, screened the film 'Where no Vultures Fly'.

The Royal Hotel, in the meantime, had a certain farmer who, during those 1950s, would commute once a month from Durban to his farm in Monzi, calling in at all the small hotels en route to catch up with friends. It was his habit to overnight at the Royal Hotel where he would hold court at the bar until late. Eventually, having over-indulged, he would routinely pull out his firearm and fire a few shots into the bar ceiling, much to the enjoyment and admiration of his fellow revellers. As this was a regular occurrence, the Royal Hotel proprietor issued an instruction that the bedroom above the bar be reserved for that same farmer on those nights, because he would be in the pub and not in the upstairs bedroom at the time of the shootings.

On Tony Balmer's first day at high school, which was Maritzburg College in Pietermaritzburg, some older boys asked him, 'What's your name?'
'Balmer,' Tony mumbled nervously.
'Barman?' they misheard. 'So you're a boozer are you?'
Boozy Balmer' stuck and Tony was even introduced
to his friends' parents by that nickname.

Being at a school so talented at rugby was extremely challenging for Tony. To watch the 1st team was like going to a test match. Tony was up against the likes of Toffee Sharp and Andy van der Watt who were yet to play for the Springboks. But then, in 1963, Tony's position changed from centre to flank, which better suited him, and he not only made it into the much-sought-after 1st team, but he also achieved his honours in rugby. As a member of the Natal schools' team he played in matches at Loftus, Ellis Park, and King's Park against the Free State, Transvaal and Northern Transvaal sides. The game at Ellis Park was a curtain-raiser to the Springbok/Wallabies match. Later, when doing military service, Tony would play flank for the defense 1st team, but the lure of his girlfriend, Paddy Hayter with the laughing brown eyes, was sometimes more important than a fixture and he chose to visit her instead. In total, he hitch-hiked an impressive total of twenty thousand kilometres, up and down, visiting Paddy in Pietermaritzburg.

In 1962, having achieved first position in high jump, long jump, pole vaulting and shot put, Tony was open champion in athletics and awarded Victor Ludorum. In high jump and pole vault there was no soft landing as you see today. They landed in a sawdust pit on the ground. Tony represented College when he competed in long jump against Paul Nash who was to become the fastest man in South Africa by running the 100 metres in 9.8 seconds. Wanting to be on the sports field only, Tony failed Standard 7 – quite spectacularly (his own words). Audrey insisted that he would not leave school until he passed matric. So Tony pulled up his socks and, in 1964, he was chosen to be head boy of the school. He was also put in charge of the cadets, in the position of officer commanding. Shouting orders at platoons marching in time to the music of the cadet band: 'turn right! turn left!' served as a great grounding for the army.

Year-end, when cadet regalia was handed in, Tony was ticking off items when the master took the check

Tony Balmer   *Paddy Balmer (née Hayter)*

sheet from him. He noticed that Tony had placed a 'C' next to some of the boys' names. 'What does the 'C' represent?' he asked.

'Query, Sir.'

'You don't spell query with a C.' So Tony changed the C letter to a K.

One of Tony's duties as head prefect was to attend functions at other Pietermaritzburg schools. After the inter-house gala at their sister-school (Pietermaritzburg Girls' High), the girls would invite them for tea. Tony did not know then that Paddy Hayter, who was part of that group, would one day be his wife. Although Tony did not know Paddy, she knew all about him since she and her family attended nearly every 1st team College match.

Paddy's Dad, William (Billy) Hayter, had fought in North Africa during the 2nd World War, but he didn't talk very much about those terrible times. He was also in Italy when they executed Mussolini and strung him up by his feet. After the war he worked in the foil department at Hulett's Aluminium factory in Pietermaritzburg, eventually managing that sector. Paddy's mother, Betty Jannet (Bobby) Hayter was a warm, happy person and always full of fun.

While Tony was taking Paddy out, he scratched a heart into the side of the wooden cupboard in his room at hostel. Apparently that romantic piece of vandalism still exists.

On 1st March 1965, Tony boarded the army train to Bloemfontein. On arrival, the atmosphere immediately changed from the friendliness on the train. Tony's troop were issued uniforms and equipment and ordered to their allocated bungalows with the command, 'Hardloop!' It was dark and they were unfamiliar with the terrain. Struggling under their loads, they often fell into the trenches with all their kit.

Stan and Audrey refused to sign the necessary papers for Tony to enrol into the parabat course, but the armoured car division allowed him to take licences in vehicles such as the Panard, Saracen and Ferritt armoured cars as well as 4-ton Bedford trucks.

After Tony's basic training and the undertaking of an officer's course, Tony held the office of 2nd lieutenant: assistant veld cornet. During that time, air force officers invited Tony, among others, to enrol for the Army Air Reconnaissance Course. This was to fly the Cessna 185 at Potchefstroom. (The Cessna aircraft was a 180 HP, six-seater tail dragger which meant it had two big front wheels and a smaller back wheel.) Hundreds applied, but only two officers from Tempe army barracks were selected. Tony was one of them.

And so, in September 1965, Tony climbed into an aeroplane for the first time in his life and started his pilot's training. To go from his low position at Tempe to being an officer at the officers' quarters in Potchefstroom, with his own batman to make his bed and do his laundry, was quite an experience. Officers also had their own watering-hole where Tony's beers, or cane and cokes, were very cheap – a major bonus.

Tony flew mostly at 16 to 46 metres off the ground, practising road landings which were smooth and farmland airstrip landings which were bumpy. Short airstrips were always a challenge. Pilots had competitions, cutting their engines at one thousand metres and gliding with no engine assistance to a line marked on the air strip. The person who landed closest to the mark won. In 1966 the South African Airways wanted Tony to sign up permanently. Tony would've gone straight to Pretoria to fly Impala jets, then on to other jet fighters or bombers. But Stan had asked him to please come home to help run the family butchery businesses. The business expanded when Stan bought both Kangela Butchery, and Cash Butchery where Pick 'n Pay stands today. He was yet to acquire Premier Butchery as well.

Tony also learned how to run the abattoir where cattle, sheep and pigs were slaughtered. Most of the beef stock came from auction sales all over Zululand. Sheep arrived by train from Colesberg in the Karoo. Mr Colley in Melmoth supplied tender young pigs. Baconers were bought from Harry Goddard of Dapplemere Estates near Eshowe.

Tony was greatly relieved a few years later, when his and Terence's brother, Donovan took over the running of the abattoir. Tony had worked solidly for five years. The only diversion from work was his annual Air Force call up. The main butchery, ZMI, was doing well, but the others were a burden. Tony took the decision to sell Cash Butchery, as well as Kangela Butchery which he sold to Bruce Kippen (who married Caryle Illing). Bruce ran it for a few years before he went farming for Radclyffe Cadman.

After a courtship of nearly six years, Paddy Hayter made her own wedding gown and the dresses for her flower girls and bridesmaids. Tony felt like the luckiest man alive. They set about renovating the rundown old house in Kock Lane for which they paid R7 500. They named that home 'Le Chaland' after the hotel they'd stayed in during their honeymoon in Mauritius. Rotten windows and doors were falling out; the corrugated-iron roof was rusting. Creating the home they wanted took years. But with her passion for gardening, Paddy soon transformed the mealie patch into a paradise.

A natural-born florist, Paddy had been winning prizes since she was five-years-old. At the age of 14, and then again at 16, Paddy surprised competitors at the Spring Show, staged by the Hilton Road Horticultural Society, when she beat all the adults in the open section. Her entry in 'Spring Splendour' was considered the most outstanding. Paddy also repeatedly won the floating trophy in the inter-school's arts and crafts section at the Royal Show in Pietermaritzburg. After school, Paddy completed the Master Florist Diploma at the esteemed Elro Braak School of Floristry in Pretoria. She came top of the course. It was during that course that Paddy met artist and fellow florist, Diamond Bozas. In Eshowe, on more than one occasion, she worked side by side doing demonstrations with him. At the age of 20, Paddy came first out of 80 applicants in the Bridal Bouquet Competition in Durban. Competitors came from far and wide, including Zimbabwe.

In 1999, at the 6th World Flower Show held at Durban's ICC, Paddy earned the 1st prize and gold medal for her mass arrangement titled 'Siyanibengelela/Welcome'. This huge accomplishment was judged by 24 judges from all over the world. Participants came from as many as 14 foreign countries. Paddy soon became a household name in Eshowe, running a florist business from her garage in Kock Lane; creating flower arrangements for weddings; and orders delivered to patients at the hospital. She regularly held six-week courses for housewives, maids and children.

Before marrying Paddy, Tony made a point of paying off his dream car, a Volvo B122S. After the wedding it went in for a touch up weld on the exhaust pipe. Returning the car to Tony at ZMI butchery (a 250 metre drive) the mechanic had an epileptic fit and rolled the Volvo in front of what is now FNB. The car burst into flames. The mechanic was rescued and the service station replaced the car with another Volvo that the Balmers drove for 25 years.

In 1968 Tony stood for Eshowe's town council and served as a councillor for three years. He was the youngest councillor in South Africa at the time. In those days, the mayor was given an allowance of R2 000 a year, mostly for entertainment expenses, and councillors were not paid at all.

In 1969 Tony negotiated with the managing director of Adams Store to put a meat market into their supermarket. Pre-packed meat was an unfamiliar concept and unfortunately the novel proposal did not interest Adams' management at the time.

When Jenny Suttie married Jeremy Hawke, his move to Eshowe benefited the store greatly. He had been working for Knowles in Pinetown and had experience in running a large supermarket. With his background knowledge, Jeremy was able to convince the Adams board that a butchery was a very necessary part of a modern supermarket*. Tony Balmer was allocated three square metres of floor space in the supermarket and three square metres in the SaveMor section of the store. In the early 1970s, the law stated that supermarkets had to accommodate black and white customers in separate shops. SaveMor served black customers and Spar was 'whites only'. Whites were allowed to go into 'black' stores and black labourers were allowed to work in 'white' stores, but they were not to serve customers.

Indeed, Tony's foothold in Adams was small. He employed just one blockman to work in the butchery workroom and a woman to pack the meat into the fridges in the supermarkets. But after a few months the meat started to move faster and the business became a successful concern.

Then the time came for Stan Balmer to retire. The businesses were shared out accordingly with a percentage of gross values paid out to Stan. Terence took the farm Rooipoort in Babanago and Donovan took ZMI and its properties. Tony got Adams Butchery.

In 1974 the Adams group bought Eshowe Spar, which belonged to Leif Dahl of Eshowe and Stan Cope from Melmoth. It was originally situated north of the Eshowe Methodist Church and is a hardware store today. Of course, they needed a butchery in Eshowe Spar Supermarket too. So when Donovan decided to sell off the ZMI butchery business, it was transferred to Eshowe Spar. That's when Tony employed Jeff Skinstad (formerly from Natal Parks Board) to help run both Adams and Spar supermarket butcheries.

Tony then had time on his hands to help run the supermarket. When the Adams company offered Tony the post of supermarkets' manager he accepted with

*Remember, Adams Store was inherited by Maggie Mikula and Jenny Hawke. Its board consisted of 'The Girls', their respective husbands (Paul Mikula and Jeremy Hawke), Dennis Brown, Walter Strachan, Deshaun Grice, Lawyers Shepstone and Wylie, and managing director Cecil Christian.

open arms. With Jeremy Hawke's help (as well as a change in the law) he was able to combine SaveMor and Adams Spar Supermarkets into one multiracial concern. And he was also put in charge of Eshowe Spar at the northern end of Eshowe.

Adams Butchery did so well that, in 1978, the Adams board decided to buy out Tony's shares. It was an offer he could not refuse, enabling him to acquire his family beach cottage called 'Crannogs' at Salt Rock. Sadly, Audrey, who so loved the beach, was to spend only one weekend at Crannogs before she died, six weeks later.

In 1982 Tony and his business partners, Pat Robinson, and Andy Craig (KV Challenor's grandson who had been mayor of Eshowe from 1993 to 1996) felt the time was right to buy out the shareholders of the supermarket businesses and the properties on which they stood. It was a daring and daunting plan since they had very little collateral – or cash for that matter. None-the- less, Tony ended up as a shareholder of the company known as A Adams (Pty) Ltd and the pressure was on to make the business thrive. Up until then, the shop had been a traditional department store divided into sections. But now it became a supermarket system with a bank of tills at the front.

Tony, Pat and Andy were soon running two large supermarkets, a bottle store and a hardware/building shop. The hardware shop was bulging with no room for expansion, so they bought the successful hardware store next to Edwards Pharmacy. It was started by Arie Van Dort, but later bought out by Cedric Du Plessis, Peter Poege and Doreen Bell – all former employees of Adams.

Later, Tony, Pat and Andy moved the whole operation across the road, next to Standard Bank where it still is today. In 1984 they sold the business to Gerald and Ian Upfold. Today it is owned by Bryan Tyack, Tony's brother-in-law married to Viv, and called 'BBS Mica'.

In 1986 unions made changes and trading hours turned into seven-day weeks. Also, Pat Robinson was wanting to go back to Durban, thus the plan to sell off each entity separately, pay the bank off, and then collect rent for the spaces that were not sold. By the end of 1986 Tony's group was left with the premises only. Today, Shoprite rents the building that was Adams Supermarket and is owned by Tony.

Tony and Andy paid Pat Robinson out. Andy, who had articled with Campbell & Craig (now C & H accounting firm), took charge of collecting the rentals and keeping the books. Tony became responsible for maintenance of the buildings.

Tony and Paddy became actively involved in community affairs in Eshowe. In 1971 they joined Eshowe Round Table and, for 16 years, thoroughly enjoyed good friendships with other members while all their children grew up together. They had become very friendly with the Hawke family and introduced them to Round Table where Tony held every position offered, including a term as the chairman*.

Eshowe Chapter of Rotary International received its

---

*Table No 24 of Round Table, in Eshowe, was inaugurated on 18th October 1953. The first chairman was Guy Taylor who had been mayor of Eshowe from 1956 to 1958. The organisation has since supported the Eshowe Child Welfare Society. They also, for a number of years, organised the Forest Noel nativity play at Bishop's Seat. In 1959 they hosted the founder of the Round Table movement, Louis Marchese of Norwich, England. In the 1970s, they obtained a site for a holiday home for the underprivileged in Richards Bay.

The Seven Balmers: Terence, Winsome, Tony, Donavan, Adrian, Sharon and Vivian

charter in 1955. They made it their responsibility, during apartheid years, to send Zulu children to the seaside and white children to field training camps. They are also part of an international exchange student program.

Fiona and Fergus Upfold, on more than one occasion, hosted students from overseas. They included my daughter, Keri's friend in her matric year, Alyssa Deutsch from America, and Franci Dattelina from South Germany. Franci refused to move on, according to the customary 'one term only' with various Rotarian families. For that entire year Fiona and Fergus Upfold were her Mama and Papa, and their children, Kim and Marc, were her sister and brother – full stop. Period

V

Fergus Upfold is the sixth child of Yvonne Upfold (née Barratt) whose parents farmed at Nkwaleni, and Stan Upfold who, during the 1950's, arrived from further north in Zululand, to work as a mechanic for Eshowe

Motors in Osborn Road. Three of their eight children (Glenda, Gerald and Jon) were toddlers at the time. Shann, Debra, Ian, Fergus and Shelley were yet to be born at the Queen Victoria Hospital.

After hours, Stan Upfold took on private work repairing farm machinery. Soon thereafter, a farmer from Gingindlovu offered to lend Stan the money to buy Eshowe Wagon Works from Harold Yardley for £4 000. The company back then involved shoeing horses, repairing wagons and making wagon wheels. At one stage it belonged to a Mr Thring.

By the time Gerald and Fergus took over Eshowe Wagon Works from their father, wagon repairs were replaced with the maintenance and manufacture of farming equipment like trailers, cranes and infield loaders for the loading of cane onto trailers.

Ian, in the meantime, went to run the family sugar cane farm in Melmoth and opened a business called 'Melmoth Farm Services' doing farm equipment repairs. He later started a lucrative concern called 'Melmoth Hardware'.

Jon took over the wagon-works business in Eshowe after Gerald and Fergus started their own industries in engineering.

Business was poor so Jon, along with his wife, Julie Upfold (née Geach) packed up and moved to Durban where they opened a clothing boutique at the Pavilion.

Julie's father was a jeweller in Eshowe. Her mother worked for Lovell-Shippey as an estate agent. They had seven children namely Robin, Adrian, Vicky, Julie, twins Sally and Anne, and Stella.

After school Julie found employment at Standard Bank in Eshowe. One day she ran into Jon at the showgrounds where Jon's simple 'Hello' set in motion a wedding in 1966 (they recently celebrated their 58th wedding anniversary) and a houseful of children namely Alec,

Back Row: Bryce Foster (married Hannah Upfold), Guy Upfold who compiled the illustrative plates for Roberts Birds; he works at Amatikulu Fish Farm, Eli Upfold works for Valleytec, Retiree Jon Upfold, Gary Upfold who owns Valleytec, Ryan Upfold, Matthew Robins (married Emily Upfold), Ian Upfold.
Front row: Retirees Gerald and Margaret Upfold, Hannah Foster (née Upfold), Leanne Upfold (married to Guy), Janine Dixon-Smith (née Upfold), Julie Upfold (married to Jon), Hayley Dahl (née Upfold) (an honorary ranger heavily involved in the Save the Rhino campaign), Emily Robins (née Upfold), Convent Teacher Charmaine Upfold (married to Gary), Retirees Fergus and Fiona Upfold, Joan Upfold.
Seated: Timber Farmer Steve Dahl (married Hayley Upfold).

Luke, Janine, Meg and Guy. Like their parents they all attended Eshowe schools.

In the meantime, the parents of Yvonne (matriarch of the Upfold family) sold their farm at Nkwaleni. Her brothers, Stanley and Harold Barratt, moved to Eshowe where they started up a scrap metal dealership where First National Bank stands now in Osborn Road. Zululand Metal is now in the industrial area and managed by Daniel Smit. Daniel's sister, Rachel, had married Stan Barratt's son, Steve Barratt.

When Stan Barratt died, his sister, Yvonne, took ill, so Jon and Julie returned from Durban to look after her. They bought a house in Leigh Avenue and Jon went back into engineering.

Between 1983 and 1992 Julie had a fabric and haberdashery shop near Coley's Supermarket which burnt down in that Four Square Centre fire of 1993.

Raising their children included many fun times like surf-fishing almost every weekend and collecting old bottles in the forest.

The buildings that today stand in Brockwell Street where once was Eshowe Wagon Works still belong to the Upfold family.

Gerald Upfold and Margaret Upfold (née Freeman) had four children: Carol, Deane and Jill (who are twins) and Gary who owns an electrical company called 'Valleytec'. Subsequent to the burning down of those premises during the 2021 unrest, Valleytec has

---

*It is interesting to note that the following Upfolds all married partners who, like themselves, attended Eshowe High School. Jon, in fact, was a founder Standard 6 pupil when the high school opened its doors in 1959. Gerald Upfold married Margaret Freeman, Jon Upfold married Julie Geach, Fergus Upfold married Fiona Dufton. Fiona was the daughter of Harry Dufton who, for years, worked at Arie Van Dort's hardware store. Her mother, Bessie owned Fashion Fantasy Boutique in Osborn Road. Ian Upfold married Joan Swemmer, daughter of the resident magistrate at the time, and Debra Upfold married Michael Rosewall (Trevor Rosewall's brother). Glenda Upfold (the eldest) married Neville Beanland who had a business, Elf Electrical, until they emigrated to Australia. Shann Upfold married Clive Craig who opened the Eshowe branch of Campbell & Craig, now C& H Accounting.

Diamond Bozas' paintings of Stanley Upfold's wagon works in Brockwell St

The same property in 2024

relocated to the industrial area.

During my early years in Eshowe, Deane (one of Gerald and Margaret's twins) owned a hairdressing salon on those wagon works premises. It was by far the most stylish in town with pitch black walls and elegant white leather sofas.

Fiona Upfold owned a florist in the small building situated between the old wagon works property and Aston Townsend's huge old house. The florist was called 'Joan's Florist' because it was started by Joan Phillips. Barbara Townsend took it over for a while before selling up and working as a secretary at Eshowe Junior School. Fiona Upfold (née Dufton) married Fergus Upfold during the 1970s after he returned from completing his accountant articles with Campbell & Craig at their branch in Durban. When I first met Fiona she was in partnership with Meg Chennells, running the most popular catering business in town. They were the best of friends who, subsequent to my divorce from Pat Brenchley, were both incredibly kind to my second daughter, Keri whose first job was working in the kitchen at the George Hotel with Meg. Meg encouraged Keri to au pair in America for a few years. After her return to South Africa it wasn't long before Keri went au pairing in London. When Fiona taught home economics at Eshowe High School, she was a mentor to my third daughter, Jodie Brenchley who also taught there and worked in the office before leaving to teach in Vietnam.

VI

After my divorce in 2003, I had the pleasure of working temporarily with Sharon Louw at Ezemvelo KZN Wildlife. I am yet to meet someone who so very much loves her line of work.

Sharon Louw (née Byrne) grew up on a farm in Melmoth. Mike Nixon had the pleasure of teaching her at Eshowe High School where she was a weekly boarder. There she represented Zululand and KZN in hockey (cudos to Rob Stuart and Les Ashley) and athletics, obtained an honours blazer and was appointed deputy head girl in 1988.

She wanted to study nature conservation, but, championing conflicting ideas of past generations, her parents did not think employment opportunities would be good for a 'girl' in this field. Along with her closest friends, she was shipped off to Durban to complete a secretarial course at Sight & Sound Business College. It was the worst year of her life. Thereafter she went on a field guide course offered by the Lake St Lucia Children's Camp, owned and managed by Bill and Cathy Fraser who were based at Fanies Island. Shortly after that course Sharon was offered a guiding position. She thoroughly enjoyed being part of an environmental awareness team which included varied school groups visiting the facility.

Subsequently, she registered for a Diploma in Nature Conservation at the Technikon of Pretoria. What followed were two exciting years of studies and field trips that included holiday work in Natal Parks Board Reserves. Those activities served to reinforce Sharon's deep love for conservation.

Sharon's 'practical' third year placement was a difficult choice between the then KwaZulu Bureau of Natural Resources and the Natal Parks Board. They each offered fantastic practical training opportunities. What eventually attracted Sharon to the Natal Parks Board was the variety of training opportunities across the province which were divided into three-month stints at various reserves. She worked and lived at St Lucia, Klipfontein Dam in the Vryheid district, Oribi Gorge Nature Reserve, Spioenkop Nature Reserve in the Estcourt district and Garden Castle State Forest in the Drakensberg. She was one of the cadets that included only two girls among their ranks, who completed their practical training with the Natal Parks Board in 1993.

In 1994, after obtaining her Diploma in Nature Conservation, Sharon accepted a post as a nature conservation technician with the KwaZulu Department of Nature Conservation.

She remembers her interview with the then CEO, Mr Nick Steele, who was most encouraging of women entering the realms of conservation.

Sharon was based in the Eshowe Regional Office and worked in the Community Conservation Division with Mrs Sarah Allan. Later, she moved across to the Research Division to work with Mrs Beryl Guy.

And so, there was Sharon, based in Eshowe where she had completed high school and was now to live, work, meet and marry Andre Louw, and raise three daughters namely Jade and twins Jordyn and Gemma. I was working with Sharon at the time we received the exciting news that she was expecting twins. There I was in the wildlife office jumping like a rabbit and prancing like a buck. After producing five children I am still in awe of the sheer wonder of a process that offers some sense of immortality. I immediately set out crocheting a baby blanket for the Louw twins, but when I picked it up to finish the final row I saw that my Jack Russell puppy had chewed her way through the very middle of it.

Now living in Mtunzini, Sharon looks back on her years in Eshowe with some amazement. She learned so much, and not only from fellow colleagues. She remembers her first meeting with entomologist Denis Eckard who arrived at her gate at 9 Poynton Place saying, 'I believe you are studying nature conservation.' This led to many years of Sharon working on projects together with local honorary officers. Buttoned up in khaki, the honorary officers were very active. Many worked weekends away at Hluhluwe-iMfolozi Park, Mkuze Game Reserve, eMakhosini-Ophathe Heritage Park and Ezeweni Farm in Melmoth. Honorary officers, including work colleagues of Sharon's, have left strong conservation legacies in the greater Eshowe area – Ken Morty originally fenced in the Entumeni nature reserve and undertook field ranger patrols on horseback. A keen sportsman, who was well integrated in the community, he was able to share critical historical information on the management of Dlinza Forest and Entumeni's Nature Reserve*.

Based in Eshowe, Sharon had the opportunity to work in protected areas all across Zululand. Her passion and commitment saw her propelling up through the ranks of technician, chief technician and specialist technician. At the University of KwaZulu-Natal (Pietermaritzburg) in 2010, she completed her masters in environment and development with a focus on protected area management. She was then promoted to regional ecologist in 2013. One of her key roles is providing support to protected area managers at Nkandla and Ongoye Forest Reserves, Entumeni Nature Reserve, Dlinza Forest Nature Reserve, Amatikulu Nature Reserve, Harold Johnson Nature Reserve, Umlalazi Nature Reserve, Enseleni and Lake Eteza Nature Reserves, the eMakhosini-Ophathe Heritage Park, including the district conservation officers in the King Cethswayo and iLembe districts. One project that stands out is monitoring the critically endangered Millar's Tiger Moth, that saw great work and friendships develop over the years with Denis and local farmers, Barry Emberton, Louis Gunter and Hugh Lee.

*Other members of the municipality instrumental in securing land for the expansion of the Dlinza Forest Nature Reserve included Chris Gerber, Neville Williams, Suzie van der Westhuizen, Gerhard de Jager, Rob Wilson, Ronel Hulley and Alderman Stan Larkan. Colleagues such as John and Auriel Tinley, Graham and Nora Keet, Dave Balfour, Yoliswa Ndlovu, Richard Penn Sawers, Amelia van Rooyen and Phumla Zulu were resident Eshowe-ites. Honorary officers, offering many skills, were Denis Eckard, Chris Pargeter, Titch and Brenda Wellman, Gavin Lawrie, John Mellet, Hamish McLaggan, James Braithwaite, Bob Turner, Rex Duke and Don Leitch.

Prof Neil Crouch, Sharon Louw and Prof Gideon Smith at Aloe sharoniae site

I might add that local farmers actively manage natural vegetation on their farms. They excitedly report rare sightings such as birding breeding sites, side-striped jackal and leopard.

Then the seeds of the tiny endangered Saunders' Grass Aloe (Aloe saundersiae), that grow at Nkandla, were propagated by Gareth Chittenden of Zululand Nurseries, to facilitate the re-establishment of an aloe colony in Nkandla Forest Reserve. (I remember doing a botanical painting of the specific plant for Sharon's private collection). Sharon emerges as an accomplished and meticulous observer of minutiae in the landscape around her. When the rhino poaching war first arrived in Zululand in the early 2000s, for security and safety reasons, delays in Sharon completing veld evaluations resulted in her photographing an unusual aloe. That aloe helped Professor Neil Crouch and Professor Gideon Smith focus attention on the species, which was subsequently named *Aloe sharoniae*, in Sharon's honour.

Chapter 7

Stan Barratt had two sons, Harold and Steven. Both were successful businessmen in the industrial area, but also full of pranks. During the good old days of the Star Theatre/Cinema in Eshowe, they waited for the audience to be entirely, absolutely and utterly engaged. Then, at the moment when Dracula flew on the big screen they extracted, from under their jackets, two large flapping roosters and flung them over the heads of viewers in the front seats.

The theatre also presented musicals such as 'The Sound of Music', 'Camelot' and 'Annie Get your Gun'. 'Woodstock' enthralled the then younger generation. Bannock and Liz Scheffer sang about the balloon seller, and Don Harding crooned 'Smoke Gets in your Eyes'. Julius the Hypnotist put on some good shows, and the Zululand Show hosted their Show Queen contests.

Most patrons for the Saturday afternoon matinees were scholars seeking entertainment while their parents played golf. During evening shows the screen was sometimes a haze through thick cigarette smoke. On one occasion, during the viewing of 'Papillon' the reels got all mixed up. Nonetheless, everyone stood up after the show, as they did after every show, for the singing of 'God Save the Queen'.

Mike Nixon didn't miss westerns like Clint Eastwood's 'The Good the Bad and the Ugly'. Fifty cents bought him admission, a coke, and a chocolate. During interval, he and his friends would pop over to the Royal Hotel for a quick beer in the new pub which had replaced the original pub that had been destroyed by a fire. The newer pub had a couple of roughly hewn black oak beams. The counter was a very solid wooden affair

Majorettes marching past the Star Theatre

2024 - If those walls could talk.

with a dark polished appearance. A heavy brass foot-rail ran along the counter with a copper trough filled with sand behind that. The counter was lined with a beaten copper kick-board and, more than once, 'Scrap' (Stan) Barratt was seen eyeing it with a professional eye.

In later years the 'S' was stolen from the theatre's signage and it read 'Tar Theatre'.

There was a spelling competition in the theatre's monthly programme. The first person to spot the misspelt word got a free entrance ticket.

I

Richard Yardley recently compiled the writings of Eddie Wellman* (Ozzie Wellman's brother).

Eddie Wellman recalls in his book titled 'Zululand Tales' that among the hotel managers that came and went in Eshowe, one of the more colourful was Ted Keey. Ted was a big jovial man who often sported a red and white striped bow tie while on duty at the Royal.

Saturday raffles in the pub at the Royal became quite an institution. Started by one of the managers who was a MOTH, those raffles were mostly in aid of MOTH Club funds.

Ted also saw other possibilities of boosting the bar turnover and the first raffle was for half a sheep. Tickets cost R1 and were numbered up to one hundred. At first the barman on duty battled to sell them all, so to help increase the number of contributors, and attract more customers, the manager decided to give everybody who had taken a ticket a free drink. Also, as an added incentive, the hotel would dish out free plates of curry

---

*Eddie's social circle included Norman 'Jackson' Freeman, Emer Reve, Eric Platt, Dick Field, Mickey Leathern, Stan Folkard, Peter Knoop, Billy and Johnny Edwards, Ronnie Martin, Norman Steenberg and John Truelock – among others.

and rice. Then a free raffle for a chicken was added. In addition, a bottle of whisky was donated by the hotel. This raffle was also free and everyone who had had a drink during the preceding week qualified because when you paid for a drink, your name was written on the back of the till chit. Come Saturday, one chit was drawn from a box. The winning person had to be present to get the bottle – if not, the draw went forward to the next week. Later still, a 4,5 litre bottle of whisky was added to the list of prizes. By then the donations cost R2 each.

One of the first winners of the half-a-sheep was Eddie Wellman's brother, Ozzie, who was not actually a supporter of the pub. It just happened that on a Friday evening after a motor traders meeting, just across the road at Natal Motor Industries, chairman Micky East suggested they have a drink at the Royal.

'Bossie' Bosman had the most incredible luck: he won five 4,5litre bottles of whisky in six weeks, plus a few more on other occasions.

Some fishermen from the Transvaal, passing through on a Wednesday, took a few tickets saying they'd be back on the Saturday to pick up the whisky. Sure enough, one of them did win it. They promptly filled their 20 litre Coleman water container with ice blocks, decanted the whole 4,5 litres into the ice and departed.

The Royal Hotel had built up quite a reputation for its meals and non-residents were encouraged to book a table. Andre Meyer, the landlord, got a phone call from Ulundi booking lunch for Chief Mangosuthu Buthelezi's party of 30, some four weeks hence. A week later that booking was cancelled. But on the original date, just before lunchtime, the party did arrive. Obviously, this caused a bit of consternation, but Andre kept his wits about him. He discovered plenty of lamb chops in cold storage and these were quickly grilled. There was also a large pot of putu (thick mealie meal porridge) originally intended for his staff. A spokesman for the party later expressed his appreciation and said that in future they would have their lunches there whenever the occasion presented itself.

The Provincial (George) Hotel in Eshowe was the rival of the Royal and had its share of loyal patrons. There were, of course, those who supported both establishments. They would drive past the one, checking to see whose cars were parked outside, then maybe drive to the other one, depending on who they wanted to see (or who they wanted to avoid).

If you add the Country Club, the Sports' Centre, the MOTH Club and the police canteen, Eshowe had six pubs. The police canteen was really a private club for members of the force, but Johnny Roux from the CID, the first honorary barman, invited some members of the public for the opening and a few of them became regular customers. Not only were the drinks cheaper than the hotels but the atmosphere was quite different. Eshowe was the first station for a lot of young constables who had just come out of training and it was a pleasure to see how keen and enthusiastic they were. Another advantage was the early closing time which meant one didn't get into trouble for getting home too late. And sometimes (accidentally) one got early warning of roadblocks and could warn friends.

The police canteen was run by members of the force and, like any hotel or club, the barman contributed greatly to the success or lack of it. One of Eddie Wellman's favourite bar-tenders was Basil Nicholson. Eddie and Basil had a lot in common, not least of which was their love for cooking. Often, Eddie would visit him for a quick beer and a recipe, then rush off to Adam's Supermarket, buy the ingredients he was short of and rush home to cook. One of Basil's recipes was for fried chicken which, he claimed, his children preferred to Kentucky. It required Aromat and crushed corn-flakes, among other things.

One evening as Eddie was driving home, he saw a helicopter hovering over the airstrip. Arriving there, he discovered an Army Puma. Mike Hill, an ex-Eshowe boy and a friend of Eddie's, was the pilot. Apparently the engine was giving trouble so they would need to stay over. They were on the way to Durban from Hluhluwe and were carrying a Nyala carcass obtained from the Natal Parks Board. It seemed likely that the machine would be stranded for a few days so they were worried about their meat. They took off again and landed in the police grounds, where fortunately, the canteen had a large cold-room to keep the carcass in. Eddie phoned Ernie Wardell, a local blockman, who agreed to cut it up. Seldom had Eddie enjoyed venison more than the shoulder they gave him. Naturally he had consulted Basil about the recipe and invited him and his wife to share in it.

Talking about food, I must make mention of those mischief makers who belonged to families that spent their holidays on nearby beaches. There was no development at Ballito in the 1950s and fishing off the rocks there was lots of shad to be caught. According to Tony Balmer, when fishermen felt crayfish clinging to their bait they would reel them in. Once the crayfish had dropped off it was the children's task to scramble about catching the crayfish before they slid back into the sea.

There existed a certain nameless opportunist who hit on an effortless way of acquiring crayfish. Aware of the many people on the rocks after dark, who were catching crayfish without the required licence, our mischief-maker walked out with a flashlight while blowing sharply on a whistle. Thinking the police were about to arrest them, those who had been catching crayfish illegally dropped everything and scattered, leaving their catch to be readily harvested as easy pickings.

II

Thanks to much fund raising initiatives over the years, the MOTH Club were able to buy a number of houses left behind by the Water Affairs Department after the completion of the Goedetrouw Dam Scheme. These houses, called 'MOTH Cottages', although prefabricated, are quite comfortable and let out at a nominal rent.

The Eshowe MOTH Hall, opposite the old wagon works in Brockwell Street, has in its time been hired out to different institutions including the Blood Transfusion Service. On those days, members wishing to go to the bar (which was housed in the back) could either sneak round the side, ducking as they passed the window, or donate blood first.

Eddie Wellman always insisted on having his left arm punctured so as not to weaken his dart-throwing one. He also ensured that at least two pints of a suitable liquid replaced his blood loss as soon as possible.

One day it was decided to install a pool table in the MOTH Hall's bar area, so the room had to be enlarged. A new counter was also fitted, which ran the length of the room and was nearly one-and-a-half metres wide. It reminded Eddie of the olden times when the barman needed the protection it offered.

Eddie used to drop in occasionally when he saw Syd Brien's car parked outside. Syd was, at 80, the oldest practising attorney in Eshowe. He was interested in the English language and music and usually discussed those subjects over a beer that he drank slowly and deliberately.

In 2024 the MOTHs Hall, opposite the old wagon works, houses a gym

Indeed, the pub was a pleasant place to spend half an hour with friends on the way home from work*.

III

The Armistice Day Parade and the Remembrance Service are attended by all MOTHs. One year even the German Lutheran minister, an ex-Luftwaffe pilot, was present. In 1944 Eddie and 25 high school pupils from around Natal spent the Michaelmas holidays as guests of Rotary, camping on the Technical College sports grounds, just off the Durban beachfront near the Snake Park. They were given lectures on leadership etc and visited factories like Dunlop's and Lever Bros. Also the Daily News where they each got a copy of the paper

---

*Among the staunch MOTH Club members were Dennis the Menace (also known as 'Plastic Bones Palmer'); Jimmy Keyes (an entertaining humourist); 'Uncle' Louis Stead (ex-mayor of Ladysmith); Oom Piet de Haas (the barman); as well as Johnnie Jewaskiewicz, Rob Chowles, Jan 'FM' Henning, borough health inspector and spare-time barber who gave haircuts in aid of club funds, Johnny Louw, Edgar Brook, Scon Bannock and brothers Harold and Steven Barratt.

with their picture in it as it came off the press.

The Flying-boat Base at Salisbury Island was also on their list and they were allowed aboard a Sunderland moored there.

At the end of their tour they were taken to the MOTH headquarters at Old Fort Road and met Charles Evenden, founder of the order. He gave an illuminating talk on how it came into being, and its aims.

Eddie Wellman's son, Alfred Wellman was a class mate of Mike Nixon's at Eshowe High School during the 1970s. Mike remembers him as an incredible sportsman as well as head boy and awarded Dux in his matric year. Alfred's younger sister, Rita Wellman, was Dux in her own matric year. Sadly, Alfred died, far too young, in a car accident in his 2nd year of studying building science at Natal University (Durban) at the same time that Mike Nixon was studying there.

IV

The very first aeroplane to visit Zululand touched down on the Eshowe Golf Course at 10.14 am on Friday, 3rd May 1918. When word got out that Major (later Lieutenant-Colonel) Allister Miller, the pioneer of South African civil aviation, was extending his country-wide visit to Natal, the chairman of Eshowe's local board was asked to send a wire expressing the hope that the major's arrangements might allow for him to visit Zululand.

Major Millar agreed to visit Eshowe if a suitable landing place, complying with certain expressed requirements, was guaranteed.

It took nearly three days to prepare a suitable ground on the golf links. Mr WA Vanderplank placed a number of his own staff at the disposal of the board. Mr A Cowley supervised the workforce in cutting grass and

filling holes. The news that the aeroplane might be expected became known, but a rumour accompanied it saying that the flight would be on Wednesday morning instead of Friday. A number of people came to Eshowe on that day only to be dreadfully disappointed.

On Thursday 2nd of May, Major Miller wired that he expected to reach Eshowe on the following morning at about 9 am.

Long before that time, a big crowd assembled on the golf links. Blacks and whites alike were eager to witness the spectacle of a flying man visiting a spot which not many years ago was occupied by buffalo and elephant.

The weather was perfect on the day of arrival. Businesses in town closed so that every person was on the golf links to patiently await the aircraft that was a whole hour late.

After 10 am, every eye was directed to the tiny object in the distant sky which gradually assumed larger dimensions, gracefully circled the ground and landed lightly on the links.

There was an immediate rush for the wonderful machine. Resounding cheers greeted Major Miller when he climbed down from his seat.

There were some white rabbits on board that the

major proceeded to auction off for war funds, raising the grand sum of £65.

Messers JY Hunter (chairman of Eshowe's local board at the time), JD Hunter, CF Adams, TG Tallantire, T Poynton, CEG Benham, Reverend A Dyre and several others received letters by 'airmail' that day for the first time ever, from Durban.

Chairman of the Eshowe local board welcomed the aeronaut: *'Major Miller, on behalf of the residents of Eshowe and district, I extend to you a very hearty welcome on this your first visit to Eshowe, and the thanks of the district are due to you, for your kindness in having gone to the trouble of visiting us today. Needless to say this will be a red letter day in the history of Eshowe, and will be remembered by both young and old for many years to come. This is the first aeroplane that has visited Zululand and it will be an education to children. It will also be a power of good to the Zulu people who see you through your travels through Zululand. Major Miller we are indeed honoured in having your presence.'*

Almost two years later, on 20th February 1920, The Zululand Times reported an account of the next aircraft to visit Eshowe: *'Early on Tuesday morning, Eshowe-ites were astir in anticipation of the arrival of the 'Natalia' chartered on a business tour by the enterprising firm of Dunlop Tyre Company, for whom the local agent is Mr Tom Poynton. The aeroplane, which is an Avro machine, was piloted by Captain C G Ross and timed to arrive between the hour of 8 and 9am. The golf course was the chosen spot for landing and a large and expectant arrival.'*

In fact, just after 10 am, a telegram was received by Mr Poynton stating that the machine could not leave Durban until 11 am. Despite this disappointment the spectators preserved their patience and stuck to their ground. At about 3 pm a small speck heading for Eshowe was visible. Flying at an altitude of about 1 000 metres, the Natalia quickly became visible to the ordinary eye and within a few minutes made its descent.

As soon as the aeroplane landed, Mr Charles Dalby, deputy chairman of the Eshowe's town board (he was to become chairman in 1921), gave a welcoming speech saying that they were there that day to greet their aerial visitors, Captain Ross, Captain Cullum and Mr Baxter, the mechanic.

Mr Dalby had personally followed the 'Natalia's' enterprise with great interest. He noted that while crossing the Drakensberg, Captain Ross had attained a height of 3 000 metres, and after striking an air pocket he had skillfully handled the drop made by his machine, manipulating it safely into Natal, Bergville. He went on to say that this was proof of the stability and safety of the modern aeroplane and he recognised that aircraft would play a great part in the future by means of bringing the nations into closer contact, and be a great factor towards the maintenance of peace throughout the whole world. He pointed out that Captain Cullum had visited Eshowe before as the representative of Dunlop Tyre Company and he was sure he was voicing the sentiments of all present that the undertaking embarked upon by Captain Cullum's firm would prove a success.

Captain Ross replied, stating it was a great pleasure to visit Eshowe. He was also hopeful of a successful mission and equally optimistic about the future of aviation in the country.

TG Tallantire, local newspaper agent for the Natal Mercury, received a parcel of the paper together with illustrated souvenirs which the proprietors of the popular 'Durban Daily' wanted distributed. Recipients endorsed the sentiments expressed that this unique event would be the forerunner of a regular 'aerial' postal service to Eshowe.

Questioned as to how they regarded the landing, Captain Callum stated the landing site at the Eshowe

Country Club was equal to that in Durban. He trusted that in the near future a syndicate might be able to procure an aeroplane to be stationed at Eshowe. He also stated that they were particularly indebted to Mr Tom Poynton of Eshowe for the manner in which he arranged the trip.

Flights were taken by several Eshowe residents at £5 per head per flip*. One and all spoke of the exhilarating feelings experienced whilst in mid-air, and the wonderful panoramic view that the flight offered.

Mr Baxter, it was interesting to hear, had won the DCM at the same time that Major Miller (who flew to Eshowe in 1918) won the DSO, both flying in the same model of machine.

I might mention that ordinary mail service had been in effect since 1911. The Royal Mail Service was started by Mr Charles Dalby at the wheel of his motor car. Post bore Zululand's own issue of postage stamps that are collectors' rarity today.

*They included JY Hunter, CH Dalby, Miss Fry, Miss Osborn, Mr and Mrs Gebers, JHA Badenhorst, E Wilkinson, Master T Hunter, KV Challenor, J Ashby, GC Haines, T Wantink, H Yardley, G Yardley, FW Paul, AW Paul, EF Nottingham and T Poynton.

Chapter 8

Please allow me to introduce my dear friend, Marian Mattinson (née Gunter) who encourages with such emotional intensity. She is the friend who has a hugely exaggerated opinion of my creative intelligence. Marian considers having worked for the bank and various accounting firms as her local claim to fame. But, as you can see by the pictures opposite, it is her phenomenal talent as a painter is what holds her in such tremendous esteem. Having no professional qualifications in art allows her, rather unfairly I think, to describe herself as a 'hobby artist' – this despite her having won prestigious international awards. The cover of my childhood memoir, 'Wars of the Weavers' is a Marian Mattinson watercolour. The original belongs to proud owners Dr Kevin and Mrs Loreen McDonald.

Marian, her brother, Louis Gunter, and their incredibly bright sister, Myrtle who was head girl at both Eshowe Junior School and Eshowe High School (the latter in 1965) grew up on a farm just outside Eshowe on the road to Entumeni. To this day Louis runs that original family farm that, during his childhood, operated by candle-light and with long-drop toilets. Their parents, Lionel Gunter and Patty Gunter (née Wiggett) acquired 'Eskom' electricity well after the children left school. Patty's weekly shopping list included the 'Daily Mirror' – an overseas newspaper bound into a book. It evolved from being the reading material to being the loo paper in the long-drop. Marian and her siblings were boarders from Class 1 to Standard 8. Thereafter Marian boarded privately with the Crawford family. In matric she boarded with Tannie Dorfling and Oom Jan. Oom Jan was Maryna Claasen's grandfather. Maryna is still a good

friend of Marian's. She married Empangeni chiropractor Willy Holder.

Marian's art journey began during her junior years when Eshowe Junior School submitted her art to the annual Zululand Agricultural Show. Lionel and Patty realised that Marian needed to pursue a form of art. Even though art was not a subject at Eshowe High School they bought her a box of professional pastels and a pad of archival pastel paper. The price (R2.75) is still on the box. She still uses those Rembrandt chalk pastels today and the paper is still in perfect condition.

Marian's teachers, recognising her talent, tried encouraging Lionel Gunter to send her to Durban to study commercial art. A small-town girl at heart, the idea of going to Durban terrified Marian, and Lionel Gunter, frankly, did not believe in girls needing formal qualifications. So it was a job in the bank until marriage and children came along.

Mike Mattinson burst into Marian's life on a huge motorbike wearing boots, black leather jacket, black leather gloves and a studded belt. He was a brave, unruly student who, on a bet, shaved all his hair off. On another occasion he fashioned his hair into a Mohawk – the Moby Dick version.

Mike and Marian dated throughout Marian's senior years at school. They got married on 14th October 1967. Their years together included romance, fun, hardships and great rewards. Mike gave his all in commitment, work, fun and kindness. Having served his apprenticeship as an electrician at Darnall, his birthplace, he moved to Mandini, following which he began working for Zululand Tyre in Eshowe. He chose to leave the company shortly before marrying Marian.

Lionel Gunter despaired at his future son-in-law being unemployed. So Stan Upfold, a very good friend of Lionel's, introduced Mike to his son-in-law, Neville Beanland, owner of Elf Electrical. When Neville moved to Australia he offered the business to Mike and Marian who turned down the offer due to lack of experience.

Lionel Gunter, not wanting his family to leave Eshowe, chose to rent out his farm to his children. This enabled Lionel and Patty to retire to their holiday home at Makakatana, near Charter's Creek on the banks of Lake St Lucia. Makakatana is currently part of St Lucia Western Shores.

The worst drought in living memory forced the end of Mike's and Marian's farming operation. And Mike went to work for the Hardmans at Eshowe Mart.

Myrt's husband, Ken Hall took up a position with Zululand Tyre in Osborn Road. And Louis continued to rent the farm that he owns today.

It was at this time, while Marian was working as a bookkeeper for Coopers & Lybrand, now C & H, that the Mattinson's got their big break. It was a case of being in the right place at the right time: Marian was doing the books for Road Island Service Station which at the time was owned by Tim Chennells who was wanting to sell. Ralph Hamann, being Tim's accountant, saw an investment opportunity which would work for both Mike and himself.

Cynthia Squires, Mike's partner in crime, was included with the business. Mike could not have managed the smooth takeover and running of the service station without her administration skills. She remains a good friend to the family and is a regular friendly face at Eshowe's Garden Club meetings.

Marian's art training (over 45 years' worth) was with Diamond Bozas. But, in 1979 she attended a watercolor workshop with artist Marj Bowan. Marian still refers to her notes taken at that workshop. She bought a little set of Winsor & Newton artists' paints and used that same set right up until 2019. Funds were few at the beginning so watercolor was not a medium she used often because paper was expensive.

Shortly after Marj's course, Marian returned to working full day as a bookkeeper for Coopers & Lybrand until she retired just before her 60th birthday. This was when she took it upon herself, with added help from the Aitkens, the Lees and the Wisemans to nurse me through my nervous breakdown.

Marian also saw to her mother, Patty who had moved in after Lionel died, and was needing constant medical attention. Patty lived with Mike and Marian for 14 years.

Marian had hardly retired when she was diagnosed with cancer. Fortunately, even though rampant, it was caught and treated timeously.

Patty died a month after Marian finished her treatment and the month after that Marian's husband, Mike had a major heart attack. They were in Kruger National Park celebrating Mike's 3rd day of retirement. Doctors in Nelspruit operated through the night to save him. It was quite traumatic for Marian to be told to say goodbye to her husband as they could not guarantee his survival. Mike was a strong man with a very positive attitude to life. He had an amazing sense of humour that saw him through many challenges.

The year 2010 was a hectic year for the Mattinsons. Mike's inherited Alpha-1 Antitrypsin Deficiency slowly took center stage. He lived for 18 years after being told he was not going to live past six months. He went into hospital often and the family could not be blamed for thinking, 'Surely, this must be the end.' Yet he rallied, overcame and conquered. Collectively they named him the 'Warhorse'.

Camping, boating and fishing at Kosi Bay will never be the same without Mike at the helm. His skill at boating around Kosi lakes, day or night, regardless of the waves, was remarkable. Also his continual efforts in maintaining Makakatana at Lake St Lucia were hugely appreciated by the Gunter family.

I

Art was something Diamond Bozas tried to keep alive in Eshowe. With his encouragement we younger members took over. While working full day, Marian Mattinson would take three days off work to help assemble stands and man exhibitions.

In 2015 Mike and Marian's elder daughter, Shelley joined the Watercolor Society of KwaZulu-Natal. In 2017 she insisted that Marian join her.

They could not leave Mike on his own as, by then, he was on oxygen 24/7. It turned out he was an amazing sport, happy to sit in the car reading, while waiting for Marian and Shelley to attend their courses. Marian thoroughly enjoyed the demonstrations and being part of an art group. She and Shelley were introduced to Grant Wood, Marion Townsend and other excellent artists.

Shelley participated in a workshop with Grant shortly after his demonstration.

Before Mike died in 2019, he made sure the art studio on their Mtunzini property was built. He was determined that 'the girls' pursue their art after his death. He encouraged them to participate in the Hilton Arts Festival. The week after his death, the email came to say they had been accepted. Marian and her artistic daughters, Shelley and Theresa felt like small fish in a huge ocean when they arrived in Hilton to set up their work. They had to remind themselves that they were doing this for Mike. However, they thoroughly enjoyed those few days and not only did they cover their costs, but they made a profit. Plus, David Johnson, a well-known wildlife artist came to look at their stand. He convinced them to arrange a pastel workshop in Mtunzini. They have since had three workshops in which they, all three, have participated.

It has been non-stop art for Marian since Mike died. She has been awarded free scholarships by overseas artists. Between her garden and art, her days are not long enough. She is most grateful to have something wonderful to wake up to every morning.

Her daughters, Shelley and Theresa encouraged Marian to join their webpage, 'Shades of Trees'. They currently have a gallery at Mtunzini that is open for viewing by appointment only as it is a working studio.

During Marian and Mike's years of membership of Round Table, the club put on a fundraiser mime act called 'SHOWTIME.' Tony and June Tucker's rendition of 'Oh doctor, I'm in trouble' is still spoken about, as is John and Sandy McHugh's stint called 'Saturday Night Fever'.

Another mime was a rendition of 'Patricia the Stripper'. Harold Champion mimed along to Chris de

Burg's lyrics while the dowah girls (including Wendy Ferguson, Trish van Wyk, Elaine Chesterton and Jenny Hawke) put on a dance show.

Marian was 'Patricia' stripping behind a shadow screen. After the show, she was reprimanded by a local headmaster's wife for being so badly behaved when she still had children at the school. Marian enjoyed a chuckle, and rightly so, for not only did she teach her children the additional three 'R's for Rights, Responsibilities and Rewards, but she also nurtured, in them, those invaluable 'F's for Fun and Fellowship with Family and Friends.

II

Dr Tom McHugh (1906 - 1984) qualified as a doctor and pharmacist in Dublin, Ireland.

When his father, a chemist in Ireland, died, Tom had to take over the family business until his younger brother qualified. That's when he saw an advert in the newspaper looking for a doctor to locum in Eshowe, Zululand, South Africa. It turned out that the person needing the locum came from the same town in Ireland as Tom.

And so it was, on 27th April 1935, that Dr Tom McHugh arrived from Ireland to do a six-month locum for Dr Eddie Holland, who had a multiracial practice next to the Queen Victoria Hospital.

After that six months in Eshowe, Tom returned to Ireland with the intention of specialising in surgery, but his efforts were hindered by the 2nd World War.

He returned to Eshowe that he'd grown so fond of during the locum, and simply picked up again at Dr Holland's surgery. The two of them flipped a coin to see who would go north to treat wounded troops. Dr Holland, who was honoured with the Papal distinction

of 'Pro Ecclesia et Pontifice' in 1956, later wrote a fascinating article about the three Eshowe hospitals that was published in The Zululand Times on 4th March 1965. I quote Dr Holland: *'When Colonel Pearson went into the laager in Eshowe on 23rd January 1879 a military hospital was established in Norwegian Mission Church* at KwaMondi. *This church was burnt down at a later date. In charge of the hospital was Staff Surgeon Norbury, RN. His staff consisted of Surgeon Major Fitzmaurice and Surgeons Thompson, RN, Wilson, AMD and Giles Civil. They evidently had a hectic time to begin with and Colonel Pearson, expecting surprise night attacks, ordered all soldiers to sleep under their wagons. Pneumonia became rife. Casualties were frequent from skirmishes and infectious disease was rampant. The death toll at 'Etshowi',* as *it was called in official dispatches, indicate that enteric and dysentery were the most common cause of death. The first civilian doctor to practice in Eshowe was Dr Balfe and he was joined by Dr Case who also saw to the surrendered or captured Boers in Eshowe's concentration camp from 1899 to 1902. The first nurse to work in Eshowe was Mrs Milne, grandmother to Clifford Tallantire. She arrived in 1886 and many a tale she related to me of her nursing experiences with Dr Balfe who was her idol. Dr Balfe was succeeded by Dr Henderson and he was the first medical officer appointed to the Queen Victoria Hospital when it was opened on 14th February 1899. It was the very first cottage hospital opened in Natal, built with funds amounting to £800 collected from Europeans and Africans. The government contributed on a pound for pound basis.* The ground was purchased from Colonel G Mansel, CMG, in Mansell Terrace. Dr GK Moberly succeeded Dr Henderson as medical officer in charge. He was medical officer to the force that moved to Nkandla against Bambatha in 1906. The casualties were sent to Eshowe. In 1910 Dr Moberly moved to Empangeni and Dr GH Wildish replaced him at Eshowe. Although no relation to author Selwyn Moberly, Dr Moberly did write two books, namely 'Zululand Romance' and 'A Square Deal'; both mirroring his own personal experiences against the backdrop of early Eshowe. Dr Wildish arrived originally in South Africa with Kitchener's Scouts in the Boer War. He served in the Great War in South West Africa and volunteered for service in the 2nd World War, but owing to the number of evacuees on the South Coast where he had settled, who needed medical attention, his service had to be declined. Dr Wildish carried out a valiant crusade against the great flu epidemic of 1918. I joined Dr Wildish, in 1925, and we worked together until 1933 when he retired to Umkomaas. Dr Wildish rendered yeoman service to Zululand. He was an excellent surgeon and a wise physician with a wide knowledge of the types of tropical disease then prevalent in Zululand. My strangest and most trying experiences in those days were calls into the reserves to deliver dead babies from dead mothers and it had to be by nature's route, otherwise the amaZulu believed that the mother would not rest in the afterlife. The recognised fee was five hard-earned pounds. In those days much travelling was done on horseback, even to the leper institution at Amatikulu. If no horse were available distances had to be travelled by foot. The very ill usually reached the surgery in a wheelbarrow if they could not sit on a donkey. The malaria epidemic of 1929 to 1932 changed the Zulus' attitude to hospitals. At first they refused injections and threw away the quinine tablets. But afterwards they would take, with avidity, a quinine mixture. Every bed was taken, tents were pitched and tarpaulins hung from the fence. We had no light in the surgery that adjoined the Queen Victoria Hospital and when darkness fell we turned the car lights on to chairs in the open and continued injecting well into the night. With first light we started again. The establishment of the malaria research laboratory under the direction of famous Entomologist D Botha and Dr de Meillon was the final round in the battle against malaria in Southern Zululand. Dr de Meillon proved a great asset to the hospital in helping to investigate other parasitic diseases as well. After Dr Wildish's departure, in 1933, I took over his various appointments. Several assistants came and went and eventually I was lucky enough to secure the services of an old family friend from Ireland, Dr Thomas McHugh, in 1935. I think it will be universally agreed that I could not have made a better choice. He acted for me, often without the help of an assistant, during the war years, and continued to be my loyal and trusted partner until I had to retire from general practice in 1958. By 1956 the old Queen Victoria had become outmoded and inadequate, so the Provincial Administration built a large modern hospital in Kangela Street, partly on the site of Shaka's Kangela Kraal. The old hospital was retained as a nurses' home. Dr M Adhams became the first full-time superintendent of the hospital. Over the years Queen Victoria Hospital had a number of outstanding matrons. The original two nurses at the opening on 14th February 1899 was Miss Clarke, and Miss Agnes Wilson who was to become Mrs Walter Vanderplank, a distinguished member (chairlady in 1922) of Eshowe's Local board, and later to achieve the distinction of being the first woman in South Africa to become the head of a local authority. She was married to the Office Commanding of the ZMR. Other matrons' names that come to mind because of their outstanding service were Miss Heine later to become wife to early Eshowe-ite magistrate Alfred Boast. She carried the hospital through the strenuous period of the Bambatha Rebellion. There was also Miss Murison who married Mr Christisen. Miss Kershaw, now married to Mr Kei Newberry, Miss Clohessey, who died while still matron, Mrs Wainwright, still matron of Durban hospital, Mrs Nan Rout for years past assistant matron and Miss Ballenden, last matron of the Queen

Vic and present matron of the new hospital. When I joined the staff Miss Murison was matron. She died when on my staff at Springfield Military Hospital during the war, a great loss. In my 30 years' work at Eshowe Provincial Hospital a series of splendid nurses served the sick and it seems invidious to pick out individuals for special mention. However, I am going to mention two: Miss Ella Beswick and Miss Betty Temple. The former I first met in Italy when she was assistant matron of the RAF. Hospital at Foggia. She joined the staff at Eshowe immediately after the war and did splendid work in charge of the non-European section. Miss Temple also joined the staff after the war. She received well-deserved promotion and the hospital is lucky to have retained her services. No mention of nursing in the old hospital would be complete without reference to Mrs Mc William who, throughout the year, was always at hand to help out in every emergency and staff shortage. In a life-time spent in hospital work and administration I have never experienced anywhere such steadfast loyalty and devotion to nursing duties as I experienced at Eshowe Provincial Hospital. Was it the high standard set by the pioneers that acted as goad and a goal for their successors? Whatever it was lightened the doctors' burdens and made the hospital 'home for the sick'. Lastly, I must refer to Mrs Mary Bartman, our coloured interpreter who seemed to know every dialect. She started in practice with Dr Moberly and Interpreted for Dr McHugh. She has since retired'.

III

Dr Tom McHugh left his beloved horses behind in Ireland and he missed game-bird shooting with a shotgun. However, in Eshowe, he still got to go fishing and to play the odd game of tennis. He was invited to play tennis at a farm in Entumeni where he met the beautiful young woman, Joan Richardson.

Dr McHugh, himself, was most attractive, always immaculately dressed and of a quiet unassuming but friendly disposition.

Dr Tom's father-in-law had been in charge of the African Contingent in the 1st World War. He was called up for service when Joan was all but three-years-old. On 21st February 1917, while crossing from England to Havre, he and over six hundred black South African soldiers drowned when, in thick fog, an American ship rammed into the South African ship called 'Mendi', sinking it to the bottom of the ocean.

Joan's mother, Dora then married Gwetsche Taylor who owned a farm called 'Arcadia Estate', which now belongs to Rob and Jane D'Aubrey. Joan Richardson was raised on that farm while attending Eshowe School. She could speak isiZulu fluently. Her isiZulu name was 'Uvendhle' meaning 'limp bones' because she was often seen practising ballet. Joan's nanny, Hlebegile, worked for Dr Tom and Mrs Joan McHugh from the day they got married in 1937. When Joan died, Hlebegile was sleeping in a bed next to her, nursing her day and night.

In 1937, with Rodney Lagerwall's contracted expertise, Tom and Joan built the house in Residency Road that Trevor Rosewall occupies today.

A quick aside here: Trevor Rosewall married Joy Rosewall (née Imbrailo) who worked with Pat Brenchley's colleague, Richard Tudor-Owen, for the Sugar Association. Joy's brother, Vincent Imbrailo, was Rory McHugh's (Tom and Joan McHugh's youngest child's) best friend at Eshowe High School. The Imbrailo family owned the complex of wood-and-iron houses situated at the hospital robots in Kangela Street. The existing 'Hospital Tea Room' was a tea room managed during the 1950s/60s by Mrs Imbrailo. She could speak English, Afrikaans and isiZulu fluently. The building that today is a funeral parlour was leased out by the Imbrailos to ZMI butchery. The third building was the family's home where Joy and Vincent grew up with their two older siblings.

Years later, living in the house that the McHughs built, Trevor and Joy Rosewall raised three daughters, Vanessa, Faye, and Catherine who is an optometrist in Johannesburg. She and her husband, Derek McCarthy are very good friends with my children, Keri and Carl.

Faye's father-in-law is Jeff Black who was bitten by a shark at Amatikulu beach during the 1960s. A large group of 20 to 30 young Eshowe-ites, including Tom and Joan McHugh's sons, would regularly go to the beach to ride waves on big tractor tubes. Looking out to sea one day, those on the beach saw a good 30 yards of red blood floating across an oncoming wave. Jeff Black's entire thigh was a large flap of flesh. He was taken to a doctor at Gingindlovu who immediately treated him for physiological shock. He recovered in Eshowe and moved on to play a nine handicap at golf. Twenty-five years after the event, he developed a hematoma the size of a golf ball on that thigh. An operation revealed a shark tooth that had taken a quarter of a century to work its way to the surface.

As a general practitioner and surgeon, Dr Tom McHugh found practising tropical medicine in Zululand so much more interesting than his work had been in Ireland. He wrote a paper on the subject of Lymphatic Filariasis, (also known as 'Elephantiasis'), that was published by the South African Medical Association. Elephantiasis occurs when filarial parasites are transmitted through mosquitoes, often in a person's leg. In 1957 Dr Holland retired and Tom Mc Hugh bought the practice that he relocated to the Sugar Building where 'Jus Glass and Aluminium' is today.

Tom McHugh was assistant part time medical officer of health to the Eshowe municipality from 1935 to 1958, which is when Dr Holland retired. He also assumed duties as medical officer of the railways, and he was the deputy medical surgeon for many years.

As well as their association with the municipality, Doctors Holland and McHugh had been the resident doctors at the Queen Victoria Hospital. That hospital had been built at the turn of the century. It was a homely, rambling establishment which would become the nurse's hostel when the hospital moved to the new four-hundred-bed facility in Kangela Street.

In recognition of Dr Tom McHugh's services, he received the highest reward that can be bestowed on any local resident person: The Freedom of the Borough Award. His contributions to the community included the opening of a family planning clinic, in 1974, and another clinic where 'handlers of food' were regularly examined.

Tom and Joan McHugh had five children: Patricia, Anne, Timothy, John and Rory.

John McHugh, their fourth child, was born in 1943. He thoroughly enjoyed growing up in Eshowe, attending Eshowe Public School in Main Street until Standard 9, before moving to the newly built Eshowe High School campus in Kangela Street.

In 1955 Dr Tom and Joan McHugh bought the Methodist Manse from author Selwyn Moberly. Moberly's family had moved to Eshowe, in 1903, when he was six. In 1953 he wrote the Forest Noel Nativity Play. With an able pen he also wrote the popular book about Eshowe called 'City Set on a Hill' that is available at Eshowe's Fort Museum's research room. It is a must-read for those particularly interested in early politics.

In the very first Forest Noel, in 1955, John McHugh, aged ten, was the 'Christ Child'. Some other actors to perform in that production included Father Herold, Herman Gebers, Vicky Kolbe and Syd Brien.

MR G S Moberly who will be a special guest at the production of 'Forest Noel.'

Altogether the full cast and crew included one hundred people. The Town Board ran a power line to the site. Local sawmills contributed timber for the building of an open-air stage. The rector of St Michael's Church led the singing. Syd Brien, a well-known attorney in Eshowe at the time, played the part of old man Simeon who recognises the baby as the prophesied saviour and takes him from Joseph. Syd was always worried about forgetting his lines so they were written out for him and pasted to the baby Jesus doll. The Forest Noel Nativity Play was a tableau specifically designed to be produced at Bishop's Seat in Dlinza Forest. Moberly felt that the towering trees represented a great cathedral with pillars and vaulted ceilings, like those in Europe.

According to the then author of Eshowe's local 'Culture Vulture' newspaper column, Ida Gartrell, in 2004, no one could ever forget the angels appearing in a blaze of light high up in the trees, or St Michael dressed in silver and white with his blazing sword defending the Christ Child from Satan who was an imposing figure of black and red, once played by Alwyn Schultz. This was all accompanied by the choir's amazing singing.

The play, which was performed every three or four years until 2008, had been recorded for radio, and, in 1991 was filmed by the SABC to be aired nationwide.

The show had been conducted in rain on more than

The clearing in the forest called Bishop's Seat

The first Forest Noel in 1955

one occasion. And once, during a complete power failure, a deafening clap of thunder saw angels scattering and one falling to the ground when struck by lightning through her metal halo.

Important angels, like Gabriel, had to climb a ladder and stand on boxes and other platforms in the 'clouds' above the stable. The overall scene included a live donkey, the owner of which played Angel Gabriel.

The play was a community service with free entry to the public who parked their cars at the entrance to the forest. They then walked along a narrow track that was lit up by lanterns, leading to Bishop's Seat.

In 1978 the play was produced by George Garside, who was also Eshowe's assistant town clerk at the time. The choir was conducted by Eunice Reeves. Mary was portrayed by Ida Gartrell opposite her then husband, Bevan Gartrell who played Joseph. Although that particular performance was played in the rain, the newspaper reported the show as being told with a rare 'dignity and beauty'*.

IV

After school John McHugh was drafted into the army for nine months, after which he attended Pharmacy School at Durban Tech for five years. He started playing golf at 14-years-old and still plays once a week with Eshowe-ite businessmen Gerald Upfold and Dave Davenport. It so happened that during his first year of studies at Pharmacy School, John was playing golf in Eshowe with pharmacist Clive Chesterton, when John asked Clive if he could please do a locum at Clive's

---

*The last production of the Forest Noel in 2008, was directed by Monica Rossouw, whose daughter, Carly was head girl of Eshowe High School in 2001. Monica, a noted mover and shaker in town, was also an Eshowe High School graduate.

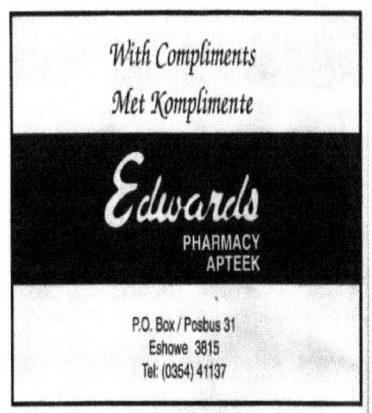

Pharmacy called 'Edwards'. After qualifying as a pharmacist John returned to Eshowe where he was permanently employed by Clive Chesterton. In 1984 he bought the branch of Edwards on Adams' Corner. He called it 'McHugh's Pharmacy' (at the time, there were 11 qualified 'McHugh' pharmacists in Ireland – male and female). Unfortunately, John's father died just one month before 'McHugh's Pharmacy' opened for business.

In 1992 a travel agent offered a special to all pharmacists who wanted to watch the Springboks play rugby in England. After that fabulous holiday, John and Sandy returned to Eshowe to hear from Sandy's mother that fellow pharmacist, Brian Langsford of Capital Pharmacy, had broken his hip after slipping on a banana skin outside Standard Bank in Osborn Road. No, this does not only happen in cartoons. My daughter, Jodie injured her wrist after slipping on a banana skin.

Brian Langsford, unfortunately, developed complications and died. Mrs Langsford chose to join her two daughters in Durban, so sold her share of Capital Pharmacy to John.

Mrs Smith of Nkwaleni told John that she knew of a young man, Linton Hackland who was a pharmacist looking for work. And so Linton joined John's business in 1992. Linton's wife, Janine was also a qualified pharmacist who locumed on occasion. Linton pulled Capital Pharmacy through hard times and, in John's

Sandy and John on their engagement in 1969

words, 'Got it running like a train'. This, before Linton and his family emigrated to the United States in 2004. John's wife, Sandy McHugh (née Lovell-Shippey) had an equally beautiful sister, Carol, and a younger brother, Barry, who was Mike Nixon's classmate at Eshowe High School. Their father, Pat Lovell-Shippey was employed as the company secretary of Huletts' Mhlume Sugar Mill in Northern Swaziland. Sandy and Carol attended St Mark's school there and have attended numerous happy reunions over the years. They came to Eshowe, in 1965, when Pat was promoted to general manager of Amatikulu sugar mill. He later started an estate agency called 'Eshowe Estate Agency' through which Mike Nixon bought the house that we still live in today.

John met Sandy at a party in Mangosuthu Buthelezi Drive at a venue then known as 'Eric Platt's Rondavel'. Only the framework survives today. Sandy, at the time, was working for Zululand Times at Tally's Corner. They dated for a few years, never missing the Christmas and New Year's Eve fund-raising parties at the Rugby and Cricket Clubs. They married, in 1971, and had three children: Sarah, Sean and Michael.

In 1977 John and Sandy bought the old Methodist

Manse in Kangela Street from John's parents, Dr Tom and Mrs Joan McHugh. In 2011 they sold it to Kingsley Holgate, who recently sold it to Stephan and Sally Schoeman. They are turning it into a bed and breakfast establishment.

Both of John and Sandy McHugh's boys, Sean and Michael, attended Durban High School. Thereafter, they both attained BComm degrees at Stellenbosch University. Sarah trained as a legal secretary and married a lawyer.

After graduating from Stellenbosch, Sean began manufacturing cosmetics. He finally sold his cosmetic concern called 'Ethnic Style' and took over 'McHughs Pharmacy' on Adams' Corner. This was after Linton Hackland left for America. Sean promptly removed all scheduled medications. He sold only patent medicines such as eucalyptus oil for congested chests, oil of cloves for toothache, castor oil for constipation, oil of wintergreen for aching joints, Grandpa Headache Powders, Vaseline Petroleum Jelly to relieve chapped skin, and blue bottles of Philips Milk of Magnesia. Condy's crystals was a solution to wash out wounds. Dr Mackenzie's Veinoids were popular for bladder complaints – they made one pass bright blue urine that was considered proof of effectiveness.

In the meantime, Sean's friend, Bruce Evans who married Penny (daughter of Dave and Ann Davenport) opened the Kwikspar Supermarket next door. Not too long after, Bruce offered the manager position to Sean who, a few years later, bought that franchise.

When the larger main Spar Supermarket in Eshowe became available, the group wanted to sell the franchise to someone who lived in Eshowe. Sean and his wife, Michelle McHugh (née Reeves) bought it. When the Gingindlovu branch became available, they bought that too. John and Sandy's son, Michael co-owns 'Build-it' hardware store with an old school friend, Steven Kewley, who lives in Ballito.

John McHugh's one regret in life, is that his children, having had such urban schoolings, never learned to speak isiZulu. He and Sandy do, however, have the joy of sharing three of their grandchildren (Murray, Ross and Marc) with Gareth and Correen Reeves of Brockwell Engineering. Nowadays the couples live just a few houses away from each other at Eshowe Hills.

John's brother, Rory McHugh (more about him in Volume 2), was the youngest of Dr Tom and Mrs Joan McHugh's children. He was an agricultural sales rep for Triomf Fertilisers. A confirmed bachelor, he was a friend with whom I shared more than one beer at the George Hotel on a Friday evening.

One day, while driving down William Chadwick Drive, I recognised Rory's little Jack Russells at a gate. Realising that this was where Rory lived, I promptly invited myself in for a cup of tea. Rory wasn't sure whether or not he owned a teapot, but he managed to locate a packet of teabags under the sink.

It was from the window in that very kitchen that Rory watched one of his dear little Jack Russells get lifted swiftly into the air by a Crowned Eagle – never to be seen again.

Although, like most brothers, John and Rory fought a lot while they were growing up, they subsequently, and often with their elder brother, Timothy, got together at each other's homes. They chatted often on the phone or when Rory popped in at the pharmacy, certain to bring John and Sandy a pocket of grapefruit each time he visited clients at the farms in Nkwaleni.

Chapter 9

Falling under the Department of Higher Education and Training, the Eshowe campus of the Umfolozi TVET (Technical and Vocational Education and Training) is one of 50 colleges of its kind in South Africa. It offers a range of national business, engineering and skills programs.

This huge campus was, until the year 2001, the Teachers' Training College. Trevor Smith was rector for 12 years, during the 1970s and 80s. His wife, Susan ran the tuck shop. During those early 1980s Trevor was also chairman of Eshowe Junior School's Parents' and Teachers' Association. His son, Alex was head boy there. One innovation introduced by Trevor Smith at the college was to get one of the two banks in Eshowe to encourage the first year students to open transmission savings accounts. When payments from the bookshop had to be made to students, instead of Marilyn Wilkinson having to write out cheques for each student, she merely wrote the amount on a class list and gave it to the bank to credit the students who could draw from the two ATMs in town.

When rector Trevor Smith left, in 1986, the new rector, Peter Cooper, abolished the wearing of uniforms. The Teachers' Training College offered an excellent structure in routine management that allowed for students to have the afternoons off from attending class. Those college students were extremely eager to learn, many moving on to university to acquire an even higher level of education. Many former students have become principals at high schools in the district. These include Mr Jo Cele from Gawozi Secondary School and Mr Lizwi Dlamini from Sunnydale Secondary School. The dedicated staff at the college included mathematics lecturers, Eddie Curtis who is presently principal of Eshowe High School, and Myra Dunley-Owen who was one of a few fellow lecturers to receive the top examination results, every year, in the whole of the country. Wally Walters was in charge of the art section. He organised a conference in Durban taking over the Garden Court Hotel, with staff from all over the country, running 12 workshops every day for a week – a great achievement for Wally and the college.

Tienie Janse van Vuuren taught at the college from 1984 to 2001 for a total of 17 years. She started with the teaching of languages: English and Afrikaans. Thereafter she taught history until the college opened a commercial department. She then taught accounting, business economics and commercial law. Of Tienie's three daughters, Lucia, Maria and Elsie, it was Lucia who walked in her mother's footsteps. She taught for three years at Sunnydale High, and briefly at Eshowe Junior School, before taking up an appointment at Ntabantuzuma High School, at Entumeni in the Eshowe district, for 20 years*.

Zanele Lushaba (née Gcabashe) worked at the college from 1978 to 2003. She started out as junior lecturer, then senior lecturer and finally head of department of auxiliary subjects. She also worked as assistant librarian to Norma Prince. She lectured religious education, covering the traditions of Christianity, Buddhism, Islam and Judaism. The goal was not to convert, but rather to prepare teaching students to relate to pupils of various religions. Zanele also lectured life orientation and practical English, and did a fair share of administration work. After working at the college for a quarter of a century, she worked with Mike Nixon at the Empangeni District Office. Zanele was born and bred in Kwa Mbonambi.

She matriculated at Eshowe College, then called 'Eshowe College and High School', situated exactly where the college still stands today. Those days one wing was for the Form 4 and Form 5 high school students and the other wing for the training of teachers.

After Form 5, Zanele went to the University of Zululand where she studied for a BA degree. Her subjects were psychology, biblical studies and isiZulu. She also obtained her teaching diploma there. Zanele moved on to teach high school agricultural science, biblical studies, life orientation, and isiZulu as a first language. She married Geoffrey Lushaba who had his honours in history as well as a teachers' diploma. Together they lived in Durban where their eldest daughter, the very beautiful Ntombi was born.

When Geoffrey obtained employment at the Eshowe

---

*Other lecturers at the college included Colin van Tooren who taught science. Marylin Wilkinson taught history and ran the bookshop. Rector Peter Cooper, William Mngoma, Gail Maytham, Alwyn Schultz, Steve Untiedt and Mike Nixon taught geography. Don Mhlongo, a published author of Zulu novels, taught isiZulu. Lettie and Gert Meyer, and Igna Vermaak taught Afrikaans. Dan Vilakazi, and Fanalake Ndlovu (who was also vice Rector) taught education as a subject. Michelle Storm and Freeman Nkosi taught art. English lecturers included Alistair Maytham (married to Gail), Cein Moll, Stella Prozesky, Pete Southey, Rob Wissing, John Goodall (married to Estelle), Bheki Zulu (who moved on to work for the South African Qualifications Authority), and Anne-Louise Gaisford who also worked in the library, headed by Norma Prince and then by Betty Wiseman. Brian Cawood taught biology as did another friend of Mike's and mine, Lynette Malan (née Spencer) who transferred from the English Department.

Geir and Ntombi Daasvand

College of Education, he encouraged Zanele to apply for a position there. Zanele was appointed and joined the Eshowe-ite staff. She was thrilled because her family home was situated only two kilometres from the campus. Ntombi was a toddler at the time.

Zanele has lived in the gracious double-story house opposite the George Hotel at Tally's Corner since 1993. Her immediate next door neighbour is Ellen Mkize. During this time, Ntombi matriculated at St Annes in Hilton and studied hotel management and food service management. But she ended up working, for many years, as secretary to local architect, Jeremy Steere. She then met and married Norwegian, Geir Moe Daasvand and moved to Norway. There she studied and qualified as a teaching assistant. She and Geir have a daughter, Maya Linda.

Zanele's second daughter, Nonceba was born soon after Zanele started lecturing at the college, followed by another daughter, Linda who would matriculate at Eshowe High School before joining the South African Police Service as a policewoman. Linda sadly passed away from tuberculosis complications in 2013. Zanele has raised Linda's son, Menzi who has autism.

Nonceba did a BA at the University of KwaZulu-Natal and is presently an academic coordinator for the Durban chapter of the School for International Training – a study-abroad programme based in Vermont. The Durban chapter hosts American students who spend a semester in South Africa studying international relations and diplomacy before returning to the States.

In the meantime, Zanele is loving retirement from her own fruitful career. She has been an active member of the Lutheran Church since 1978. She loves gardening and is a prolific reader of non-fiction on anything scientific – such as agriculture and animal husbandry. Her one favourite is the ever-popular 'Farmers' Weekly' magazine.

I

Lynette Malan (née Spencer) lectured at the college for a total of 18 years, from 1984 to 2002.

She met her husband, Kevin Malan in Durban after she had graduated with a BSc in botany and zoology at the University of Natal. Her friend (also a 'Lynette') had previously been on a blind date with Kevin.

Kevin came across both Lynettes spending a day on the beach. While Kevin was chatting to the Lynette he knew, her boyfriend arrived: a towering broad-shouldered six-footer.

Kevin was instructed to quickly move over and sit next to Lynette Spencer. Thus began a courtship that resulted in 50 years of marriage. The Malans had three children: Terence, Tamryn and Garth. During Kevin and Lynette's 18 years spent in Eshowe, Kevin commuted each day to Melmoth where he managed the Metro Cash & Carry there.

I became friends with the Malans when their youngest son, Garth dated my eldest daughter, Lara right through high school and beyond, for a total of seven years.

Mike had become friends with the Malans during his own years of lecturing at the college from 1997 to 2000. Prior to transferring to the college, Mike taught geography to Tamryn Malan at Eshowe High School. Geographer Daphne Untied taught Terence, the eldest Malan, who was an excellent sportsman. He was also head boy and awarded Dux in 1994.

Mike remembers Tamryn Malan being an exceptionally hard worker, and of course he remembers Garth, the youngest Malan, who played such a significant part in my daughter, Lara's life. The entire Malan family were incredibly supportive of Lara during my divorce from Pat Brenchley and subsequent nervous breakdown*.

During Lynette's time at the college, Trevor Smith was succeeded by Peter Cooper. He was married to Faye, the librarian at Eshowe High School. When Peter and Faye Cooper relocated to the Natal Midlands they sold their home in Pearson Avenue to Dave and Barbara Freer. Pat Brenchley and I bought that lovely old house with the Oregon pine floorboards and encompassing verandas. It served as the very first nursing/maternity home in Eshowe during the late 1800s (before the Queen Victoria Hospital was built). Unfortunately, my family never got to enjoy the house because it was sold towards the divorce settlement.

Lynette Malan's father, Jack Spencer lived in a granny-flat in the Malan's garden in what was then Melmoth Road. Jack enjoyed excellent health in his retirement. After his driver's licence was cancelled, when he turned 90, he could be seen walking briskly into town to do his visiting rounds.

Those on his route included previous mayoress, Betty Waters, who lived just down the road, Geraldine and Peter Wright who kindly organised a helicopter ride for Jack on his 90th birthday, Annette Leitch at Crystal

*If you or anyone you know is battling with mental illness please read my book: 'One Green Bottle'.

Jewellers where Steers is now, Irene Strachan, Henry and Val Truter, Andre Schnetler, Ozzie Wellman, Dr Baldassini and Mali Govender. He periodically stopped in at Gary and Renée Lagerwall's home where staff served him tea and biscuits whether the Lagerwalls were there or not.

Friends remember Jack's gifts: meringues or biscuits delivered in chicken liver containers that he always wanted back. He was also well known at the Bowling Club which served his favourite meal, tripe and onions, once a week.

Jack had led a varied life that always made for interesting conversation. He was born in Johannesburg, in 1912, and as a young lad earned five shillings per service for pulling the bell chords at the Anglican Cathedral.

Boxing was a compulsory school sport those days. After school Jack joined Ernie Eustace's Boxing Academy in Booysens. He entered the South African championships as a lightweight and reached the finals, being beaten only by Teddy Brawn who later became an Olympic champion.

During this time, he qualified at the Johannesburg Trade School with an engineering diploma. His first job was a five-year contract serving an apprenticeship as a diamond cutter and polisher. A parcel of six large polished stones once went to the wash in his overall pocket.

He then exchanged the fine-precision work with diamonds for much bigger, but equally complex, aircraft engineering and thus served a second apprenticeship.

Jack took up flying while based in Kimberley and qualified for his pilot's licence, flying up-side-down over the big hole. It was there that he met and married Phyllis Metzger with whom he had two daughters, Valerie and our Lynette.

When the 2nd World War broke out in 1944, Jack became an engineer officer in the SAAF where he worked on Dakota and Ventura aircraft.

At the age of 48 he left the skies to work, in Cape Town, for Barlows on their Caterpillar and Nuffield tractors, hysters and escavators.

Another change brought Jack to Durban to work for the Illings McCarthy Rodway Group, agents for Komatsu, Haitchi and Mazda cars and trucks. During this time, he visited Tokyo and Osaka in Japan where he was taken on a test drive of the very first rotary- engined Mazda cars and trucks. On his return he stopped over in Sydney, Adelaide and Perth, where he persuaded those Australians to buy Japanese tractors and excavators. In his travels Jack met Frank Sinatra and Judy Garland in New York and Maria Callas at the Worms Opera House in Germany.

Jack died in Eshowe at the age of 95.

We miss him.

Terence Malan, Lynette Malan, Jack Spencer, Tamryn Malan, Garth Malan and Kevin Malan

II

My third child with Pat Brenchley was an unexpected but wonderful surprise. We called him 'Colin'. Shortly after Colin's conception I retired from working for Dr Eric Brits. At the time Eric was setting up his museum collection of antiquated medical instruments in a room outside of his consultation rooms that are situated diagonally opposite Eshowe Provincial Hospital in Kangela Street.

I was delighted to find recently, after Eric's 34 years of private practice in that corner house, that he has rearranged all the cabinetry into the actual consultation rooms, where, apart from paging through magazines, patients are usually at a loss of what to do with themselves.

But not anymore.

After a turn to the left and another to the right – left, right and centre, one comes across Oregon pine and glass cabinets filled with all sorts of ominous curiosities (medical paraphernalia), some from well over a century past. I have watched patients let their eyes wander over those displays and shake their head to express mystification and, in my case, a heartfelt gratitude for modern medicine with its delicate little syringes and charming little test tubes and vessels. Dr Eric Brits, himself, when showing me the collection for the purpose of this book, runs his fingers over those showcases with a blend of admiration and awe. His collection includes a metal item measuring two inches square with a trigger that expels a dozen razor-blades to penetrate the patient's skin, in two neat rows of six slits. Leeches, during the 1800s, were then attached to 'extract' the bad blood that was thought to be the cause of an otherwise inexplicable illness.

Eric started collecting these antiques during his army services at mission hospitals that were largely run by nuns. One, Sister Oberholzer lived to be 104-years- old.

The curator of Addington Hospital's museum in Durban was Thelma Blair-Hook, a retired matron. Sadly, that museum was badly vandalised by criminals who stole precious collectables and furniture (pieces of solid oak) that they used as firewood. Mrs Blair-Hook kindly donated Eric duplicate items that were no longer in use. His collection also included things that he searched for, far and wide, in antique shops.

Where Dr Eric Brits' private antique collection is not the only exhibition of historical interest in Eshowe, neither is the Museum Village the only 'site' of historic value.

There is the military cemetery that has a memorial listing of 48 burials, and a further 34 graves of unknown soldiers. It was established in 1879, after British forces occupied the abandoned KwaMondi Mission Station in Eshowe, following the Battle of Nyezane on 22nd January 1879. The mission station was renamed 'Fort Eshowe'.

British forces dug deep trenches around the perimeter and converted the church into a hospital for those wounded in battle. Within a matter of days, the British found themselves besieged there for ten weeks during which 28 British officers and soldiers died, due to the lack of adequate medical provisions. Many died of disease rather than wounds of war, with dysentery, enteric fever and sunstroke claiming the majority of the victims.

The military cemetery was in use for about 20 years. Today the deep trenches dug by the British are all that remains of the fort. There is a granite memorial at the Museum Village listing the names of those soldiers who could be identified.

III

Martyr's Cross is a memorial standing high on Mpondweni Hill outside Eshowe.

After his coronation, King Cetshwayo who believed Christianity spoilt the fighting spirit of his warriors, knew he could not forbid missionaries from doing their work in Zululand, but he made it clear that any of his soldiers who became Christians would die.

Despite the great risk, Maqamusela Khanyile (1850-1877) enrolled for the baptism class at KwaMondi, the Norwegian Mission Society Station that had been permitted by King Mpande, Cetshwayo's father.

Maqamusela Khanyile's neighbours called him 'Umuntu wesonto' meaning 'church goer', because he prayed aloud among them. Unlike other Christians, who abandoned their home and their Zulu customs, Maqhamusela continued to serve in the Zulu royal house. He remained a polygamist and continued to wear his head-ring (the Zulu symbol of manhood).

When warned of the danger when others overheard the order to kill him, the church goer said, 'If they kill me because I believe, let them do so. The Lord will receive me. Has not Christ died for me? Why would I be scared?'

Four men were given the task to kill Maqhamusela. They were Mjejane Mpungose, Ngcelu Mpungose, Nyamalala Zondo and a Swazi man by the name of Hwayimbane. They went to the home of Maqhamusela on 9th March 1877, but he was away visiting his grandmother. They left a message for him that he was summoned at Mpondweni hill.

When Maqhamusela got the message he went to the hill with a strong suspicion of the fate awaiting him. With permission he prayed for himself, his family, the slayers themselves, for the Zulu king and his community. He warned the executioners that a great thunderstorm was coming. He told them to run for shelter after their deed was done.

According to his murderers, Maqhamusela was not at all afraid. Nyamalala Zondo aimed his old fashioned muzzle loader and misfired.

Maqhamusela said 'You, my kinsman, you must not slay me'.

Hwayimbane took the muzzle loader and shot Maqhamusela in the head.

A terrible storm broke immediately and the slayers fled for shelter, abandoning the dead church goer. After the great storm, Reverend Ommund and others searched for Maqhamusela's body but to no avail. There were no signs of it being dragged or eaten by animals.

His sons and wives fled and returned only in 1881.

Maqhamusela was 70 years old at the time of his death. To Zulus he was regarded as a rebel who disrespected the king. To Christians, Maqhamusela remains an inspiration and a symbol of hope, put to death for refusing to serve in the king's army. Thus Maqamusela Khanyile was the first South African Christian martyr. The cross on the hill near Eshowe's Gezinsela Township marks the spot where he met his tragic death.

IV

In the years following the Anglo-Boer War that took place from 11th October 1899 to 31st May 1902, British employers in Natal had difficulty recruiting African farm workers, partly because of increased competition from the gold mines of the Witwatersrand. To pressure Zulu men to enter the labour market, the colonial authorities introduced a poll tax payable by all adult males in addition to the existing hut tax payable by every kraal-head. In addition, they were to pay a dog tax for those hunting dogs that were so valued by the amaZulu*.

This triggered the Bambatha Rebellion of 1906 led by Bambatha kaMancinza (1865-1906), leader of the Zondi clan of the Zulu people.

Bambatha had occasionally opposed the Natal Colonial Administration so authorities suspected that he had joined with other chiefs in expressing discontent over the new tax. But the new tax was not the only reason for the rebellion. Other causes included the sale of sugar farmland to whites in Zululand, and that blacks did not have the vote in the all-white government.

When Chief Bambatha was summoned to Greytown in Natal, he fled to Zululand instead. This act of defiance attracted the support of other Zulu leaders. When he returned to the Mpanza Valley to discover that the Natal government had Valley to discover that the Natal government had deposed him as chief, he gathered

---

*It is said by some that indignation arose mostly from the fact that the kraal-leader's dignity would be diminished if every youngster were given the privilege of being a tax-payer.

together a small force of supporters to launch a series of guerrilla attacks, using the Nkandla forest as a base.

And so, in 1906, the Bambatha Rebellion broke out. When a column of police was sent to the district to rescue fearful white families it was ambushed and those police were killed. But British troops succeeded in getting face to face with the rebels at Mome Gorge that is still, today, seen as one of the most ravaged war zone areas. As the sun rose they opened fire with machine guns and cannon on those equipped mostly with only assegaais, knobkerries and cowhide shields. The British army killed Bambatha and six hundred of his followers. Of the British that were killed some were mutilated for medicinal purposes. These included Messers ETN Brown, A Powell, Sangreid and OE Veal.

When it was reported that Bambatha had been killed in action by Natal government forces the claim was disputed by his supporters who believed that he had fled to Mozambique.

Then on 13th June 1906, a Nongqayi policeman pitched up at the government camp with the severed head of Bambatha.

On 30th July 1906 volunteer troops were disbanded, bringing a final end to the rebellion. Altogether, between three and four thousand Zulus were killed, more than seven thousand were imprisoned and four thousand flogged. The war cost the Natal government £883576 (equivalent to £101 million in 2021).

The government put prisoners to work at the harbour, on the railways or on the roads.

After that rebellion had been put down, King Dinuzulu was accused of having ordered Bambatha to start the rebellion in the first place. Although he steadfastly protested his innocence he was put on trial for treason and found guilty of sheltering Bambatha's wife and children for 14 months. He was fined £100 and sentenced to four years' imprisonment, in March1908.

On a separate occasion he was also tried for treason and sent to St Helena (more about that later).

In 2006 the centenary anniversary of the rebellion was commemorated in a ceremony which declared Chief Bambatha a national hero of post-apartheid South Africa. His picture appeared on a postage stamp and a street was renamed in his honour.

It's interesting to note that the hip-hop musician, Afrika Bambaataa, takes his name from Bambatha, the most famous rebel in South Africa.

V

In view of the upcoming photos of Eshowe school headmasters, one of the first friends I made in Eshowe comes to mind. She was retired teacher, Ruth Harold, who lived around the corner from Pat Brenchley and me. Her partner, Aston Townsend had been mayor of Eshowe from 1974 to 1975, and again in 1979.

Ruth told me how she had arrived from Johannesburg to the tree-lined haven of Eshowe back in August 1960. She was to teach at Eshowe Junior School for 28 years. Prior to her arrival the Eshowe primary and high schools were one single school known as Eshowe Public School in Main Street where, today, those old redbrick buildings house only the junior school. In 1949 the director of education, Mr Banks, planted a Natal Mahogany in the grounds to mark the school's 50th anniversary. This tree, together with its memorial plaque, still stands in the parking lot.

As previously mentioned, the very first school in Eshowe was opened by Anglican Bishop WM Carter in

Past Headmasters

Eshowe School

Mr T.H. Atkinson
1896-1904

Eshowe School

Mr I. Burton
1904-1913

Eshowe School

Mr T.D. Wilson
1914-1926

Eshowe School

Mr G.W. Watmough
1926-1929

Eshowe School

Mr W.N. Newell
1929-1942

Eshowe School

Mr J.H. Anderson
1942-1945

Eshowe School

Mr P. Hardaker
1945-1951

Eshowe School

Mr L.W. Dwyer
1951-1953

Eshowe School

Mr R.W. Martin
1953-1958

Eshowe School

Mr C. Griffin
1958-1959

Eshowe Junior School

Mr C.J. van Niekerk
1960

Eshowe Junior School

Mr P.R. Kay
1961-1963

Past Headmasters

Eshowe Junior School
Mr J.G. Hattingh
1963-1965

Eshowe Junior School
Mr J.C. Ware
1966

Eshowe Junior School
Mr D.P. van Zyl
1967-1969

Eshowe Junior School
Mr Mr K. Nixon
1970-1978

Eshowe High School
Mr G.M.N. Goodwin
1960-1967

Eshowe High School
Mr D. Vosloo
1968-1971

Eshowe High School
Mr Beaumont
1972-1977

Eshowe High School
Mr H.H. Johnstone
1978-1983

Eshowe High School
Mr J.D. van Coller
1984

Eshowe High School
Mr C.J. van Tooren
1985-1991

Eshowe High School
Mr B. Pfister
1992-1993

his home in the 1890s. A lady teacher was brought in from England, but soon after she left to join a religious order in Pietermaritzburg. She was replaced by Reverend Langdon Davis.

After operating from the town's public library (since 1896) the school relocated to the building in Main Street, when it was completed in 1902. (The separate Eshowe High School campus in Kangela Street was built and launched half a century later, in 1957).

Two events of enormous significance to the future of education occurred, in1915, when government schools received a circular, from the Department of Education, ordering principals to refuse admission to mixed-race children, and to expel those already attending the school. Also, compulsory school fees were abolished. Seventy-seven years later, in 1992, public schools assumed state aided or 'Model C' status. Mixed-race, Indian and black children were admitted for the first time and compulsory school fees were reintroduced.

After the first decade of serving as resident hostel teacher, Ruth Harold bought a plot in Dalby road – this on a female teacher's salary. Females earned substantially less than their male counterparts those days. Just one year later, Ruth and her son, Michael were living in their newly-built house.

Ruth absolutely loved teaching young children. I remember how she laughed when relating some of the definitions children gave her for certain words. Here are some examples: 'monotony': in Christianity a man can only have one wife – This is called 'monotony'. 'Celibacy': celibacy is a crime a priest commits when he marries. 'Census Taker': A census taker is a man who goes from house to house increasing the population. 'Monologue': A monologue is a conversation between

Eshowe Public School that serves today as Eshowe Junior School

two people, such as husband and wife. 'Chivalry': chivalry is the attitude of a man towards a strange woman.

Ken Nixon, Ruth's principal at Eshowe Junior School, once made the mistake of asking her to take the B Class. This resulted in a deputation from a number of angry parents.

Things have certainly changed since then. Ken Nixon remembered Mrs van Rooyen, the special class teacher, who was well over 70, but kept on because the department could not find a replacement. He overheard her, one day, reprimand a mother for daring to come to the principal's office wearing sandals. Another character, Mrs du Plessis, the senior Afrikaans teacher, stood no nonsense from the pupils but had a delightful sense of humour.

Mrs Kolbe was known for her fantastic hospitality, sometimes throwing dinner parties for no less than 50 guests. She was a playwright in her own right and wrote the passion play called 'The Road to Calvary' that was produced at the Star Theatre in 1964.

In the early 1970s, work alterations were carried out on the school buildings, including the construction of the senior primary block. Senior pupils were not impressed with having their woodwork classes carried out in the morgue of Eshowe Provincial Hospital. I'd like to make mention here that principal Ken Nixon personally made the little chairs for the dwarfs in the school play, Snow White.

Following the building alterations, it was wonderful to have a well-equipped hall for assemblies, music classes and other events. Previously, the whole school had to walk to the Town Hall for concerts and prize-giving ceremonies.

At the official opening of the new school hall the school choir sang the song, 'Food, Glorious Food', from the musical 'Oliver'. This was considered by one parent to be a communist song and in turn he reported the matter to the aspiring National Party candidate in the forthcoming elections. He used the term 'the hair-raising activities at Eshowe Junior School' in his speeches at various centres (but not in Eshowe). For some years after, Eshowe residents jokingly referred to Ken Nixon as 'Comrade Ken'.

Comrade Ken had fantastic support from the advisory school committees. Some chairmen of note were Herman Gebers, Barry Parker and Brian Wynne (married to Jan). Brian enabled the school to purchase a new school bus, in 1978, which cost just over R11 thousand. In the same year the swimming pool was built at full cost to the school. Previously, galas were held at the public pool.

After Ruth Harold's retirement from teaching she painted the loveliest pictures of birds that sold like hot cakes at the birding weekend's art exhibition.

VI

It so happens that, in the very year I arrived in Eshowe, Tony and Linda Warren rose to the challenge, received the required training and started the independent Eshowe Christian School at the Community Church.

Dr Jon Larsen was on the church leadership as assistant pastor.

Joyce le Fevre had been a member of this church in Eshowe while her mother, Margaret Warner lived frugally on a government pension in England. When Margaret unexpectedly received a settlement from an insurance policy pay out she donated the money via her daughter, Joyce to the Eshowe Community Church. The favourable exchange rate allowed for the exact amount needed to start up the Accelerate Christian Education – ACE school. The 'Margaret Warner Compassion Trophy' goes each year to the learner who most demonstrates kindness.

In 1997, Eshowe Christian School, a ministry of Eshowe Community Church, with Linda Warren as principal, opened its doors to 45 learners including my daughters, Lara and Keri van Schalkwyk. The school provides, through ACE, a methodology which is based on behaviourist therapy and proven results using approaches of mastery-based learning. My girls were leaving their father and their friends behind in Mpumalanga, and they had our new family arrangement in Eshowe to which they needed some adjusting. Thus the ACE 'learn-at-your-own-pace' method appealed to me. The plan was for them to eventually graduate, at Grade 12, with accredited certificates equivalent to matriculation, from the School of Tomorrow.

In the beginning, the school was housed in the church hall in Kangela Street. Every Friday the learners at the ACE school would close up their desks, move the furnishings out of the way and set up for the Sunday Service, after which, members of the congregation would reverse the process. This weekly ritual of packing and unpacking was quite a task. Everyone was delighted when

<u>Back row: the talented artist and mathematician Mrs Erna Bester-Wade (Gr7- 8), Mrs Margie Neen (senior learning centre, married to yet another of Pat's colleagues in the sugar world, John Neen), Pastor Tony Warren (administrator), Mrs Linda Warren (principal), Mrs Jan Wiltshire (Gr1-2), Mrs Wendy Sherrard (monitor)</u>
<u>Front row: Miss Cynthia Bishop (Gr5-7), Mrs Joy Latham (Gr 3-4, who previously taught at Eshowe Junior School for 30 years, Mrs June Naidoo(secretary) and monitors Mrs Elise Lawrie and Julia Neen (Margie's daughter).</u>

in 2012, the church built the existing spacious and airy learning centre.

From the year 2000, Jan Wiltshire headed the Computer Centre. On several occasions she ran the Computer Graphics Course attended also by students from other schools and some adults. Kevesh Govender and Gerrie Wagenaar took over when Jan left in 2016, to concentrate on her Coffee Break magazine. Jan's son, Steve Wiltshire, an ex-pupil, owns a computer repair business in Eshowe called 'Mactron'.

Some learners of the ACE School, starting with Cynthia

Bishop, in 1998, attended the annual All Africa Student Convention where ACE learners from all over the world compete in a wide variety of events including sport, academics, stage performance, preaching, art, photography, carpentry, engineering and handwork.

For a number of years, the Eshowe Christian School held the School Spirit Trophy. Many learners obtained Northern Coastal Colours, KZN Christian School Colours and even South African Christian Colours in a variety of sporting codes. Back at the beginning, Lara attained ACE Natal Colours for hockey, swimming, middle distance running and shotput. Keri excelled at swimming and squash, beating the matric boys when she was only in Grade 7.

As with any school, they certainly put up with their share of mischief makers. There was the incident on a lovely sunny day when most of the students were out playing sports at another school. The remaining staff members and students in the classroom heard a loud explosion. Rushing outside, they discovered a team of workers who had been digging a trench staring open-mouthed at a cloud of blue smoke wafting through the air. The workers snitched on a particular student who had planted the time-delayed fuse so that he could be far away from the scene of the crime. Shreds of red paper identified the make of firework as a gorilla bomb, a particularly large firework. Grateful that this was no more than a prank, the principal telephoned the prankster's father who happened to be an army officer. Following a stunned silence, he asked, 'A guerilla bomb?!' And what a laugh when a student blended two scriptures to come up with 'Lies are an abomination to the Lord (Proverbs 12:22) and an ever-present help in times of trouble (Psalm 46:1).'

Chapter 10

In the meantime, my little daughter, Jodie Brenchley attended Sharon Yardley's 'Donkey School', a delightful little playschool on Dave and Sharon Yardley's farm where, at the age of four, Jodie finally accepted that it was socially expected for her to wear clothes.

The earliest Yardley to set up this farm was George Henry Yardley, born in 1869 in England. In 1894, he married Mary Major (also known as 'Polly') from the nearby village of Ball Green. The following year their daughter, Ethel was born. In 1896, at the age of 26, George Henry left his young wife and daughter and joined 275 passengers aboard the 'Gothic' in the port of London, and set out to South Africa. While away, his second child, George Yardley Jnr, was born. This was followed by another son, Harold, after George Henry returned to work as a coal hewer in England.

In 1903, answering to a longing in his heart for the Africa he'd left behind, George Henry boarded the 'Avondale' Castle in the port of Southampton.

In Cape Town he was delighted to be granted a permit to once again enter and reside in the Transvaal at the Witwatersrand goldfields some fourteen hundred kilometres away. Putting his English coal mining experience to good use, he worked underground operating pneumatic machines used for drilling holes where explosives could be laid.

George Henry sent for his family a year later. But, suffering from Miner's phthisis in his lungs, George took his family back to England where he set about building a shop and a row of houses in Ball Green. After having enjoyed the South African climate, the family found it difficult to settle down.

In 1907 George Henry joined 118 fellow passengers boarding the 'Norman', a 4 005-ton ship of the Donald Currie & Co steamship line, and headed back to South Africa where, in 1911, he bought two farms in the Eshowe district.

The two farms, Gratton and Norton, were adjacent to one another on the northern outskirts of Eshowe. There is an interesting history of ownership: In 1908 a Certificate of Allotment was issued in favour of W Storrie and a year later, on 25th August 1909, it was sold to Samuel Bath of Verulam.

The Yardley family arrived in Eshowe when the only form of public transport was the ox-wagon. In the area of Mangosuthu Buthelezi Drive was the outspan where oxen were un-hitched from their wagons and allowed to graze.

Most of the houses were down Main Street near the courthouse. There were a few houses in Kangela Street, as well as St Columbia's native church, the cemetery, a polo ground and a racecourse.

A few of the families that were here at that time were the Wantinks, the Clauses and the Ashbys.

Eventually, when he could afford it, George Henry bought a horse and trap. Mr Nottingham and Mr Dalby later had a car that they used to run the post up to Melmoth. A separate horse or mule-drawn post-cart service was at Bond's Drift on the Thukela which was operated by Messers J Colenbrander, and S Offer who served twice as chairman of Eshowe's local board, during the 1920s. Later the postal service was carried out between Gingindlovu and Eshowe by Mr Offer alone.

In 1907 Mr Offer experimentally put an old-time traction-engine (steam road-locomotive) on the roads in Eshowe. The vehicle had wide steel wheels that rolled and compacted the road rather than tearing it up like wagon wheels did. But they were slow and did not take off.

In 1908 the first motor-car was spotted in Eshowe when the governor of Natal, Sir Mathew Nathan, made an official visit to the town.

Two years later, the Zululand Times reported seeing a motor-bike and two motor-cars in Eshowe.

The first motor-car to be owned in Eshowe belonged to the Royal Hotel, owned then by Mr White (no relation to attorneys Hlope, David and Don White).

The Yardleys found life on the farm terribly uncomfortable as they were living in a wood-and-iron house with no running water or electricity or gas. To make matters worse, livestock often died of disease until, in 1912, George Henry applied for a loan to build a dipping tank.

His lungs wracked with disease, George Henry died at the age of 45, only three years after settling in Eshowe. During her life in Eshowe his daughter, Ethel recalled: *We sold everything in England and came to South Africa in 1911. We sailed in the 'Edinburgh Castle' which was, of course, quite modern and up to date. We arrived in Durban in June 1911. Dad met us there and showed us all around. It was not as it is today. Where all the hotels and tea-rooms are at the beachfront, was all beach sand, no benches, just two poles with a plank across them and you sat on those. The promenade was all sand, right up to West Street. We looked around for three days and then boarded the train for Gingindlovu, where Mr Offer kindly met us and drove us to Eshowe by wagon. We didn't have a very good train journey up to Gingindlovu. Gingindlovu 'means 'Swallowing the Elephant'. That area was named by King Cethswayo after he defeated his brother (Mpande's eldest and favourite son, Nbuyaze) in battle. He slept at that area the night after and told his followers that they had helped him to 'Swallow the Elephant'. The engine broke down and they had to get another engine from*

Stanger, so we had to sit and wait for it to arrive. On the train with us were people that we would get to know better once in Eshowe. They were Mrs Una Adams with Mrs Suttie and Mr KV Challenor. From Gingindlovu we travelled to Eshowe on Mr Offer's mule wagon. What an experience, oh. After England then seeing this country. We just could not imagine what sort of life we would have here, but we came to love it very dearly. On the old mule wagon were all our cases, Mother's hand sewing machine and her china tea-set. We had to outspan half way up, had tea cooked on a fire in all that open space that seemed to carry on and on. Then we were on our way again. The river crossings were all right because it was winter and there was only the one anyway. It was dark by now, so they covered us three children with blankets. Dad woke us up to see the first lights of Eshowe, which was the gaol. After that it seemed like ages before we arrived at the farm, which we eventually did at 2am on 1st July, 1911. Once it was daylight, we looked around. Well, in England you can see your neighbour's farm in the distant but here we were and not another farm in sight. It was an adventure for us children but poor Mother, how she must have felt. There she was with her sewing machine and china tea set and not another person or farm in sight. I was 16-years-old, and wasn't very impressed I can tell you. I had left all my friends behind in England and they would write to ask when was I coming home. On Sundays we went to church – a walk of four miles from the farm Gratton, on the road to Melmoth. Of course we got used to it, but the roads were so narrow and muddy. I eventually managed to get a bicycle which was all right in dry weather but in the rain it was a case of slip and slide. Having a bicycle in those days was quite something, when you consider that it's only just recently that women have taken to driving cars. That was unheard of when I was young. When we arrived in Eshowe there was only one car and that was driven by Tony Wantink. Our house had been built about six months before we arrived. We had paraffin lamps and a wood stove. We got our water from rain-water tanks. We had to heat

Harold Yardley in army uniform in about 1916

the water on the stove in big paraffin tins which Father had made handles for. You would take two cloths, one for the top, one for the bottom, and lift it off and carry it to the bath. No just switching on the tap. In 1914 my father died so George managed the farm with Mother and myself. We grew black wattle, sweet potatoes, madumbies and mealies. George, Harold and I would take it in turns to sell the produce to the natives. Not being able to speak a word of Zulu, this was quite a job. Otherwise, I would spend time doing needlework. Sugar magnate and lawyer, George Hulett, was our closest neighbour. He lived where the Pennefather's farm now. They had a daughter my age so I would walk from Gratton, across the Umlalazi River, and on up to where the William's farm now is. There I would be met by the Huletts' horse and trap, and I would spend the day with them. I met my husband, Albert Paul at the Methodist Church where I was introduced to him by my father. It was then called 'The Wesleyan Church'. On the way out to our farm was the coloured transport camp. There were four or five coloured families living there. They ran the transport so that's where they outspanned the wagons and had their camp. The coloured cemetery is still there. Sunnydale only came into being much later. I was married to Albert Paul from 1917 to 1941. The Zululand Times reported our marriage as follows: A very pretty wedding took place in the Wesleyan Church, on Tuesday, 27th February. Ethel Yardley, only daughter of Mrs H Yardley and the late G Yardley, of the farms Gratton and Norton, to Albert W. Paul, of Greenhill Farm, both of the Eshowe District. The Reverend J Edgcumbe Smith officiated. The bride was given away by her eldest brother, George. Bridesmaid Miss Zieglar an old friend of the bride. To Harold Yardley was entrusted the duties of best man. Both bride and bridesmaid carried beautiful bouquets made by Mrs Agnes Vanderplank. Friends had very prettily decorated the church with flowers and evergreens. Miss Wantink presided at the organ and played 'The Voice that breathed o'er Eden' upon the bride entering the church and the 'Wedding March' when the ceremony was over. The wedding cake was made by Mrs Schmidtmann 'a real beauty.' A motor car was supplied by Mr White of the Eshowe Hotel. A reception was held on the farm, Gratton and in the evening dancing was kept up until the small hours in the morning. Wedding presents were numerous and some were exceptionally good ones. The bride's dress was white satin pailette trimmed with shadow lace, bodice to match, bridal wreath and veil. Bridesmaid's dress was Grecian poplinette trimmed with white ninnon and satin. White crinoline straw hat to match. The mother of the bride was gowned in Saxe blue satin pafette and white straw hat and ostrich feather. Dresses were made by Mrs Ashby. The happy couple left by motor for Gingindlovu to catch the train for Maritzburg where the honeymoon is to be spent.' (I might mention that the Wesleyan Manse in Kangela Street was where John and Sandy McHugh lived prior to moving to Eshowe Hills).

Ethel continued: 'Albert built a house on our farm mainly of stone, which he had to blast out near the river on the farm. This was about four miles to the south-west of Eshowe. We named it Greenhill because when I first went to see it, it was a green hill looking so lovely. After we started farming sugar cane, we would stand on the top of the hill to look out on miles and miles of lovely green lush sugar cane waving in the breeze. We eventually had two farms: Greenhill, and the other was Whitfield (an old English name). As newlyweds we didn't have much money and farming was not the profitable business that it is today. We slowly bought oxen, then a plough. Albert would do the ploughing himself with a little 'voorlooper' in front. He planted sweet potatoes, madumbies, *mealies, wattle and gum trees. It was very unsatisfactory farming; the right crop for this area hadn't been discovered yet, which is of course sugar cane. Many farmers left because they felt hopeless, but Albert was determined to make a success of it. In 1919 our first child was born, a daughter, but we lost her. Our daughter Gladys was born in 1920, then Sheila was born in 1924. Albert always remembered Sheila's birthday because that was when he worked his very first sugar cane crop. He was among the first to plant sugar cane in Eshowe. Pulling out the old crops and slowly planting sugar cane was especially hard where we had wattle and gum trees. Unfortunately, I was not happy living out on the isolated farm. This resulted in Albert building a large double storey house in Main Street. Albert drove every day to and fro between the farm and Eshowe until we sold the farm in 1971. In town we would often spend a Saturday afternoon playing tennis at the courts behind the Police Station in Main Street.'*

Below are a few paragraphs extracted from letters written over a long period by Ethel to relatives in England. These give an idea of life in Eshowe during those times:

'20 Dec 1950: The congregation have built a new Methodist Church in Eshowe, the windows were donated by members of the congregation. Harold and I donated one in memory of Mum and Dad, under each window there is a brass plate with the names inscribed.

16 Oct 1952: We have had very dry and windy weather over here. It is so dry that we are restricted our water supply in Eshowe, we can't use it for the gardens. This is the first time that we have been restricted like this and we need a lot of rain to fill the dams.

16 Oct 1952: Eshowe is growing very fast, any amount of new houses and business places have been built these last few years, it isn't the small place that it was when we came here many years ago, it is beautiful little town though. It is kept so nice and clean.

22 Mar 1956: Is there still a brass band at Norton? We have two orchestras here, that play for dances.

22 Mar 1956: We shall have a tarmac road from Durban to Eshowe in a year or two's time, it will be a much straighter road with not so many bends. The tarmac road is over half-way now; we still have to travel about 40 miles on the old road. Two of the main streets in Eshowe are tarmac. These roads are nice, there is no dust.

4 Feb 1959: I was so thrilled to hear your voices again over the phone. I could hear you all very clearly. The reception over here was excellent, could you hear me clearly? I wanted a nine minute call this time. I was so disappointed when the calls office told me I could only have six minutes on Christmas day, the time seemed to pass so quickly.'

I

In 1974 Ethel wrote in a letter to Douglas Holdcroft: *'Eshowe is a beautiful little place, of course having been here so long, it has been interesting to watch the town changing from a little village with a couple of stores, a butchery and a few houses, mainly wood-and-iron, to the well-kept borough it is today. Of course today it has its modern buildings, houses, new schools and government buildings. We love the place and cannot think of living anywhere else. We have fairly hot summers, but it is cool at night. The winters are lovely, sunny days, no rain, no snow but can get quite chilly if the wind blows off the Drakensberg mountains that do get snow in winter.'*

I

Ethel and Albert Paul's daughter, Gladys was born in 1920, in Eshowe. She married Amyias (Whiskers) Larkan (1909-1980) in 1941. They built 'Central Stores', a grocery store catering for the housewives and a trading store for the Zulus in the centre of Eshowe where First National Bank is today.

The previous photo is of Whiskers Larkan, in about 1968, with his award from the Zululand Show for growing prize vegetables.

After Whiskers' death, Gladys moved from her house in Cetewayo Place to a town house at Azalea Place, down the road from the Bozas' residence, where she spent the last decade of her life.

Ethel and Albert's second daughter, Sheila (1924-1984) married Percival Scrooby in 1953. Percival (1919-1996) and Sheila had one daughter: Shirley who was deputy head girl, in 1974, at Eshowe High School. For 42 years she worked for the Standard Bank in Eshowe. A dedicated member of the Eshowe SPCA, she devoted most of her spare time to the care of animals. In the year that I arrived in Eshowe (1996) Shirley was awarded a much-deserved certificate of merit by the Rotary Club of Eshowe for 'Devoted and Unselfish Service Above Self to the Community'. During the early 2000s, she adopted a daughter, Caroline, who does her proud.

George Henry Yardley Jnr was almost 18 when George Henry Yardley Snr died. Being the eldest, George Jnr ran the farms for 24 years until 1938 (eight years after the death of his mother), when he sold his shares to his younger brother, Harold, for £250.

During the 1st World War, George and Harold joined up with the Zululand Mounted Rifles.

George married Kathleen (Kay) Jubber in 1927. They had one daughter: Ivy, but she died at five days old of jaundice. Medicine, those days, went so far and no further. George, like his sister, Ethel, was a good correspondent and included here are a few extracts from letters he wrote to England during the 1930s: *The fields out here are not hedged like at home; just vast open spaces where one can see for miles. This vastness is coloured by belts of forest which gives the country a beauty unsurpassed; save by an English spring which, in my opinion, is nature's perfection, or is it that spring at home is more attractive to the eye after a dreary winter? The vegetation out in this part of the world could almost be termed perpetual, it never dies, and the weeding required to grow crops would shock the modest British farmer.'*

'I will be cutting 2 500 tons this season and every stick has to be cut by hand with a cane knife, loaded onto wagons, transported three miles to the railway siding, and then loaded again into railway trucks, then it is carried 50 miles to the sugar mill. We have good prospects now of getting a mill in Eshowe, when we shall all be very pleased as we shall save the railway charges which are very heavy.'

'You would open your eyes in wonder to see the extensive agricultural development out here; you can travel 50 miles and see nothing but cane as far as the eye can see on either side, with homesteads dotted about, and large sugar mills at intervals. During the cutting season, which starts in May and finishes in December, these mills never stop crushing day and night, except on Sundays. So you see South Africa today is not the wild country it was. When we came here 20 years ago it was quite barbaric.'

'Tis a wonderful country for instance the one day you can be in the heart of the big game country where all kinds of big game roam at large and the same night be in a city as modern and up to date as any in England. The motor-car, of course, has made this possible. I have bought a motor lorry to transport the cane to the station, it is better than the wagons.' 'There must be great changes around Norton. You will be quite up to date when you get electric light. Eshowe townships are thinking of installing it.'

'As I write the wireless is giving us beautiful music from Durban. I have a nice little set, I get Joburg, Durban, Cape Town, and other places in the world when conditions are right.'

'Time flies. Here we are on the threshold of another Christmas. I suppose you are not sorry to see the end of 1932. We are still going through a terrible commercial upheaval. Well to get to

something homelier and pleasant. The Toe H Branch in Eshowe are holding a concert on December the 1ˢᵗ and I am taking a big part in it. We are also learning Christmas carols to sing in the church. Oh, but Christmas here is very hot, really too hot to enjoy anything.'

'We in South Africa have had the greatest happening; the whole country has received a thorough soaking for which it was greatly in need. In times of drought it brings home to one how utterly helpless we are without God. Thousands of cattle died, the natives who were the principal sufferers were, in some parts, absolutely starving. The government came to their aid and distributed mealies in all the famine areas. We in Eshowe seem to have been more fortunate than others, we did get a shower now and again which kept the cane alive. I have just been appointed as secretary of our Church Trust Committee and Kathleen has taken over the duty of organist.'

George Yardley Jnr died in Luanshya, Copperbelt, where he and his wife, Kathleen had bought a trading store and small-holding.

The youngest of George Snr and Polly's three children was Harold Yardley (1898-1953) whose isiZulu name was 'Sandhlana' which means someone who is good with his hands. His sister, Ethel Paul, related further: *'When Harold worked for Mr Miller, Mr Michael East Snr was working there also and from there they both went over to Poyntons because it was a bigger garage. Harold worked as a mechanic with Michael East and Ken Newberry. The Zululand Garage was opposite Van Dorts, this was much later of course, but it was where the Eshowe Centre is. It was part of the centre from Milton's SA Perm on the Adams side as the garage, and it later became the Barclays Bank. Before that it was Goatleys house and grounds, his house is still there at the back of the Zululand Times offices. There was also later a house at the back of the Royal Hotel where confirmed bachelor, KV Challenor, brought up the family of five Howells children he*

Poyntons Garage, in 1925, where Harold Yardley served an apprenticeship as a mechanic

The building later became the Hardmans' Eshowe Mart

adopted after their parents drowned in a boating accident in 1917. Next to that were the tennis courts and the bowling greens, this went right down as far as opposite the Town Hall you see. At the Town Hall site was a big kraal which had the name Esibaweni meaning 'The place of the horse fly'. All who went to drink there carried a small brush wood to keep the horseflies off. Then came the garage, Goatleys house, Zieglars Butchery then Goatleys store (Storekeeper Mr AE Goatley was chairman of the Eshowe Town Board from 1935 to 1938). Harold went as an apprentice mechanic over at Atshades Garage that still stands there along the way from Eshowe Mart to Tally's Corner. He was in the Workshop Brigade during the war and afterwards he went to Millers Garage that was at the back of the Royal Hotel in those days. Further down, towards Gingindlovu, was Swarps (Ellen Weid) then came Brunners Store facing towards Gingindlovu. White's Hotel (The Royal) at that time was just wood-and-iron. On the left of that was Adams Butchery, then Garrads store which was called 'Central Stores' and they lived at the back. It was back off the road about where Adams bottle store is now. There was a house behind Adams Store as well, where the staff lived at different times. From there you would go along Main Street, down the dip where the railway bridge is now, and on up to the courthouse, post office and officials' housing. On the other side of town in Mangosuthu Buthelezi Drive (then Melmoth Road) there were no houses, just outspan areas, then Adams Camp Store, then Cox's house. JB Cox arrived from England, in 1901, to manage Adams Camp Store. He served on the Local board and in other positions in the community. He was a keen supporter of the Country Club. In 1938 Harold bought the garage from Mr Tom Poynton who had arrived in Eshowe in 1915. He married Gladys Cobb, and together they had three children; Tom Jnr, Jack and Bunty. The business was the first motor repair garage opened in 1916. Tom also took over the farms from our brother George and moved into the original homestead on Gratton. In 1948 Harold bought the Eshowe Wagon Works from Mr

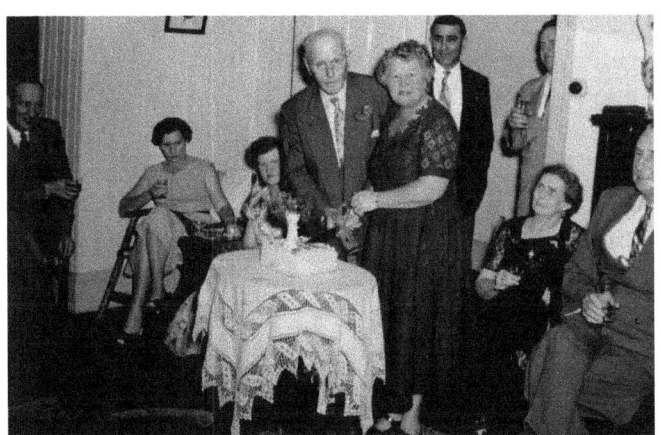

Albert and Ethel Paul's Ruby wedding anniversary on 27th February 1957

Proom. It was a small blacksmith and farrier shop that specialised in making horse traps and wooden trailers to cart sugar cane. He built a motor garage adjoining the wagon works and introduced the first hydraulic hoist and greasing bay to Eshowe. He joined the Zululand Mounted Rifles and was in the Workshop Brigade during the war when he was sent with our brother George to East Africa. Because of their mechanical knowledge they were responsible for keeping the military vehicles on the road. Harold got Enteric Fever (Typhoid) and George got malaria, suffering an attack every afternoon until he grew out of it. The officials in East Africa wouldn't accept that you could contract malaria and didn't supply quinine. Afterwards, Harold lived in a house in Main Street, adjacent to the railway bridge. He was accidentally knocked over by a motorcar in 1950. There was a case over it and Harold won his case. He still limps a bit yet. He later sold the Wagon Works (Lot 644), in 1951, to Mr Stanley Upfold for £4 000. As a result of his accident Harold Yardley developed Buerger's disease, a toxic condition which attacks the arteries and veins. He died three years after the accident, in 1953, aged 55. Harold Yardley's first wife was Kathleen Newberry (1900-1925) who died at age 24, and like all the Yardleys of old she is buried in Eshowe's cemetery. They had one daughter, Mavis (1925-1998) who was a member of Diamond Bozas' Monday morning art class for many years, enjoying the company and banter of the other ladies. Her special friends from school days were Maureen du Plessis and Bubbles Bozas.

After school Mavis worked as a clerk, for many years, for Barclays Bank in the building that is now the offices of WE White Attorneys.

After marrying Arthur Baytopp, a classmate of Diamond's, she became a farmer's wife until Arthur sold and moved into Eshowe. As Mavis aged and was unable to fend for herself it was her caring niece, Shirley Scrooby who nursed her. After Harold's first wife, Kathleen died he married Agnes Hawxby (1901-1977). They had five children: Desmond, Norman, Margaret, Roland, Lester. Desmond was born in 1928 in Eshowe, and died in 2020 at age 92. In 1948 he started work for Natal Estates where he spent much time on horseback. It was the only means of transport there at the time. He was thrown from his horse and critically injured when kicked in the head, but he recovered after surgery. Desmond married Evelyn Packham (1931-2016). They had four children: Richard, Dave (married to Sharon of Donkey School), Angela and Andrew. Two weeks after his father's death in 1953, Desmond resigned from Natal Estates in order to return to Eshowe and run Gratton and Norton until 2004. In 1953 his mother, Agnes, wrote: *I'm very lucky to have Desmond here to run the farm, we have had a terrible drought and the cane hasn't been too good, but the rains have started and I'm sure within the next two years, we will be well away. Desmond is getting married on 28th November. Margaret is one of the bridesmaids, there are three and Norman, my other son, is groomsman. I think they are sending out just over 200 invitations.'*

Desmond told a story of when he had just started farming on the Umlalazi in the early 1950's, and was called to assist the locals with a problem they had below Mandawe. On arrival he was directed to a thick patch of bush that was surrounded by very excited assegai and knobkerrie wielding Zulus with their yapping dogs. All of a sudden a large and very irritable buffalo with assegai wounds came charging out of the bush, caught a local and gored him to death. By now everyone was up trees until Parks Board tracked down the buffalo and shot it.

In 1964 Desmond purchased an adjacent farm called 'The Mill'. At this time Agnes Yardley wrote to Roland Yardley in England: *'We are having far too much rain here lately, as a matter of fact floods in some areas, wash-aways and rail derailments. Desmond can't get on with his planting, the fields are very wet, and there are springs all over.'*

Desmond bought the farms 'Gratton' and 'Norton' by paying out his brothers, sister and stepsister. In 1978 Desmond was re-elected as chairman of the Eshowe Farmers' Association. Here is an excerpt from his address to the association at the AGM in 1979: *'Ladies and Gentlemen, I wish to welcome you all here to an occasion to bring members and their wives together, and also the opportunity of meeting representatives of various departments associated with this association. Until recently we were one big happy family, sending the final product of our sweat and tears to the Gledhow Mill. Somehow the Millers managed to change this state of affairs, and now we have, I hope, two happy families. I wish to welcome Mr Mike Hulett and Mr Bill Warner of the Amatikulu Mill. It is with regret that we have to bid farewell to Clive and Shan who are leaving us for New Zealand. Clive met and married Shan in Eshowe and introduced the firm known as Campbell & Craig, which has been recently taken over by Coopers & Lybrand. Bill Lee has lived in Eshowe since 1917 and after managing for Frank Chennells he farmed on his own account since 1937 at Brocklee. He has served as this association's chairman and secretary for a number of years, and for many years on the executive committee. Nothing has ever been too much trouble for Bill when it came to serve this community of ours. I think it is fitting to call on Mr Boet Fourie to present to Bill a Certificate of Merit, awarded by NAU to mark it in respect and appreciation for the service rendered by him to this our association and to the local community.'*

In 2000 Desmond stood guarantor on the purchase of a neighboring farm, Gebersruh, for his son, Dave (Sharon's husband) who took over the running of the farms. Unfortunately, for various reasons it was decided to sell. In 2003 Gratton, Norton and The Mill were sold to a Mr Cele. Gebersruh was sold to Mr Steenberg who already owned a farm that initially belonged to the Ashbys.

6th April 2004 Desmond and Evelyn finally moved off the farm some three generations and 93 years after George Henry Yardley and his wife, Polly arrived in 1911. Harold and Agnes's second child, Norman Yardley, was born in 1929. In 1960 he married Phyllis Low. In the late 1960s they managed 'Jabulani', a trading store belonging to the Jenkinsons, which was situated across the road from Eshowe Provincial Hospital in Kangela Street, next door to Dr Donald Clark's practice. A few years later Harold's brother, Desmond, bought a trading store up the road from East's Service Station: KwaZandhlana, managed by Norman and Phyllis into the mid 1970's. After it was sold Norman and Phyllis worked for Spar in Eshowe. Thereafter, Norman worked, until his retirement, for Browns Wholesalers in Gingindlovu. In 1986 he was victim of an armed robbery. A press article gives more detail: *'A Gingindlovu businessman was shot during a R13 000 robbery at a store in the town yesterday.*

Mr N Yardley and Miss K Pillay of Brown's Cash and Carry were on their way to the bank when the robbers struck, a police spokesman said. Two black men demanded that Mr Yardley hand over the money, but he refused. One of the robbers fired a shot which hit Mr Yardley in the left foot. The robbers grabbed the moneybag and fled, escaping with R13 480. Police have not made any arrests.'

In the early 1990's, Norman was stabbed during another robbery while he and Phyllis were relieving at the Irons' trading store in Ubombo. Fortunately, he recovered without complications.

Harold and Agnes' third child, Margaret Yardley (1935-2005) married Ronald Ireland (1930-2009) in 1957. Harold and Agnes' fourth child was Roland Yardley (1936-2015), called 'Rusty' due to his auburn colouring. His boyhood was spent on the family farm, having fun with his brother, Norman, driving their father, Harold's tractors and 1934 Ford truck. Rusty married Maureen Anderson in 1965.

Harold and Agnes' fourth child was Lester Yardley (1941-2013). Lester was great friends with Des Shuttleworth who wrote recently in 2020: *'I remember 'Eshowe Motors' being where Poynton's Garage is depicted in your photo. In later years it became 'Eshowe Mart', next to 'Quicke's Tea Room', now Absa Bank. The building on the left, in my time, was a sports shop run by Harold Streek with a flat upstairs.*

Hoo Foster Motors (Maurice Hoo-Foster) was further to the left, opposite Edwards Pharmacy/ old Post Office, now Pep Stores and many other businesses. There was a house next to the sports shop which was demolished to make way for the building of Hoo-Foster Motors. Mr CE Hoo-Foster was chairman of Eshowe Town Board in 1930). I recall as a youngster in Barclays Bank DC & O (now attorneys WE White's office) buying a bicycle

The Mayoral Chambers next door to the Town Hall was built in 1934 to serve as Eshowe's second Post Office. It also housed the Telephone Exchange, then the Town Library, and the Vukani Basket Collection before it relocated to the Museum Village

The glazed tiled panel depicting life in old Zululand was created by British artist Alfred Palmer (1877-1951)

from Harold Streek for £12 and I had to get my father's written permission to pay it off over three months. Was earning £27 one shilling and eight pence at the time. I later bought a Buzz Bike from Durban Glass Works, the same as Lester Yardley', and also paid that off at £3, 7 shillings & 6 pence per month. The Buzz Bikes were 49cc Gino Bartelli's. I have a pic somewhere of both our bikes together on the farm near the pools and the .22 rifle leaning against Lester's bike saddle and Simba his dog next to it. I visited the pools a few years back and was sad to see that they are reduced to a narrow stream, and standing there so many memories came flooding back from weekends spent at the farm with Lester. Like

<u>Very first matric class at Eshowe High School in 1959:</u>
<u>Back row: Nicholas Steynberg, Paul Otte, Dougal Thompson, John le</u>
<u>Roux, Lester Yardley (head boy), David Stead.</u>
<u>Front row: Irene Language (head girl), Hazelanne Hirsch, Aletta</u>
<u>Pearce, Hazel Gardner, Pam Goodwin, Penelope Atkinson, Avrille Schroder.</u>
<u>Absent: Esme Krause</u>

the times when Des and Eve were away for the day and we would steal the Ferguson tractor out of the garage and go for a joy ride around the farm. We used to make canoes out of flattened out corrugated iron and stalk each other with our .22 rifles shooting at the waterline in an effort to sink the canoes. At the farm we would place a wooden block on our heads and take turns shooting it off with the .22's from about 15 paces. Such was the trust in each other's shooting, until one day Lester's brother, Des, caught us and gave us a good talking to.
Fishing at the pools brings back many memories of activities there with Lester. The Hadidahs, Cattle Egrets and Herons used to roost in the branches overhanging the pools and a Hamerkop had a huge nest in the fork of one of the trees. Lester preferred to use putu for bait to catch Scalies, while I preferred to catch grasshoppers for bait.'

Lester Yardley was one of the first matriculants to enrol for their last year of school at the newly built Eshowe High School, which opened in January 1959, on the spot where British troops once played polo.

Irene Strachan recalls that she and Lester were co-head prefects in 1959. Irene's own daughters, Cindy and Monti Strachan were to matriculate at Eshowe High School in 1987 and 1989 respectively.

Lester Yardley married Eris Dedekind in 1965. Lester's nephew (his brother Desmond Yardley's son), Dave, was married to Sharon. It was from Sharon Yardley's 'Donkey School' that my little Jodie Brenchley transferred to Holy Childhood Pre-Primary School. There, she and her younger brothers yet-to-come (Dale and Colin Brenchley) would spend their earliest schooling years with teacher, Paris Sumner.

Paris was married to Doug Sumner who took over from his good friend, Ken Nixon, as principal of Eshowe Junior School. Thereafter, Doug was principal of John Wesley School at the Methodist Church.

II

In 1963 Doug Sumner's 1951 Morris Minor barely made it up the hill to Eshowe when he was appointed to teach mathematics and arithmetic at Eshowe High School. Those days the boys had to do mathematics. Girls could choose between mathematics and housecraft. Doug earned the Zulu name 'Isikhova' meaning 'Owl' because he was said to see in the dark, spotting truants who'd been raiding the Balmers' orchard bordering the Dlinza Forest where the Volbrechts now live.

Later, Doug was to become principal of Eshowe Junior School for 17 years. During that time, he met and married Paris who would teach with him at the junior school before relocating to the Convent.

Andre and Alison van Schalkwyk

The other pre-primary class next door to Paris' at the Convent was occupied by Alison van Schalkwyk's class. Wee Scottish lass, Alison van Schalkwyk, speaks with a charming accent. Helen Braatvedt, unable to make head or tail of what her child was talking about, eventually asked, 'What on earth is a booing?'

'It's the fastest aeroplane in the world.'

My personal favourite is when Alison offers dessert, 'Anyone for poooding?'

Alison van Schalkwyk and Paris Sumner had taken over Sister Carina's and Sister Birgitt's classes respectively. Alison's husband, Andre van Schalkwyk was the 18th principal of Eshowe High School, from 1993 to 2016, for a period of 23 years. Mike Nixon served as his deputy before transferring to the college.

In 1996, the year I arrived in Eshowe, Eshowe High School celebrated a centenary of quality education. An iconic educationist to his core, Andre wrote in his foreword for the celebratory magazine: *'Facing all the changes in 1996, during the centenary celebrations, it was emphasised that the elements of the traditional school system, being the qualities of courtesy, discipline, honesty and courage, will never become outdated'.*

Back to the Convent: Thanks to financial donations from overseas, the present pre-primary school building

was completed in 1972, by builder Mr Norman Wilson. Benedictine brothers built the playground. In January 1959 the new sign was put up outside the playground: Holy Childhood Convent Nursery School. Sister Carina had 50 children in her class and Sister Birgitt had 55. During that first year the children participated in the school concert called, 'Ladies and Gentlemen out of Fashion'. They had their first sports day where they showed their skills in flat race and doggy walk. In 1965 the school adopted a little lamb called 'Black Beauty'. In April 1979 they celebrated the recognition of the school by the Department of Education in Natal.

Previously, in 1955, the Director of Education had refused the Convent's application to be registered as a government aided school, their reason being that there was within two kilometres of the school a government school which could well accommodate all the children in the area.

The purchase of the school grounds was initially resisted. Father Balgeri mentioned to Alexander Bozas that the owner of that land (Mr Briggs) refused to sell to

Catholics. Eventually, Alexander Bozas, whose bakery was just across the road from the Convent's grounds, bought the property and then sold it to the Catholics at no profit.

The Holy Childhood School recently celebrated 60 years of service by the tireless commitment of the Franciscan Sisters of Oberzell, missionary nuns from Germany whose one apostolate was the education of children in Eshowe*.

And so the school was established in 1954. After Sister Martina retired as principal, Sister Theodeland was principal for seven years until her tragic death in 1998. She had gone missing while returning from a visit to the Mbongolwane Mission. Eventually her car was found abandoned. After a massive search, her body was discovered about 30 kilometres from Eshowe. There was a bullet wound in her head. Shocked, shaken and disbelieving, everyone wondered who on earth would want to hurt a servant of the church. The attack was widely publicised overseas. Pope John Paul II mourned Sister Theodeland's death, as did the German government. Lindy Lawrie (married to farmer Steve Lawrie), was involved in a children's tennis tournament when a child reported to her that there were men running down the road with policemen chasing after them and shooting. Like everyone else in Eshowe, Lindy was shocked to learn of the escape of those three apprehended perpetrators. Chairman of the Parents' and Teachers' Association, pharmacist at Edwards Pharmacy, Gerald DeBeer expressed collective horror and outrage. Sister Theodeland was laid to rest at the Holy Cross Mission.

The Convent is actually one of very few that still has a Catholic mass every week that the whole school attends and is open to the public. A final folk mass is held at the

*The nuns who served with so much self-sacrifice and devotion over the years were: Sister Alberta Fasel who arrived in 1951; Sister Mary Daria Heppt who was the first principal of the pre-primary school in 1953 to be followed by Sister Cordula Bundsschuh in 1958; Sister Cordula who was principal until 1966 when Sister Carina Leschinger took over the reins; Sister Prokopia Hergenhan arrived in 1953 as first principal of the Holy Childhood Primary School; music teacher Sister Dolores Engelhardt arrived in 1955 as did future principal, Sister Martina Worner, who was principal for 24 years. She had graduated from Durban Training College in 1958 and taught Standards 4 and 5. In 1957 Sister Kunhilde Wenninger undertook the position of matron of the boys' hostel and also taught religious education; Sister Fidelis Schramm arrived in 1963 and was to work at the school for well over 50 years. Sister Carina Leschinger, who arrived in 1966, undertook the duties of principal of the pre-school after Sister Cordula and also taught handwork to boys; Sister Edith Hepp was in charge of the girls' hostel; Sister Liboria Ehler arrived in 1969, an Edgewood graduate who taught Standard 3 and woodwork to the boys; Sister Birgitt Loch arrived in 1971, a qualified preschool teacher and organist. She wholeheartedly took over as principal of the pre-school in 1995 because Sister Carina was suffering health issues. Each time I ran into Sister Birgitt, over the past two decades plus, she asked after Jodie, Dale and Colin Brenchley by name. She retired at the end of 2012 when management of the pre-school was amalgamated into the primary school system. However, she continues to be the organist for St Benedicts Cathedral. IsiZulu teacher, Sister Mary Innocentia Blose, joined the Convent in 1986. Sister Gregoria Lutter arrived in 1996 specialising in domestic science, needlework and home economics. Sister Fidelis Schramm was Class 2 teacher from 1964 until 2006, but continued to teach religious education while serving as convent superior. Sister Theodeland Schreck obtained her teaching diploma at Edgewood College of Education and undertook the duties of Standard 4 teacher specialising in science and computer studies.

Past Principals

Sister M. Prokopia Hergenhan
1953 - 1966

Sister Martina Wörner
1966 - 1990

Sister Theodelind Schreck
1990 - 1998

Mr. Karl Schmidt
1999 - 2004

Mrs. Margie Salter
2005 - 2012

end of each year, at which each child hands over a gift for a less fortunate child.

The first school fête took place in 1958, opened by mayor, Guy Taylor. Stalls included eats, games and dancing entertainment. In 1959 swimming was introduced.

As one of the class-mums of the Grade 1 class taught by the kind and gentle Connie Dunn for 12 years (from 1998 to 2010), I spent many a happy hour with the likes of fellow class-mum, Natalie Dicks (wife of pharmacist, Grant Dicks, of Edwards Pharmacy) teaching children to doggy-paddle across the shallow end. Amid squeals of delight at small victories, there were the times that a child let out a tremendous sneeze, sending us all dashing to escape the avalanche of green floaters. Nevertheless, much fun was had and with the help of swimming trainers such as the athletically gifted class- mum, Trevlyn Palframan, the school has produced some champion swimmers.

Trevlyn's daughter, Justine represented South Africa at the IAAF 2013 World Championships and in the 2016 Olympics. Specialising in the two and four hundred metres, Justine won the four hundred metre event at the 2015 Summer Universiade.

The Convent also boasts two tennis courts that nurtured the likes of the champion Lagerwall family. Gary Lagerwall and his brother Trevor would go on to win the Zululand junior tournaments for under-15 and under-18s. Their grandmother, Winnie, father Basil, and uncles, Rodney and Roy all played for Zululand. When off the court Basil, Rodney and Roy Lagerwall were property developers. Their thirst inexhaustible, they built the Star Theatre Complex, the Eshowe Centre Sibuyile, Eshowe Mart and many more. Included in their projects

Roy, Rodney and Basil Lagerwall in about 1930

Winnie, Roy, Basil, Rodney and Oscar Lagerwall at Winnie and Oscar's 50th wedding anniversary

THIS PLAQUE COMMEMORATES
THE LONG ASSOCIATION OF
THE LAGERWALL FAMILY
WITH TENNIS IN ESHOWE AND THE
FINE CONTRIBUTION THEY HAVE MADE
TO THE WELFARE OF THIS CLUB
UNVEILED OCTOBER 1967

were the rebuilding of the Royal Hotel after it accidentally burned down in the 1940s (this is where the Ithala Centre stands today). An old man who frequented the pub at the Royal knocked on owner, Mr Steer's door to report the fire. Mr Steer thought he was joking. He gave him a shilling and a sixpence and said this, 'This one's on me'. And the hotel burnt down. It had caught alight when someone left a petrol iron on.

Electric current from the first diesel power station, situated behind what is now WE White's building (Barclays Bank back then), was switched on in 1933. An additional engine was added to the plant in 1941. But soon the town outgrew that diesel station and a steam power-plant was installed in 1949. But it was not ready for opening until extensions to Nkwaleni and Gingindlovu were completed in 1958. In 1965 Eshowe closed down its own power station and joined the vast national network of the Electricity Supply Commission. Currently, Roy Lagerwall's daughter, Lynne is playing tennis for South Africa veterans and her granddaughter is in the USA on a tennis scholarship. That makes five generations of Lagerwalls succeeding on the tennis court.

Stan Larkan, mayor of Eshowe when Pat and I arrived in 1996, was also an Eshowe-ite tennis player to be reckoned with.

Every year, for decades, the Tennis Club had a fundraiser party at which your ticket number stood to win thousands in a lucky draw. In 1999 the many tickets in the hat were reduced to Charles Cadman's and mine. We decided to split the winnings, but a final fun-draw revealed that Charles would have been the winner. Poppy Larkan had us in stiches when playfully clapping her hands on the way out saying, 'Make way for the mayor!'

Let's not forget those ladies of the tennis court: Stan's wife, Poppie Larkan, and Stan's own mother, Stella Larkan, the club's number one player*.

III

The Convent had their very first sports day on 12th September 1959. Mayoress Mrs Reid encouraged the children not only to run between the parallel lines on the sports field, but to walk between the straight lines throughout their lives.

The uniform and the motto was created by 1964 as was the school badge.

In 1977 the pre-primary and primary schools were opened to all races. Of the 203 pupils on role at The Holy Childhood School in January 1977 there were three Indian, four mixed-race, and one African child whose name was Dumile Zungu. Dumile spent a lot of time at Brocklee Farm riding horses and playing cops and robbers with the Lee twins. She later became CEO of the Durban Chamber of Commerce and Industry.

The change at the Convent, to include children of colour, was a brave and bold decision made by the South African Catholic Bishop's Conference, in complete opposition to the policy of the South African government at the time. Although a noble decision, it was one which came with consequences. Eshowe Junior School, where Ken Nixon was principal, was one of very few white government schools to participate in

---

*Other ladies worthy of mention are Bossie Hattingh, Lois Parker (wife of Barry Parker), Jan Wynne (who would play tennis right up to her 83rd year), Dora Wainman (who also played into her 80s), Eve Yardley, Barbara Maggs, Eileen East, Ann Skinstad, Marthie Bester and Barbara Townsend.

tournaments against the multiracial Convent schools. This lasted for 11 years until finally overturned in 1987. Sister Martina and Ken Nixon became good friends during that time, sharing Ken's home-brewed beer after hours. They must be applauded for aiding church and country towards healthier, happier relationships among races.

By then there were over two hundred children on the Convent's role. It became necessary to take on new staff members. Mrs Loueen Chittenden (married to Hugh Chittenden) and Mrs Karen Black joined the teaching staff. The school's first full-time male member, Mr Morcon joined the school, in 1990, when Sister Liboria Ehler was promoted to deputy principal.

The senseless murder of Sister Theodeland Schreck necessitated the appointment of a replacement principal; Karl Schmidt became the first lay person to fill this role and he did it well for five years. In his final speech he expressed the greatest faith in the new principal, Mrs Margie Salter who had been teaching at the school since 1978 (for 31 years – half of her life on earth at that time). Margie encouraged the children to never give up; challenges are there to develop character. At that time the school's own challenge was the ever decreasing pool of external funding. School management and the fundraising committee continually developed new methods of generating funds. These initiatives included the take-over of the birding weekend event from the Bird Club and Farmers' Conservancy. Also golf days, talent shows and the Mgoje trail run. The timeless school fête continues annually as a favourite school tradition.

The year 2012 saw another change with the retirement of Mrs Salter. Mrs Meg Kennedy, who had arrived at the school to relieve Dot Gilson's Grade 3 class, in

2003, was promoted to principal.

Back to earlier days, Trevor Lagerwall recalls reciting poems and participating in the Eisteddfods. The children were even taught how to lay out a tea tray. They created craft work each year for the Zululand Show that was a huge annual event. It was established in 1916 at the old golf links with Mr W T Brockwell, the pioneer farmer, as first president. Those days' women displayed their entries on trestle tables in a hall where the Country Clubhouse now stands. Not much is known about the early years of the show because a fire, in 1938, believed to be started by vagabonds, destroyed the home-industries hall and all the records.

The following year the show was held in the Eshowe Town Hall where an evening ball was convened. It was the only building in Eshowe that had electricity at the time, besides the Royal Hotel which had its own generator by then.

In 1940 the show was cancelled due to heavy flood losses. No shows were held during the war years, until 1948, when the venue was moved to the military camp in Osborn Road.

In 1958 the Zululand Agricultural and Industrial Show opened on its new premises: 81.6 acres of ground leased from the Eshowe local authorities, on the Entumeni Road just north of Eshowe that had previously been a racecourse. After two years they were to fence in an area of 42 acres to be retained specifically for the show.

Mr Batchelor was president. Bill Lee was senior vice president between 1965 and 1983. During those years he had the honour of escorting president JJ Fouche around after he opened the show in 1971. He also had the pleasure of parading with the show queen and her princesses after their coronation each year. He stood as president in 1984, and as senior vice president for the two years before his resignation in 1986.

According to Mrs DM Marsh, the show's secretary in 1986: 'Last year's show was fully booked by commercial outlets and much interest was shown in the horse section and the Nguni cattle.'

In his 60 years of service to the show committee, Bill Lee watched it grow from a tiny one-day event to a jam-packed three-day occasion.

IV

Ten Lagerwalls attended the Convent (Cheryl, Dawn, Gary, Trevor, Lynne, Geoffrey, Colin, John, Dayle and Debbie). Trevor remembers the nuns' excitement when 'The Sound of Music' came to the Star Theatre in Eshowe. The whole school went off to see it and for years afterwards they sang 'My Favourite Things'.

Candice Webb (née Pett) remembers when her class, in 1994, was selected to be part of a project to educate fellow pupils about the importance of the natural environment. Together with Natal Parks Board game ranger, Glen Holland, her class took a walk in the forest behind the school, studying the roles of indigenous tree species, fauna and flora. Then they created a musical play aimed at highlighting the importance of protecting forests. Candice went on to became environmental manager for one of the largest pulp paper mills in the world. She puts it down to that year when her love for the environment started, and that one day she would make a career out of it.

The Chennells family have had a happy three-generation association with the Convent starting with Jono, son of farmers Guy and Win, in 1955 under sister Martina. The second generation was under Sister Theodelind, and the third under Mrs Meg Kennedy.

In the 1960s, Win Chennells used to teach swimming to the children together with Hillier Lawrie, mother to farmers Gavin and Steve Lawrie. Jono remembers learning to play the triangle when not much musical ability was evident, just to be included.

We must not forget 'farmers in the making' Shane Pett and Gavin Lawrie, who, as boarders at the Convent, decided to build a den on the school grounds that would serve as their smoking parlour. Using spades borrowed from the vegetable garden they dug a hole measuring approximately 1.5 metres deep with a circumference of a metre. They then tunnelled a good six metres towards the Country Club. The project took them about six weeks to complete while packing soil into bags and spreading it evenly around the property. After lining the tunnel with banana leaves they lit up Lucky Strike cigarettes bought from the 'Corner Café' across the road, and they spluttered themselves into a suffocating frenzy. They returned after the school holidays to discover that their den had caved in and was covered over.

The Petts and Lawries continue to pursue adventure together. Recently, while camping in Botswana, they photographed the lion, pictured above, passing directly between their tents.

Chapter 11

Pat Brenchley and I were expecting our second child, a son called Dale, when we moved to the bottom end of Main Street, an extension of Osborn Road that runs directly through the middle of town, past Tally's Corner and the George Hotel, to join up with Fairley Road at the junction near the beautiful Mpushini Waterfalls.

Local businessman and property developer, Trevor Rosewall, was already letting one of his A-frame houses to the Sugar Experiment Station for Pat's colleague, Martin Eweg and his wife, Coral.

Watching our house, next door to the Ewegs, being built from the foundations upward was very exciting. Although, in Eshowe, one may experience all four seasons in a day (beginning with misty early mornings), it is mostly of a climate cooler than down at the coast nearby. Enjoying the 'champagne weather' that is sunny yet cool, my three girls and I would picnic among the marijuana seedlings, that are sometimes the brick-layers' crop, sprouting all over where Pat (with farmer Charles Cadman's help) was yet to plant our very own indigenous forest.

It was a spacious and well lit double story house, allowing for Lara and Keri, who had grown into striking (but precocious.) teenagers, to have their own spacious quarters upstairs. And the Indian Ocean was visible on a clear day. The new house was also closer to the public pool where my girls were to spend many happy summer afternoons.

I

About the public pool: between 1883 and 1899

The public pool as the big pond it was in the beginning

The same pool as it was for decades thereafter

the stream that still flows past the public swimming pool was dug out by British troops to form a dam in which they could swim. According to Tony Balmers book, that dam originally had a tree growing out of it. Its various branches proved useful as diving-boards. Later, in 1896, the tree was taken out and a proper swimming pool, measuring 50 X 25 yards was built by the Public Works Department. The pool was kept full by that same little stream running from the station side. It ran through a number of old-fashioned filter systems until the 1960s when a proper filter system was built. The middle area where the tree had been remained shallow (about 1.2 metres deep) so if you dived off the side you bumped your head on the bottom. It cost a tickey (2½ cents) to have a swim, but children often avoided the main entrance by sneaking in from the forest side.

Once we had relocated to Main Street I was also pleased to note that the beautiful Anglican Cathedral of St Michael & All Angels was situated within comfortable walking distance. In fact, this part of town had formed the original nucleus of Eshowe – The bulk of the Main Street houses were originally occupied by government officials while younger bachelors were accommodated in a cluster of rondavels behind the courthouse, opposite St Michaels. Apart from the traders' wagon routes and the military roads through the forest, Main Street was the only road that could be called an actual road.

Ever since the building of St Michaels (aside from when the wind whistled in August) one could hear the tolling church bells ringing at midday each day, five days a week. That same bell was previously, way back during the 1880s, hung from a wooden tower standing in front of the Post Office, the ringing of which was the signal to townsfolk that their mail had arrived. When the Post Office was moved to its next site (now the Mayoral

Chambers) in 1934, the bell was moved to the Anglican Church.

The Anglican Church in Eshowe served as the seat of the first black diocesan bishop in Southern Africa. It is still the seat of the bishop of the Anglican Diocese of Zululand. I had just missed the deanship of Reverend John Salt who was elected to serve as bishop of St Helena. This delightful cigar-puffing, whisky-quaffing priest was somewhat of a legend in Eshowe. He silenced his critics with the observation that he never drank at home, so the occasional pub shots were all he ever drank, and that the men he met in the pub were far more in need of his counsel than the church-going faithful.

I started attending St Michael's in 1999, the very year that Reverend Dino Gabriel arrived to serve as dean. He was a man with an exuberant personality and generous with big bear-hugs and hearty laughs. He could speak isiZulu fluently, albeit with a charming Italian accent. His and his Swazi-born wife, Elizabeth had a daughter, Charis who was my Jodie's bestie at the Convent. In 2005 Dino Gabriel was elected as bishop of the Anglican Diocese of Zululand. His deanship was succeeded by Reverend Lewis Gumede, a humble, kind man for whom I would be privileged to serve as secretary in the parish office during 2009. (Yes, I've had a lot of jobs.)

Because Mike Nixon and I were both previously divorced it was necessary to seek the blessing of the bishop before the church would marry us in 2007. Upon Bishop Dino Gabriel's blessing I immediately, and presumptuously, served him with a wedding invitation.

At our wedding in August 2007, Father Lewis was about to say 'Go forth and multiply' when he looked again at my five children and Mike's son, Travis. The look on his face prompted a burst of laughter and much applause.

Attending our wedding were many Anglicans whom I'd befriended since my shift to Main Street in 1997. To name just a few: The Wisemans, Gaisfords, van Toorens, Bozas', Jan Wynne, and Jenny Hawke who had kindly thrown me a pantry party at her spectacular home designed by her brother-in-law, Paul Mikula.

As the person who best knew both Mike and me, we asked Gavin Wiseman to give the speech at our wedding. I had spent many lovely excursions walking through the local hills and forests as a member (like him) of Eshowe's Ramblers Club. Gavin had also served as the chairman of the governing body at Eshowe High School during the time that Mike Nixon was deputy principal there. The foyer at the high school is appropriately named in Gavin Wiseman's honour. In the school's centenary magazine Gavin congratulated the school, that was born out of the early administrative, military and trading population of Zululand, for having grown through the fluctuating fortunes of the territory into the fine educational institution that it had, by then, become. Gavin's wife, Betty has an interesting history: as a born and bred English-speaker she capably taught Standard 2 children in the Afrikaans medium at Mtubatuba Junior School. Thereafter she lectured Latin to law students at the University of Zululand. Later she taught Afrikaans as a second language to college students at the Eshowe Teachers' Training College where she also served as librarian. In other words, Betty's mind is one to be reckoned with – as is her efficiency in managing the Girl Guide movement since 1987, eventually serving as commissioner and trainer.

One year, the Girl Guides were challenged to serve tea to someone special in an unusual place. They invited the then mayor of Eshowe, David White to tea on a raft at the Ehlazi dam. David White, always game for a challenge, took off his shoes, rolled up his trouser legs and perched himself on the raft made of thin branches tied together. The raft began to sink, but the mayor sat fast, enjoying his cuppa before wading back to shore. This activity did not go down with the then town clerk, whose concern it was that the precious mayoral chain, made by the SA Mint in 1958, might well have sunk and been gone forever.

Returning to our wedding: Betty and Gavin Wiseman's daughter, Ruth Rhodes is an extension officer employed by the South African Sugar Cane Research Institute. It came up in the speeches that Ruth and other girls, who were taught geography by Mike at Eshowe High School, particularly enjoyed those classes when Mike turned to write on the black board; that position offered splendid views of what they thought to be rather a 'neat seat'.

Denise Schultz, another big character in this small town, moved among the guests checking to see if the groom's 'neat seat' was to be outdone, and the seat of the bishop of the Anglican Diocese of Zululand, Dino Gabriel, was not exempt from a firm pinch.

Denise and I share grandchildren, since her eldest son, Carl married my second daughter, Keri. I could not wish for a more hands-on, fun-loving and affectionate Gogo with whom to share little Graeme and Rachel Schultz.

II

The Schultzes ancestry is colourful. Alwyn's forebears were Germans who arrived in the emigration wave of the mid1800s. they settled in the Frankfort area. Denise's ancestors are English/Maltese on her father's side and Dutch/Indian on her mother's. To explain the latter

Denise and Alwyn Schultz

Angela, from Bengal in the historical region of the northeastern part of the Indian subcontinent, was one of eleven slaves who arrived at the Cape of Good Hope between 1652 and 1657. One of her several owners was Jan van Riebeeck. After Angela was freed from servitude she married the Dutchman Arnoldus Basson and bore him seven children. All the Bassons in the country originate from this union. Denise's grandfather was a Basson. Denise's grandmother, Anna Catherina Basson (née Smuts) was a second cousin of Jan Smuts, the renowned South African statesman of Dutch descent.

Anna and Jan Smuts were born in the same room on a farm in the Cape. Their grandfathers were brothers – this makes for what will one day be interesting conversations with our mutual grandchildren who live and learn in a very different South Africa today.

When General Smuts visited Eshowe in 1922, farmers paraded their prized cattle while folk lunched under trees. At Kosi Bay Smuts galloped his horse on the beach, and to the horror of everyone present, he took a long swim, in the nude, in the crocodile infested Pongola River.

I might add that at least two prime ministers have visited Eshowe including General Smuts in 1922, and Mr BJ Vorster two decades later.

Alwyn and Denise Schultz arrived in Eshowe in 1979, having both been assigned teaching positions at Eshowe Junior School. They decided they would stay in this rural town for two years before applying to schools elsewhere. Since they knew not one soul (and both being theatric and gregarious by nature) they joined the Zululand Society of Arts and the Dramatic Society in which, for many years, they played active roles.

Neil Moore, a colleague, introduced them to the 'rugby crowd' and soon they were having the time of their lives.

They decided to stay for four years rather than just two. And Alwyn joined the Hockey Club. Today he and Mike Nixon love reminiscing about fun times there*. Mike Nixon was also a keen rugby player and apart from playing, mostly wing, at the Eshowe Rugby Club, he coached at the high school from 1981 to 1997.

After two years at the Junior School, Alwyn Schultz took up a position as a geography lecturer at the Teachers' Training College, and most importantly, he bought his first landrover.

When four years were up the Schultzes decided that there was no better place to raise a family than right

---

*Fellow hockey players were Michelle and Hugh Browning, Tim and Sandy Scott-Barnes, Sharon and Andre Louw, Richard Gartrell, Richard Garside, Rob Raw, Monica and Pierri Rossouw, Gavin Archibald, Cheryl Swart, Ron Milne, Joe Venter, Greville Oscroft, Tots Oscroft, Dave Dyso, Ivor Morris and Chris Storm.

here in Eshowe. Over 40 years later, Eshowe is still considered a wonderful place to raise children.

And so, during the 1980s, Carl and Galen Schultz were born into an era of landrover jaunts, camping trips and general shenanigans.

In 1985 Denise applied for a transfer to Eshowe High School, to hold the position of guidance counsellor, and later, also as an English and history teacher up to matric level. Apart from the classroom and organising matric dances, Denise is probably best remembered for the comedy mime show she put on, which involved all staff members bar two, and for shaving off all her hair to raise money for cancer.

Alwyn's love of nature saw him actively involved in environmental matters such as the planting of many indigenous trees around the town and at the dams, eradicating alien species, and as I have told you, saving snakes from obliteration.

Alwyn, as did Mike Nixon, remained in the college's employ until its closure in 2000 after which all remaining staff were assigned to administrative positions in the Education Department. They were required to travel to Empangeni, 65 kilometres away, and back each day. Alwyn, like Mike, was unhappy working under these conditions and opted for early retirement.

After 26 years of service to the high school, which included a short stint of teaching in England, Denise also opted for early retirement. She soon discovered, however, that she missed the classroom, and she took up a position at the TVET College in Eshowe, as an English lecturer. She taught for a further five years before retiring for a second time.

In the meantime, both Carl and Galen completed their education at Eshowe High and went off to universities where they completed their degrees: Carl in engineering and Galen in journalism.

Although both boys have taken up employment elsewhere, they maintain many friendships that were forged in Eshowe and they remember their childhood years as happy ones.

The Schultzes have travelled a good deal since being retired, both abroad and throughout Southern Africa. Other than travel, Denise has many pursuits that bring her joy, notably gardening, painting and writing. And, of course, being Gogo to little Graeme and Rachel.

Alwyn likes to potter in their (mostly) indigenous garden with a beer close at hand. He and Denise love the people of this town with whom they share a history and of whom many have become close friends. Forty-four years on they still find no compelling reason to leave Eshowe.

III

Among other guests at our wedding, (pictured here), were my friends Mali Govender and Tootsie Govender (no relation to each other) who bring me to write about our local Indian community.

What impresses me most about South African Indian people is their unending generosity. When they visit, they inevitably bear loads of treats. Be they Hindu, Muslim or Christian, each shares kindly with the other. I love Mali and Tootsie's spicy cuisine, and their colourful sparkling fashion.

When sugar cane farming took off in Natal, several decades before it crossed the Thukela River into Zululand, Natal farmers required large numbers of labourers when cane was harvested and had to be quickly refined. The Zulu people did not volunteer in sufficient numbers, largely because they considered agriculture to be women's work.

What resulted was Law No 14 of 1859, which made it possible for the British colony to bring workers from India on a five-year contract. Just over 150 thousand indentured Indians were to arrive in Natal, between 1860 and 1911. Most were young single men.

In the 1870s a new class of immigrant arrived: 'Passenger Indians' (also known as 'Free Indians') who had paid their own passage to South Africa. They were mostly Muslims who set up shop as traders.

After serving their contracts, the early indentured Indians were given the choice between re-indenture, a free passage home to India, or citizenship and a small plot of land. They mostly chose the latter.

By 1910, only a quarter of indentured men had returned to India. The rest stayed to constitute the forbearers of the majority of present-day South African Indians – a diverse community of different origins, languages and religions.

Anti-Indian legislation intensified when South Africa became segregated. In 1891 Act No 25 withdrew that original offer of land and citizenship. Already, by 1888, Indians had to carry passes and could not own land, vote or live outside designated areas. Three years later they lost their parliamentary franchise. Neighbouring Boer states forbade Indian settlement inside their borders, and any movement across borders without a pass. Apart from the few Indians working on farms in Zululand back then, Indians could cross from Natal into Zululand for only 24 hours at a time.

In 1893, with the number of Indians in Natal now outnumbering the number of whites, the Natal government disfranchised Indians. In 1896 the further immigration of Free Indians was restricted; the subsidy of £10 thousand towards the cost of bringing indentured workers was withdrawn, and an annual tax of £3 was imposed on all indentured workers (including wives and children), who entered the country after 1895, and who did not return to India at the end of their contract.

The 'Free Indian' immigrant group of traders clung to their businesses, some became landowners and, deciding to use education as their weapon, many of their sons took up professional occupations.

Although the number of Natal-born Indians continued to grow, by 1904 only 33% of the entire Indian work-force was under subsequent terms of indenture. In 1905, however, at the start of the post-war depression, re-indenture became necessary due to rife unemployment rates. As the rate of re-indenture increased, so did the percentage of workers signing up for agriculture. Labourers were expected to work for as many as 17 or 18 hours per day during the overlapping crushing and planting seasons.

Three years after the Union of South Africa was formed in 1910, the South African government introduced the Immigrants Regulation Act: Indians, with the exception of their wives and children already resident in South Africa, were prohibited from entering the country. By then the main avenues of employment for indentured labour was not only on sugar farms, but also on coal-mines and the railways

In 1925 the Class Areas Bill and the Areas Reservation Bill allowed for Indians to trade or own property in certain areas only. The government of India was invited to appoint an agent to facilitate effective co-operation between the two governments. Thus, for a time, South African Indian fears were put to rest.

In light of the bigger picture, allow me to tell you about India's enigmatic sage, lawyer Mohandas K Gandhi (also known as 'Mahatma Gandhi'), who came to South Africa by ship in 1893, to handle a case pending in Pretoria. He was thrown out of the 1st class carriage of a train en route to the Transvaal and later forced out of a stage coach, beaten by the driver, then denied a hotel room and a seat in a restaurant. To top it all, he was pushed into a gutter in Pretoria. That mistreatment was a turning point in Gandhi's life, kindling his latent interest in social activism. As he was about to return home, in mid-1894, he was persuaded to stay on to fight a proposal to deny Indians a vote in Natal's Legislative Assembly. By then indentured Indian labourers outnumbered the European population of the colony. Working class whites were particularly angry at their jobs being taken by cheap Indian labour. For the next two decades Gandhi was the undisputed leader of Indians in South Africa, forming the Natal Indian Congress to protect the rights of Free Indians as subjects of the British Crown.

After a trip home to India, where he became a well-known figure, Gandhi returned to South Africa in 1897, to be met on the Durban docks by a shouting crowd of whites determined to halt Indian immigration.

He was badly beaten and fortunate to escape with his life. Colonial secretary, Joseph Chamberlain, ordered the prosecution of those responsible, but Gandhi refused to lay charges. He had come to believe that nonviolence was the supreme virtue of the brave and manly. He also resolved to remould his personal life according to the rules of 'chastity, poverty and menial service'. During that time, he took two hours out of every day to work at a hospital learning to tend to patients. This was to stand him in good stead when he served as a stretcher-bearer in the Anglo-Boer War which broke out in 1899, and again during the Bambatha Rebellion in 1906.

In 1903 Gandhi founded the Transvaal British Indian Association. When the Legislative Council passed a law that required all Indians to register and to carry passes, Gandhi embarked on defiance and, in 1906, the Indian community pledged to defy the law.

'Satyagraha' was born: the technique for redressing wrongs by fighting your adversary without the use of violence. For over a decade, Gandhi prepared numerous petitions, led deputations to the authorities, and visited India and Britain, to promote support for Indians in South Africa.

Even as he prepared to confront the Transvaal authorities following his failure to have the British government restore the franchise to Indians, when the amaZulu revolted in 1906, Gandhi proposed an Indian Ambulance Corps. That proposal was sent to the colonial secretary who accepted Gandhi's offer to let a detachment of Indians treat wounded Zulu soldiers. Gandhi urged the Indian population in South Africa to join the war through his columns in the Indian Opinion:

If the government only realised what reserve force is being wasted, they would make use of it and give Indians the opportunity of a thorough training for actual warfare.'

That Ambulance Corps of Indians, many of whom were indentured labourers, are said to have actually identified more with the Afrikaners (the British being the oppressors of both), but Gandhi believed that alignment with the British would help the Indian cause as proof of their claim to British rights. When Queen Victoria died in 1901, it was Gandhi who lead a crowd of Indian mourners through the streets of Durban.

Earlier, during the 2nd Boer War, Gandhi recruited a splendid corps of eleven hundred Indian stretcher bearers of all religious persuasions. His closest Christian friend then, was the Anglican, Dr Lancelot Parker Booth who served as medical officer of the corps.

And so the first Satyagraha began in 1907 when about 150 South African Indians courted imprisonment by defying restrictive laws. This initial campaign ended, six months later, when an agreement was reached between Gandhi and General Smuts that Indians could voluntarily register. Then the Satyagraha was resumed another six months later after the government failed to deliver changes. Between 1908 and 1911 over two thousand Indians went to prison in order to defy the restriction of inter- provincial movement by Indians.

Gandhi threatened the South African government with peaceful revolt on an ever-widening scale, accusing it of planning to 'wipe out the resident Indian population' by 'refusing to validate non-Christian Indian marriages'. Despite these warnings, the government and the white minority were taken by huge surprise when, in November 1913, under Gandhi's direction, indentured labourers went on the first-ever strike in the country's history. Some two thousand workers downed their tools.

Gandhi led phase one of the great march that same day,

heading some two hundred strikers out of Newcastle with the intention of crossing into the Transvaal to confront the government. Within three days the number had swelled to about four thousand.

Gandhi was charged with 'aiding and abetting illegal entry into the Transvaal'. While he was incarcerated, between fifteen and twenty thousand Indians joined the strike. Police shot five strikers at Mount Edgecombe for brandishing homemade weapons.

Gandhi was released from prison in an effort to cool tempers. Early the following year a Bill was passed whereby the infamous £3 penalty tax was finally abolished, and concessions were made with regard to non- Christian Indian marriages.

Matters were by no means resolved to everyone's satisfaction, but Gandhi believed he had achieved whatever he could under the circumstances. So, on 18th July 1914, he set sail from Durban for the last time, destined to become leader of India's struggle for independence.

Gandhi had spent 21 years in South Africa. In recognition of the work he did, many places, such as buildings, streets and parks, are named after him. These include the Mahatma Gandhi Memorial Hospital, a 350-bedded hospital that opened its doors to the public on 7th March 1997. There is a bronze statue of Gandhi in Durban city centre and an excellent new Gandhi museum located at the Phoenix Settlement where Gandhi lived for nearly two decades. It features a display of his most famous quotes such as 'An eye for an eye only ends up making the whole world blind'. Gandhi Square (formerly van der Bijl Square and Government Square) is a plaza located in the central business district of Johannesburg.

In 2015, a statue of Ghandi was added to those of Winston Churchill and Jan Smuts in London's Parliaments square: three men who helped to shape South Africa. Two of them, Smuts and Gandhi, visited Eshowe.
In this photograph is Gandhi with Sonia Schlesin who started her service as Gandhi's secretary, at the age of 17. She ended up leading the Satyagraha almost singlehandedly.

Mahatma Gandhi was assassinated on 30th January 1948, at age 78, in New Delhi.

His assassin, Nathuram Godse, was a Hindu nationalist who shot Gandhi in the chest three times at point blank range. Godse felt that the massacre and suffering caused during the partition could have been avoided if Gandhi and the Indian government had acted to stop the killing of the minorities (Hindus and Sikhs) in West and East Pakistan.

Indian immigrants in South Africa, previously divided on lines of language, culture, tradition and religion, found a basis for Indian unity through Gandhi's teachings. When Gandhi left South Africa in 1914, just months before the 1st World War broke out, the leadership of the Indian community fell to 'moderates' who believed their interests would be best served by compromising with the white government. But then, in 1939, a new radical leadership emerged with the conviction that the Indian community could only be defended by struggle and sacrifice. In 1946 the 'radicals', having seen that the government's idea of a negotiated compromise was to strip Indians of the remaining rights they still had, once again invoked Gandhi's philosophy of political struggle to redress Indian grievances. When the Asiatic Land Tenure Act and the Indian Representation Act came into force in 1946, a nation-wide passive resistance movement was launched under the leadership of Dr GM Naicker in Natal and Dr YM Dadoo in the Transvaal. The campaign involved the defying of those two acts by having Indians willfully court imprisonment by crossing the provincial borders without permits. Nearly two thousand men and women were voluntarily imprisoned for non-cooperation. Although the 1946 Passive Resistance Campaign was considered a failure, it led to the Natal Indian Congress making common cause with the African National Congress. In 1947 Naicker (NIC), Dadoo (TIC) and Xuma (ANC) grew up an agreement that mandated the Indian and African organisations to work together for the end of discrimination. Prior to 1950, Indians, coloureds and Africans had been fighting their battles separately, but now the Defiance Campaign joined them into one united force. Thousands of volunteers refused to obey segregationist rules at bus stops, train stations and post offices. Between June and November 1952, over eight thousand people were voluntarily arrested. But in terms of any impact on the implementation of apartheid by the National Party after the 1948 elections, the Defiance Campaign was ineffective. But there were other gains: the formation of the Congress of Democrats (a small but active group of white democrats), the Coloured People's Congress and the South African Congress of Trade Unions. ANC membership soared from seven thousand to over one hundred thousand.

In November 1952, the Minister of Justice banned all meetings of more than ten Africans. A Criminal Law Amendment Act was passed, allowing judges to sentence resisters 'on the spot' to floggings or three-year jail terms; the government redefined 'Resistance to Racial Segregation' as 'Communism', then they drove the party underground by charging leaders with treason.

Alone among the South African states, only Natal welcomed Indians. There were no Indians living in the Eshowe district until the 1930s when some of those families in Natal were brought in to work for the Entumeni Sugar Mill. There they worked and lived for many years in homes built by the Saville family who owned the mill.

Derek Pillay (pictured opposite), and SV Naicker who was born in Entumeni, were most instrumental in getting the South African government to provide land for the establishment of the Indian settlement in Eshowe known as Mpushini Park.

Derek Pillay, along with others, worked day and night to get funding to build that suburb named by Pam Pillay, daughter of Derek and his wife, Asodhi.

Many occupants of the new suburb suggested names but Pam's was chosen as best suited, based on research she did on Eshowe's beautiful Mpushini Waterfalls.

Pam Pillay attended Little Flower and Holy Childhood Convents. Due to apartheid, she was not permitted to attend Eshowe High School. Derek's employers, Win and Guy Chennells, kindly sponsored Pamela's boarding at St John's Girls High School in Pietermaritzburg. She later met and married her husband in Johannesburg, had two children, and emigrated to New Zealand.

Derek and Asodhi's younger daughter, Karen attended preschool at the Holy Childhood Convent prior to attending Eshowe Junior School. By then government schools were multiracial. She excelled at Eshowe High School, both in the classroom and in sports: swimming, hockey and cricket. She was also president of the student union. After high school she spent a gap year in England working as a sports coach at a private school before returning to South Africa to studied law at Stellenbosch University. While there, her father, Derek Pillay died, which led to her moving to New Zealand where she runs a business with her husband, Ivan. They have two children.

Pam and Karen's mother, Asodhi Pillay (née Moodley) was born in Tongaat in 1941. After completing her schooling there she moved to Empangeni where her parents lived and worked.

Asodhi worked as a nanny for Mr Pope who was manager of the Umlhalhuz Valley Sugar Farm, which is where Derek Pillay worked at the time. The two inevitably bumped into each other – on a soccer field in fact. They got married two years later and lived with Derek's parents on Sprat's Farm for almost five years.

Derek became interested in politics, but in order to join Eshowe's Town Board he needed to further his education. Completing Dale Carnegie's course opened doors for Derek in Rotary, the Provincial Hospital, Child Welfare, the farming board, and the local Town Board where he became a councilor.

Derek Pillay and SV Naicker fought tirelessly to rezone the educational site in Mpushini Park for religious purposes. Their efforts resulted in the two beautiful Hindu temples and churches. The second temple (Sisteri Ganesha Kovil) was completed with the help of localite Devon Palaver of the Mall Pharmacy, and the Chinsamy families of Mpushini park. The foundation was started by Jerry Chetty, but due to lack of funding it remained at window height for a whole decade. It was about to be demolished by the municipality when the community got together to complete the temple into what it is today: the Sisteri Ganesha Kovil Temple that was consecrated by Swamis from India.

Derek Pillay's interests involved managing the soccer team, Young Everton Football Club in Sunnydale. He also collected antique cars and furniture.

Another prominent person from Mpushini Park was Reggie Moodley who played a pivotal role in helping Indian pensioners to register as grant recipients. He used to walk all the way to the social welfare offices in town to obtain forms for his elderly neighbours to complete.

IV

I have shown you a photograph of Mali Govender and Tootsie Govender taken at Mike's and my wedding. Back in the year 1999, distracted by my two toddlers in Pat Brenchley's Toyota Venture at Pick 'n Pay's parking lot, I managed to dent the fender of the sedan parked beside me. Dreading having to report this mishap to Pat Brenchley, I flirted with the notion of slowly reversing, inventing an illness if I was stopped and insisting on going to the doctor's rooms (where I actually worked at the time) where I would no doubt insist on a sedative to calm my nerves. However, little Jodie and Dale were fully aware of the goings on. Looking into their big brown eyes I decided to 'do the right thing'.

Ten minutes later, Mali Govender arrived with a trolley-load of groceries. She, in fact, did not even notice the ding in her car. I got out of the Venture, approached her to introduce myself, apologise (profusely) and of course, offer to pay for the damages. It so happened that she worked for Calvin Dunn's Eshowe Motor Restorers in the industrial area so I got off with a substantial discount. At home Pat Brenchley responded by merely turning his hand in the air with his usual 'I give up on you' flourish.

Mali and I have since been friends for over 20 years. There was a time, after my divorce from Pat, when Mali and I walked together in the early mornings and drank together in the early evenings, always seeing the merit in having another glass of wine when toasts were made not only to friendships, but to panel-beaters and bottle stores and every other worthy facet of life we could think of.

Then there is my friend, the much-loved Tootsie Govender, a dear woman who, for many years, has instructed yoga classes, free of charge, in the Hindu Temple and the Mpushini Park community hall. We

 actually became friends when she was working at the dentist's rooms for Dr Droes Andrews, neighbouring Pat Brenchley's 'sugar office' at the Healthmed Dental & Medical Centre in Kangela Street. Three of my own paintings hang on the walls of Tootsie Govender's quaint little home in the Mpushini Park suburb.

Today there are sisters, Michelle Winnaar and Daphne Maharaj: Daphne owns a hairdressing salon at Eshowe Hills on the golf estate, where one may undergo a total transformation beneath the delicate snipping of her scissors while she keeps conversation going, or loses herself in her craft. My ultimate treat is a full-body massage by Michelle at her beauty parlour called 'Beauty by Michelle' situated opposite the Museum Village. Michelle also does fabulous catering for events.

Then there are Preggie and Val Moonsamy who own adjacent businesses in town: 'Jus Glass and Aluminium', and 'Valz Take Aways' that Mike and I patronise for the best curry in town.

Ladies, please treat yourself to being served by the very handsome Cedric Reddy, who has been going about his business with friendly efficiency at the Mall Pharmacy for over 15 years. Alas, since 2000 he is spoken for by Veni Reddy (née Chetty). In the photo above, they are accompanied by their two children: Vayna, and Chad who was awarded Dux in Grade 7 at the Convent. Two of my three daughters, Lara and Jodie worked at the Mall Pharmacy during their high school holidays, for owners, Aunty Shilla and Uncle Devon Palaver. One day a customer returned to Lara after buying a bottle of Enos salts, and asked for some effervescence: 'This label says I must drink this after effervescence and I don't have any effervescence.'

Another member of our professional Indian community is soft-spoken gentleman, Dr Krish Murugan, who arrived in Eshowe in 1988, to take over rental of consultation rooms, situated at the bus rank, that were previously occupied by lady doctor, Winkie Humphries. From there, Dr Murugan relocated to Sugar House which is the building at the southern end of Osborn Road adjacent to the railway bridge where Main Street begins. Those rooms were previously occupied by Drs Hilton Horsley and Don Hogan who had taken over from Dr Tom McHugh in 1978.

In 1992 Dr Murugan purchased property across the road that his practice occupies to this day. This is where he came to own the very first X-ray machine belonging to a private practice, and the very first ultra sound machine in town on which the first images of my own grandchildren appeared.

And then there's the well-known Indian carpenter, renowned for the quality of his workmanship, who awaits release from prison for the crime of passion committed when he entered ZT Stationers in town and shot his romantic interest, who later died in hospital. In recent years we have had an influx of Muslim trading businesses spring up in town. Each day for the past few years we, in Eshowe, hear the Muslim's creating a lovely exotic effect when their call to prayer is broadcast from a most powerful microphone in the Old Mutual building downtown.

Chapter 12

Hugh Lee's grandfather, Albert William Lee was bishop of the Anglican Diocese of Zululand and Swaziland from 1935 until his retirement in 1946. Albert was the second son of church warden Henry Lee, a man of humble means living in Nottingham, England, close to the Iron Mission Church of St Catherine's where young Albert, an alter server and choir boy, was confirmed. Albert later trained at the missionary college, Burgh, in Lincolnshire, England. There he met a Zulu man, Philip Mkhize, who had been sent to the college by a former missionary priest from Zululand.

Albert wrote of Philip: *'His description of life in Zululand, rough, adventurous and varied together with his own attractiveness, led me to finally make up my mind that Zululand and the Zulu people were definitely my choice.'*

Allow me to quote here, French Naturalist Delegorgue's description of the amaZulu: *'I say the Zulu are civilised because they live together in societies governed by laws, which, even if they are not written down, are at least known to all. I say they are civilised because these laws constrain them to respect each other, even when their customs already teach them to help each other, for hospitality is one of their virtues'.*

Once Albert Lee had completed his two-year course, in 1901, he was ordained deacon at St Paul's Cathedral. Thereafter he completed the Livingstone Medical Course in Stratford while working at the Eton Mission in London. This limited medical and dental course stood him in good stead when he later worked in remote rural mission stations in Zululand. Albert sold his sole possession, a bicycle, to buy his fiancée's engagement ring. In 1903 he finally set sail to South Africa, leaving his fiancée behind in Nottingham. She was to join him later.

Albert was instructed to report to archdeacon Charles Johnson at St Augustine's, a huge cathedral-like church that the archdeacon had been building for some five years. It is situated in the Nqutu district some 160 kilometres from Eshowe.

Reverend Albert Lee's first assignment was to take charge of the Isandlwana Mission in St Vincent's and four sub-districts. Because he had studied isiZulu grammar at college, he soon became sufficiently fluent to enable services preached in isiZulu.

Reverend Albert Lee moved from Isandlwana to Hlazakazi where the bishop soon thereafter approved his plan to build himself a small house.

Albert married Edyth Ann Oscroft from Nottingham on 5th November 1903. Edyth was of a practical nature and, together with Reverend Albert, she settled down to the rural life with only horses to ride from place to place, including the fetching of supplies from the nearest store ten kilometres away. With the help of local Zulu women, she dug the little spring on which they all depended for their water.

A daughter, Mary Edyth was born in 1905 followed by a son, Hugh Oscroft Lee (also known as 'Bill') in 1906. When six months pregnant with Bill, Edyth visited friends in England. In Zululand, at the time, there was a frightening civil upheaval. Zulu men prepared to join the Bambatha Rebellion against the imposition of the new poll tax and the demarcation of certain areas for farming by Europeans in Zululand. Edyth returned to South Africa, in July of 1906, after British colonial troops put down the insurrection in the Nkandla forest.

Despite threats to his life during those frightening weeks, Reverend Albert Lee continued to minister to the community. After five years at Hlazakazi, he was transferred to minister to a divided community of isiZulu and Sesotho-speaking people. It was during that year of 1908 that their third child was born, a second daughter named Catherine. Each of these children were given Zulu names by the Zulu congregants. Mary became known as 'Babazile', Bill as 'Umlindwa' and Catherine as 'Thokozile' (The Placid One, The Awaited For and The Cheerful One).

After only one year at Telezini, Reverend Albert Lee was invited to take charge of the teacher's training college at Isandlwana which is 150 kilometres from Eshowe. His own thoughts, which he only wrote of many years later in his autobiography under the title of 'Once Dark Country', were as follows: *'The offer was not attractive to me or very welcome. Its acceptance meant giving up free, open air life we had hitherto lived, with its constant riding and wide touch with humanity, and settling down to a more or less sedentary life of teaching. But the Episcopal invitation is to all right-minded priests the equivalent of an order, and my wife and I, though with somewhat heavy hearts, felt that we must do what we were told.'*

It was during the years of Isandlwana, from 1909 to 1913, that the three children grew up with Zulu children, learning to speak isiZulu fluently. Their mother, however, insisted that they speak English in the home.

Bill recalled how he loved to join his Zulu friends out in the veld herding their father's cattle (the mission also had their own cows to milk and oxen to plough). His first schooling was with those same boys where they used simple slates on which to learn to write.

Many years later, Hugh Lee accompanied his father, Bill, aged 75 then, to Isandlwana where he actually met up with one of his friends from those earlier years. They were two boys recalling the fun they had experienced together as children. They were later taken to see Bill's nursemaid at the Ngobese Kraal. She was in her 90s and completely blind. She ran her hands over him calling him by his Zulu name and saying in isiZulu, 'Oh my child you have grown now to be such a big boy' – an emotional moment never to be forgotten.

Stories which Bill shared with Hugh have been recorded in a book called 'Rivers of Life' that follows the Lee family for three generations. It is a record of their origins and the adventures they experienced in Zululand, since 1903. This includes holidays into wild and wonderful places like camping trips in Lesotho, Namibia and Botswana. There was the enormous elephant, at Savuti, eating off their camping table as they scuttled back into the truck; the lion keeping them holed up in their tents, and the long-drop toilet which had a window to look through for lions that would seek out the cool cement floor when temperatures reached 45 degrees.

After four years spent at Isandlwana, Reverend Albert Lee transferred to KwaMagwaza outside Melmoth, which is 50 kilometres from Eshowe, where he took charge of the mission, the newly-built school, the farming operations, and the Good Shepherd Church.

Bill recalled the wonderful holidays the Lees and Oscrofts spent together at the beach. Each year they travelled by ox-wagon from KwaMagwaza to Gingindlovu. From there they would catch the train to Umhlali where they camped for the two weeks that were the annual holiday taken by all missionaries after Christmas services. The wagon journey from KwaMagwaza to Gingindlovu took three days. During this time, they would spend two nights in the wagon together with their supplies which included live hens for eggs and several roosters and a sheep for meat. It was Bill's duty to look after those animals.

In 1914 Reverend Albert Lee began building St Mary's Hospital at KwaMagwaza with money he managed to obtain from England which, at the time, was engaged in the 1st World War. During this time a second son, Phillip, and a third son, Michael were born.

After four years at KwaMagwaza, Reverend Albert Lee transferred, as archdeacon of Eastern Zululand and rector of Eshowe, to St Michaels Church. The railway line had finally reached Eshowe, enabling children to attend formal church schools in Natal. They would return home for the July and Christmas holidays only. Reverend Albert Lee served as parish priest in Eshowe for ten years. He also continued to serve the outlying mission churches, travelling on horseback, or even on foot. It was during his time in Eshowe that Reverend Albert Lee accompanied the bishop on horseback on their annual tour of the diocese during the July winter months. Bill, still a school boy, accompanied them during the holidays. He recalled the trip from Eshowe up to KwaMagwaza via 'Bull Run' farm and store, and then later on to Mahlabathini, Nongoma and Mkuze. From there it was onward to Ngwavuma up on the Lebombo Mountains before descending down to Swaziland, Piet Retief and back via Vryheid, Nkandla and finally back to Eshowe. It took many days of riding because the bishop would spend time addressing the pastoral needs of the clergy as well as receiving reports from each parish. He also conducted evening services. Between overnighting at such parish stops they dropped in at local stores where they were kindly received.

Some years later the bishop obtained an open model T-Ford which replaced the horses on his tours of the diocese. On one occasion, the bishop and Reverend Lee were crossing the stone drift at the Mkuze River when the bishop unfortunately missed the edge, capsising the car into the river together with all their vestments.

The congregation became worried when the bishop was well overdue, so they dispatched a group who found him, and Reverend Albert Lee, sunning themselves with all their clothes and vestments festooned on bushes.

In 1927 archdeacon Charles Johnson retired. Since 1880 he had established over 30 missions. He had also built many beautiful stone churches in addition to the magnificent church at St Augustine's.

He had requested from the bishop that Reverend Albert Lee should be sent to carry on the work that he had built up over that time. And so it was that Albert Lee returned to the place where he had begun 24 years previously. Realising that the medical needs of the large area could not be adequately met, he applied for, and received funding from England to build a suitable hospital in the centrally situated town of Nqutu. The Charles Johnson Memorial Hospital (also known as the 'Charlie J') was a fitting tribute to such a wonderful man. In the year 1935, Bishop Aylen, who had taken over the diocese, elected Albert Lee as the sixth bishop of Zululand. Bishop Albert Lee was the first isiZulu-speaking bishop to be consecrated in the diocese and done so at his beloved St Augustine's by the archbishop of Cape Town. Clergy and some two thousand laity spilled out from the packed church.

As bishop of Zululand and Swaziland, Bishop Albert Lee moved into the bishop's house in Vryheid with St Peter's as his cathedral.

In his retirement in 1946, Bishop Albert Lee came to finally settle at 'Cascades' on Brocklee farm, Eshowe.

Hugh was eight-years-old when Bishop Albert Lee died of cancer at the age of 73 in 1951.

Bishop Albert and Edyth's daughter, Mary married Aubrey Wynne and had two children (one of whom was attorney, Brian Wynne, married to Jan).

Bill married Hugh's mother, Doris Brockwell and had four children. One of whom is our farmer Hugh Lee.

Albert Lee's novel 'Zulu Knight' was published thanks to the generosity of David Durham who is the son of his eldest granddaughter, Yvonne Durham (née Wynne). His wife was an Oscroft so he is related to Hugh Lee on both sides of his family. David also reprinted Albert Lee's previous two books 'Once Dark Country' and 'Charles Johnson of Zululand'. Both books give the reader a delightful and informative insight into the exemplary work of the missionaries and teachers who came to Zululand. David Durham, a renowned entrepreneur and owner of Orange Grove Dairy, was chosen by South Africa's first premier of KwaZulu-Natal, Dr Frank Mdlalose, to chair the premier's portfolio in our provincial parliament.

To recap: Hugh Lee's father, Bill was born just after the Bambatha Rebellion. His family moved to KwaMagwaza in 1913. In 1917 Bill's father, Bishop Albert Lee moved his family to Eshowe.

The railway line extended to Eshowe in 1917, so Bill was able to go to boarding school at Cordwalles in Pietermaritzburg followed by Michaelhouse*, the famous church school in the Natal Midlands. Priests' children attended church schools at greatly reduced fees.

In 1923, at the age of 18, Bill came home to Eshowe and worked for the newly formed Nkwaleni Valley Cotton Company.

Large tracts of land were cleared for the planting of cotton. Their first cotton crop was ready to be picked in

*During recent years, head boys of Michaelhouse included Anton and Belinda Lees' son, Robert, and Christopher Brits (Dr Eric and Liesel Brits' son). Michaelhouse is a private boy's high school in the Natal Midlands previously attended by authors Wilbur Smith and John van de Ruit. John's book *Spud*, which was also adapted to the screen, recounts his experiences there.

March 1925. It rained solidly for two weeks and all the burst cotton bulbs were washed out. Other buds rotted off. Rainfall recorded was the highest rainfall in South Africa at 600 millimetres within 24 hours. Of course the cotton company went broke, and all staff ended up unemployed.

At the end of 1896, Frank Chennells employed Bill to establish sugar cane fields on his farm, The Chase. It was a time of severe drought and cattle died of rinderpest. To assist hungry Zulus, they delivered maize from America on a steam ship called 'Gertie'.

Bill Lee was a keen tennis, rugby and cricket player, and loved dancing on Saturday nights at the Royal Hotel. There he met, and finally became engaged to the youngest daughter of the Brockwell family, who had come to Eshowe in 1893 to work in Earnest Brunner's store.

In 1906 the family acquired the farm, Croisdale where Doris was born at 5 am on 5th December 1911. She was home-schooled during and after the 1st World War by her elder sister, Sybil and her mother. Her schooling was followed for a few years at St Mary's in Kloof, but she had to come home to the farm due to financial hardship when their dairy cows died of East Coast fever (tick fever). And the price of wattle dropped dramatically.

Doris was a fine tennis player who played for Zululand. But, in 1953, at the age of 42, she had a stroke on the tennis court that left her somewhat handicapped. Bill and Doris were married two decades prior to this incident by Bill's father, Bishop Albert Lee, in 1934, at St Michael's Cathedral.

Bill started out on a new job as manager of Uphulu Properties in Empangeni. In 1937 the farm adjacent to 'Croisdale' (the Brockwell's farm) was bought by Doris Lee (née Brockwell), using her portion of her inheritance from her father who died in 1933. On her behalf, her brother, Harley Brockwell planted the farm up to sugar cane. As avid conservationists, the Lees, to this day, retain a third of the farms' land as indigenous forest.

During those early days' cane wasn't cut until it was two-years-old. Bill cut 50 acres' worth when he and Doris moved to the farm they called 'Brocklee', in 1939. The South African Sugar Association had made a rule that the farm had to produce 3.5 thousand tons of cane per year. Brocklee had that by 1940, after which Bill went to Ladysmith Natal to join the Mounted Regiments. General Smuts, at the time deployed men of 50-years-old and upwards to guard road and rail bridges throughout Africa because the Ossewabrandwag* (The Afrikaner nationalist organisation with ties to national socialism that was formed in 1939), were blowing them up.

Bill Lee was promoted to sergeant and, because he could speak isiZulu well, was sent off to Sonderwater, north-east of Pretoria, to guard Italian prisoners. His isiZulu speaking group were then sent to Eshowe to train the African artillery. During this time Doris had to drive the cane trucks to keep the farm going. This is when Ralph and Neels Nielson sold the neighbouring farms, 'Cascades' and 'Neswick', to Bill Lee and his relation, Aubrey Wynne. Both farms, now called 'Lee & Son Farming' were also planted up to cane. They would plough and plant new steep lands with the help of two spans of oxen and a hand-held ox- plough. On that land the Nielsons also had a stone crushing plant and a brick yard. Kilns were fired with wattle wood and the bricks were sold for the building of houses in Eshowe.

When Albert Lee retired from being bishop of

---

*The Ossewabrandwag included 350 thousand members lead by Johannes van Rensburganer who, during the 2nd World War, opposed South African participation in the war.

Zululand and Swaziland he and Edyth lived at Cascades' for five years. Then he died of cancer in 1951. His son, Bill Lee died in 1989 at the age of 83. Having been very involved with St Michaels as church warden, lay minister and chaplain to prisoners in Eshowe's gaol, Bill received the 'Award of Simon of Cyrene' by archbishop Desmond Tutu in recognition of his service. This is the highest award that the Anglican Church can bestow on a lay-person.

He served the Zululand Agricultural and Industrial Show Society from 1923 to 1989, becoming president. He was a member of the Eshowe Farmers Association from 1937 to 1989, becoming an honourary life member. He was awarded the 'Rotary Chairman's Award for Outstanding Service to the Community'. He was also president of Eshowe Tennis, Rugby and Cricket Clubs, and chairman of the Zululand Home for the Aged. For many years he was groundsman for the Cricket Oval* which was built by British soldiers in 1895.

Doris Lee, known for her lovely smile and laughter, died on 5th December 2002 at the age of 91. Her daughter, Diana gave up six years of her own life to care for her mother with tremendous love and diligence.

---

*During the first decade of the 20th century, one sugar cane farmer, Harry Addison, son of Captain Addison, found the George V cricket field (also known as the 'Oval') too small for his best strokes. Using his own labour, equipment and wagon he arrived from his farm at Amatikulu and enlarged the grounds by cutting into Dlinza forest and levelling it. Unfortunately, he relocated to East Africa – a huge loss to the cricket community of Zululand.

I

On Hugh and Renée Lee's 55th wedding anniversary in 2022, Hugh paid tribute to Renée and their children.

Renée's ancestors on both her parents' sides came from Prussia, now modern Germany/Poland. They sailed for South Africa in 1858, on the ship 'La Rochelle', which took 87 days to finally reach East London. There they were settled on small farms around King Williams Town.

Renée qualified as a nursing sister from Grey's Hospital in Pietermaritzburg and obtained a post in Eshowe.

Hugh first met Renée at the Anglican Cathedral in Eshowe, then again, after a hockey game held at 'Cascades', his then bachelor unfurnished home on his farm, 'Brocklee'. 'Brocklee' is situated within a delightful forested rural area just outside Eshowe.

The morning after the hockey game's after-party, Hugh discovered a pair of dainty sandals that someone had left behind. Hugh checked out the young teacher's quarters and then the nurse's home where, Bingo! he found Renée.

Today, we tease Renée, speculating as to whether or not the sandals had strategically been left behind. (Or perhaps Hugh had purposely hidden them to give him an excuse to look her up afterwards.)

Hugh was shattered when Renée was given a post as a nursing sister at the frontier hospital in Queenstown. It was hard going until he received an invitation from her to attend her elder brother's wedding in Komga. Passing through Durban, en route to the wedding, Hugh popped in at a jewellery store and bought an engagement ring.

Immediately after the wedding, the ring was placed on Cinderella Renée's finger. Like the sandals, it fitted perfectly, and they were married three months later.

II

Hugh and Renée's eldest son: Ryder, after becoming a white badge prefect at Michaelhouse, studied business management at Durban Tech. He was called up to the army where, after training, he was sent to Intelligence in Uppington where he became fluent in Afrikaans. He came home to farm not only at 'Brocklee', but also to run neighouring sugar estates establishing new cane areas for Tongaat-Hulett Sugar, in an effort to save the mill. He became fluent in isiZulu and befriended many. He was then offered a management position in Kenya to run a huge sugar estate just next to the Masai Mara, close to Lake Victoria. There he developed sugar cane lands, roads and zones for a Mauritian-owned mill. He learnt Swahili and spoke it well. In fact, he became so popular that the people wanted him to represent them in local government. Hugh and Renée visited Ryder in Uganda, at Jinja on Lake Victoria, where the Nile River begins. Ryder rode the rapids down the Nile – a hair-raising experience. It was far away from home and family which he missed. Thankfully, he was offered a position

Hugh and Renée Lee in 1967

by his cousin, David Durham to join his brother, Anton Lee, at Orange Grove in Dundee, KwaZulu-Natal.

Major Ryder Lee continues to serve with the Umvoti Mounted Rifles and has completed the tough course and exams to become a colonel. Studying for an MBA, he continues to deal with HR at Orange Grove, including the defusing of union strikes and threats.

III

Anton Lee, after Clifton and Michaelhouse, studied mechanical engineering at Durban Tech. In the army he was placed in the Tiffy section dealing with the repairs and maintenance of army vehicles. Anton spent time in America with his good friend, Peter Morfopolus, working, and touring in an old Kombi. They also visited Europe before Anton came home to run the dairy. Anton's first love was always animal husbandry. He turned the dairy into an excellent business supplying Amasi of the very highest quality. However, although the dairy turned over good revenue, due to the ever increasing animal feed costs, profits were slim. Cousin David Durham invited Anton to run the Empangeni depot for the Orange Grove Dairy. Anton did so well that he was invited to take over the Orange Grove factory in Dundee. His duties include artificial insemination, calving and all hands-on husbandry required for those beautiful Jersey cows. He has also built up a fine processing factory and a covered feeding shed for two hundred cows. Presently, the dairy has 30 huge refrigerated trucks that deliver countrywide.

Many Eshowe-ites have heard the story of Anton delivering his and Belinda's youngest child on the road when they were on their way to hospital. Anton took the delivery in his stride and drove on to hospital with mother and newborn baby.

My own cousin, on his farm outside Bulawayo, delivered his youngest daughter on the side of the road en route to the hospital. They aptly named her 'Savannah'.

Hugh and Renée's saddest time was when they had to sell off their own herd and close the dairy. It was heartbreaking for Anton and Belinda who had to leave their lovely home and garden at 'Croisdale' which is the oldest farmhouse in the district, built by Hugh's grandfather, Thomas William Brockwell, in 1910, just after the Eshowe/Entumeni farms were settled. In 1972 that farm was awarded the Ian Sclater Trophy for soil and water conservation and land utilization – the best conserved farm in the whole of KwaZulu-Natal.

IV

Hugh and Renée's daughters, Cara and Nicci are identical twins. One is outrageously outgoing and the other not so much. Each other's mirror image, one is right-handed and the other left-handed.

Cara and Nicci schooled at 'St Annes' in Hilton. Those six years combined with Ryder and Anton's schooling at Michaelhouse, ran up huge expenses. There were also the demands of eight special events to attend each year. Thereafter, thankfully the twins joined the boys at the Tech where Cara studied food and service management and Nicci studied fine art.

Once graduated, Cara excelled in running the George Hotel. She next worked in Durban, and finally at the waterfront in Cape Town. Cara's true loves, however, were always the great outdoors; running, cycling, swimming and gyming – so much so that she ended up representing South Africa in the triatholons in New Zealand and Madeira. She also joined the Wild Adventure racing group which took her through treacherous areas and over remote mountains covered in snow. On that occasion she slept snuggled between two team mates to avoid hypothermia, which may have proved fatal.

Afterwards she was given the responsibility of organising adventure racing trails around South Africa. A notable one was home-based and started at the dam on 'Brocklee Farm'. It required running overland to the Umhlatuze River, then up to Khomo mountain from where they had to abseil with their bikes strapped to their backs over a precipitous kranz before riding their bikes to the Thukela where they then canoed down the river to the next stop below Mbongolwane. Then they had to run back to the starting point at the dam. It took the front team all day while other teams struggled through the night – arriving at all hours.

The next challenge for Cara to conquer was the International Ironman in Hawaii. Nicci accompanied Cara to this huge challenge: swimming 3.8 kilometres in the sea, cycling 180 kilometres, and running a 42 kilometre marathon. After 13 hours of toil in the Hawaiian heat of over 40 degrees Cara succeeded despite a broken toe. Cara also opened a swimming coaching business in Hout Bay and then took up, of all things, boxing. She had nine fights with nine wins, becoming Cape Town's champion. Cara is married to Taryn who has a son, Mathew. Together, they adopted a three-month-old Xhoza girl, Maddison.

V

Nicci Lee tore a muscle off her hip which was a serious setback to sporting achievements. She was appointed a prefect at St Annes after which she studied fine arts. After Tech, Nicci set out with a friend to work at a kibbutz in Israel, where she soon showed her farming background by being promoted to tractor driver (rather than work as a labourer shovelling manure). After this experience they set off to visit Europe, but their travels were interrupted with the news of Ryder's upcoming marriage to Carmella, and Anton's engagement to Nicci's ex-flatmate, Belinda van Tooren (daughter of Colin and Mary van Tooren).

Nicci returned from her travels to Greece, Switzerland and England and went on a game-ranging course at Hoedspruit. Soon after, she met Jackie. Together they took over Windy Ridge timber farm, converting it, with Ryder's help, to a sugar cane farm.

During their time at 'Windy Ridge', Nicci and Jackie's love for animals manifested, resulting in the fantastic care of many wild animals – birds, including hammerkop and spotted eagle owl, donkey, wild pig, zebra, caracal, genet, jackal, duiker, bushbuck and banded mongoose. They cared for over two hundred animals, most of which were released back into the wild.

Nicci took over more responsibility on the farm, handling management of labour such as weeding gangs, supervising the application of chemicals and fertiliser, overseeing the cutting and loading of cane. She manages the burning of cane, making ready for the cutters, and for the important allocation of cane to be transported by truck to the mill. She is up at 4 am each day transporting labour to their posts.

Nicci's wife, Jackie manages all finances, labour payouts, SARS and everything else requiring her computer skills.

The Lee family enjoy memories of riding on horseback from Eshowe to Hilton, night walks in the forest, holidays in Botswana, hikes in the Berg, camping by the river or on the beach.

My compilation of a scrapbook to mark Hugh's 80th birthday is what sparked my interest in writing this very book.

Chapter 13

Lara and Keri's keen competitive natures threw them into playing too much sport at the expense of their academic progress. So I transferred them to Eshowe High School where the traditional South African academic curriculum had been forcing children to keep up with their other interests for over a hundred years. In addition to the usual curriculum, photography, chess and an Achievers Club were on offer. The school has sporting grounds and facilities worthy of international 1st world standards including large sports fields, squash courts, tennis/basketball courts and a swimming pool. Other than the usual sporting activities the high school has had rock-climbing and even sword-fencing. At Eshowe High School, Lara van Schalkwyk became captain for the hockey and swimming teams. And house captain to boot.

As if there wasn't enough to do in Eshowe*, blow me down if there wasn't an internationally recognised school of drama practicing in the high school's hall.

Keri thought it would be fun to join Ida Gartrell's drama studio. During a dress rehearsal I watched my tall daughter, Keri with her long silky black hair, gracefully cross the stage. Pausing still, finger in the sir, she said dramatically, 'I've forgotten my lines!' She and I traded anxious looks, for just a moment, before Ida broke out with laughter and thunderous applause. But a career on the stage was not to be when it turned out that

*Yoga lessons, dance classes, garden, bird, rambling, art, book, bridge, chess, music, history and various sports' clubs, as well as MOTHs, Free Masons, Round Table, Rotary, Lions and Women's Institute.

Eshowe High School before extensions

The Eshowe High School Cadet Band marching through the centre of Eshowe in 1954. Those trees and palms eventually made way for the Eshowe Centre. Picture curtesy of Diana Hale whose husband, Matt Hale was the Drum Major

what Keri thought would be 'good fun' was also 'jolly hard work'. And that was the end of that.

To date, for four decades, Ida Gartrell (née van Schalkwyk), has taught speech and drama at various schools* where she also designed and facilitated a child abuse prevention programme.

Years ago, Ida was project manager of the 'Prince

*Eshowe High School, the Holy Childhood Convent, St Catherine's School, John Ross College, Sagewood Preparatory School, Gingindlovu Primary School, Gratton College, Little Flower and Mtunzini Primary School.

Dabulamanzi Trail School Birding Project' that involved eight schools, and thus began our friendship.

I also met Ida's good friend, Patti Joshua, whose children, Adelaide, Brett, Arthur and Karl were all active members of Ida's drama studio. Ida became very involved in creative development training for adults at Patti's NGO Senzokuhle CBO Network, a community upliftment organisation located in Henry and Val Truter's old house in Brockwell Street. Using creative techniques to facilitate development, this 'Community development through Drama' migrated to the King Dinuzulu Township and surrounding Eshowe areas.

The Joshua family were indeed one of the many noted families living in Sunnydale, Eshowe. Patti started out as a hair-dresser, and married Trevor Joshua, which is when Ida first befriended her. But Patti's good-natured humanitarian attributes were to send her off in a completely different direction, culminating in her bringing Buddhism to Eshowe.

Sadly, Patti was fatally knocked over by a passing vehicle in 2016. She leaves a big gap in meeting the charitable needs of Eshowe's less fortunate communities. Ida Gartrell (pictured above) was one of our daughters born, in Eshowe, to Elvira Maria van Schalkwyk (née Baasch) and Daniel Hartman van Schalkwyk. Daniel was a policeman transferred from

Mbazwana.

Due to a genetic heart condition only Ida and one of her sisters, Elda, survived childhood.

Those days Azalea bushes lined the road from beyond Tally's Corner all the way to the end of Main Street. Some have survived more than a century, flowering clusters of white or magenta flowers in late spring.

Ida's mother wanted to live in that beautiful setting, so they bought the house that Ida still lives in today. The garden is shaded by flat-crowned albizias that Ida's son, Geordie planted as a 16-year-old in 1990.

Ida's house, built by Mr Ashby Snr in 1889, belonged to Dr Balfe, the very first civilian doctor to have arrived in Eshowe to service British troops, in 1887, after the defeat of King Cethswayo. The name and date of the house is written on a beam under the floor and inside the roof. Ida continues to discover old medicine bottles on the property. These she adds to the extensive collection lining the window sills in that charming old house.

Ida's family spoke German and Afrikaans at home and English at school. I include two excerpts from Ida's diaries: *May 1956 (Standard 4) This afternoon when I came home from school I did my homework, then my Problem corrections. 'I listened to all the programs on the wireless too. After supper Elda, my father and I sang a lot of songs and then we went to bed.'*
'October 1960 (Standard 8) Elaine and I were late for school today. At last the girls and boys are allowed to mix at little break. They have lifted the apartheid rule. I am now going to take dancing lessons on Fridays. I don't have to go to music anymore but I have to go to German once a week. Rene did not have her shorts at school so she had to do PT in her pants and bra, and so did a few other kids. School was so boring today. I was yawning all the time.'

The wood-and-iron house that Ida still lives in today

Today, one finds it difficult to believe that Ida was an extremely shy child. When called upon to play the piano for visitors she would hide away in her bedroom. She did, however, obtain a certificate from the Trinity College of Music (1953-1959).

After matriculating from Eshowe High School, Ida obtained certificates from the South African Academy of Modelling and Deportment (1965), the Paris Model School (1965) and in Speedwriting American Shorthand (1967). She worked at various occupations including newspaper reporter, librarian, town councillor and secretary, during which time she joined the Eshowe Dramatic Society.

The Eshowe Dramatic Society group included Vivienne and George Garside, Jean White and her brother-in-law, Don White, the Carnegie family galore (Carnegies coming out of their ears), Glen Stevens and Lionel Murcott.

Pouring themselves into their performances, they practiced wholeheartedly in a prefab building on the property of the old nurses' hostel in Mansell Terrace,

The Old Queen Victoria Hospital became the Nurses Hostel (Home)

previously the Queen Victoria Hospital. This was prior to migrating to Eshowe High School's hall.

Ida became good friends with director, George Garside (town clerk of Eshowe at the time), and his wife, Vivienne Garside who encouraged Ida to study drama for a professional certificate.

And so Ida found her calling that remains her passion to this day.

In 1983, while working as town librarian, Ida started up her own private drama studio called 'Ida Gartrell Studio of Speech and Drama'. At one point she taught Afrikaans and Drama at Eshowe High School. However, certain parents did not approve of her liberal free-spirited principles, so she left in order to maintain her independence.

Ida continues to travel extensively and has had more than one car accident on the way. The first required the center of her face to be sewn back in place. Fortunately, she does not scar.

Youthful, agile and petite, Ida practices dancing every day (as do I) in an effort to stay fit. She readily passes for one years younger than her age.

Ida has worked extensively in a partnership with psychologist, Alison Sampson in treatment programs for adult sufferers of trauma and abuse, called 'The Confidence Clinic'.

During 1997, she trained and practiced 'Theatre of the Oppressed', a means of drama that tackles social problems. This included the participation of audience members who would shout 'Freeze!' and step onto the stage to contribute their idea of a solution to the theme problem being addressed that particular day. The play would then, of course, take off in unexpected directions that resulted in raising many controversial concepts.

This and other seemingly liberal theatre work reached a point where, in 1993, Ida's name appeared on a political hit-list. Fellow townsfolk were terrified by association and some would turn around when coming across Ida, and quickly head off in the opposite direction. Prior to that disturbing incident Ida had in fact served as a town councillor for eight years, during the 1980s and 90s.

Ida took over the costumes department of the drama society and continues to hire out outfits, too varied in styles to mention. She caters to film companies, theatre productions and private functions. This service has added much fun to local 'themed' party fundraisers.

Ida, Adelaide Joshua and Pierre Rossouw created a cast to be known as 'The Absolutely Fabulous Artistes'. All three performers workshopped the performances. I attended more than a few of their plays that were carried out mostly on the Eshowe High School's stage and at the George Hotel.

Ida also does practical stargazing for children, and has written television scripts for children's educational programmes on YOTV (Urban Brew) 'Zenzele', 'Team Green', 'A.C.T. 1' and 'Mvubuand Friends'. She has been interviewed on radio and appeared on more than one television programme including 'Forever Young', in 2021. She and an ex-prisoner, musician Bongani Sithole, performed in a play called 'Rattling the Cage' at the Grahamstown Festival in 2011. Ida met Bongani when she worked as senior facilitator and project co-ordinator of Phoenix Zululand, a restorative justice programme in prisons. There she directed the 'Voices beyond the Walls' programme, creating and recording plays workshopped from the prisoners' own life experiences, for broadcasting on community radio.

Ida locumed for the Speech & Drama department at the University of Zululand, in Ongoye, where she served as examiner for third year drama students.

Apart from her involvement in acting, directing and scriptwriting, Ida is in the process of writing a book called 'Stories Have Feet' about the fascinating creatures from Zulu mythology.

Together with the Vukani Museum and wireworker Dumisani Mthethwa (who also painted the colourful drums on the sidewalks outside the 'Atrium' and 'Super Spar') she has had stories published in 'Lighten Up' and 'Le Petit Dejeuner 3'.

Ida loves history, art and beadwork as much as she does acting, music and dance. She was the chairperson on the board of the Vukani Museum of Zulu artefacts and, since Vukani's amalgamation with the Zululand Historical Museum, she is deputy chairperson of the newly declared Fort Nongqayi Museum Village. She was vice chairperson of the annual Eshowe Heritage Festival and a board member of the Eshowe Environmental Education Centre. A mover and shaker of note, she is also on the board of the Dlinza Forest Aerial Boardwalk.

I

When requiring the services of an attorney to handle

my divorce in 2002, I found my way to Dave Gardner's office at Wynne & Wynne. This traditional house of law was founded by Walter Vanderplank in the 1940s. Back then it was housed in what is now the Anglican diosesan offices. Presently it is situated in a stylish old house, in Osborn Road, belonging to attorney Johan Goosen, a partner in the firm.

My divorce took so long that Dave (a fellow Anglican) and I became friends in the interim. A man of integrity, he was a trusted confidante relied upon to give the very soundest of legal (and fatherly) advice. I was also the recipient of his stern 'lawyers voice' on one or two occasions – matched only by Mike Nixon's 'headmaster's voice' when he reprimanded our children. Of course our grandchildren get away with murder.

Dave Gardner grew up on a farm in the Natal Midlands. After graduating at the University of Natal (Pietermaritzburg) he heard from his uncle, who was a friend of Brian Wynne's, that Brian was looking for an attorney to join his firm, Wynne & Wynne, in Eshowe.

Not long after his arrival in Eshowe, Dave heard that there was a beautiful blonde radiographer, Anita Geyser who had just started working at Eshowe Provincial Hospital. Anita had come from Harrismith where her father managed Old Mutual and her mother gave violin lessons. Both were avid art-lovers who took Anita and her sisters along to many viewings of exhibitions.

As well as a library of books about various artists, Anita, an avid music-lover, houses a fine selection of opera and jazz performances.

The Gardner home is a museum of beautiful furnishings, many previously collected by Anita's father, who, when offered the choice between a fishing boat and a magnificently carved cabinet, chose the latter. It now graces the Gardners' living room as do various other

Anita and Dave Gardner

collectables from those elaborate eras gone by. Dave told me that because he loved to attend the 'big' rugby games, he happily indulged Anita's love for the ballet. After they married in 1970, he took her to see 'Swan Lake' in London. Anita told me that afterwards he commented that never before had he noticed the muscularity of the male species' buttocks. This was overheard by other patrons who fell about with laughter. Dave and Anita have two sons, Simon and Philip, and then a daughter, Caroline who is the same age as my daughter, Lara.

Simon was born in 1973. An excellent rugby player, he played in England and America.

Philip is a writer and filmmaker. Mike Nixon played a small role in his movie 'The Killing Floor' that was filmed in and around Eshowe during 2017. The scenery truly does our district proud. Leading roles were played by Jonathan Pienaar of 'Blood Diamond' fame and award-winning actor, Patrick Ndlovu who acted in the previously-mentioned 'Shaka Zulu' series filmed outside Eshowe.

When Dave and Anita relocated from Thornley's House in Mansell Terrace to Eshowe Hills, Anita took to feeding the birds in her magnificent indigenous garden that is marked out with pathways and large potted plants.

At 4 pm each day she throws out an assortment of chicken giblets within the distance of a mere few metres. To watch the many woolly-necked storks, hammerkops and yellow-billed kites descend is quite an experience. It's not just visually exciting, but also noisy with the thumping of huge flapping wings and amplified calls.

After Dave and Anita moved to Eshowe Hills, their eldest son, Simon took over the family's previous spacious residence called 'Thornleys', situated near the courthouse among those spacious colonial residences of old. Simon runs Thornley's as a very successful events venue hosting musicians from far and wide.

Simon's friend – she with the long red hair and ready smile, Sonja Kruse, runs the bed and breakfast aspect of the property. Sonja is the daughter of Billy and Minnie Kruse, active members of the Ramblers' (nature lovers') Club. Also, Billy has been Club Singles Champion at Eshowe's Bowling Club for a few years in a row. He and his lovely wife, Minnie arrived in Eshowe, in 1991, when Billy was promoted to operations manager by Telkom. In his retirement he oversees the caretaking of the buildings and grounds of John Wesley School and the Methodist Church from which he also runs Eshowe's soup kitchen. But back to his and Minnie's daughter, Sonja Kruse. Blessed with a fabulous sense of adventure and faith in humanity, Sonja has lived many interesting chapters starting with her (never-a-dull-moment) upbringing in Eshowe. In 2009, at the age of 33, Sonja quit her job at Rhino River Lodge in the heart of Zululand and gave her car away. Without a tent, sleeping bag or bank card she set off on a year-long country-wide journey with little more than a backpack, camera, phone and a R100 note. Off she went, with an unusually determined expression, to prove that the spirit of uBantu in South Africa is still alive. 'Ubantu' is an ancient African word meaning

'Humanity to Others' reminding us that we are who we are because of who we all are together. In keeping with this spirit, Sonja fell into the habit of presenting new hosts with a gift she had received from her previous hosts. This included, among other gifts, half a bag of onions and a bottle of homemade jam.

Sonja's resulting book, 'The uBantu Girl', is largely her final gift to those 150 families from 16 different cultures who opened their hearts and homes to her, a total stranger. Those homes included mansions in affluent suburbs as well as shacks in dusty townships. She used long-drop toilets and bidets.

In her travels she learned so much about the diverse cultures of our country, taking snapshots of the turbulent political times better than any politician. Her book includes thirteen thousand images taken with her camera. That works out to a picture per kilometre because she travelled for over thirteen thousand.

Maintaining the rules of a lady properly brought up (a refinement of manners practicing the polite terms of address, table etiquette and proper decorum), Sonya's book is a proper account of her traveling through an unplanned route of 114 towns in nine provinces of South Africa – this despite constant warnings of the country being too dangerous for a young lady to travel on her own through townships, and hitching rides from strangers.

Refusing to surrender her power to the odd rejection, or to someone else's opinion, homeless, carless and jobless, Sonja's first night was spent in a rural home.

Her very last night was spent in luxury, after meeting the only white induna who serves in the official Zulu Royal House.

She experienced the lifestyles of Christians, Muslims and Rastafarians of all races, and ranging from hunting lifestyles to vegetarian. Traditional meals ranged from spicy curries to crispy chicken feet. Experiencing the joy of them all, Sonja learned firsthand about the boundless generosity of the human spirit. She ended her experience not only physically, but psychologically and spiritually stronger.

Before deciding to return to her home town, Eshowe, Sonja spent a few years living in a caravan at Kommetjie in the Cape. During that time, she taught young children while continuing to give inspiring motivational talks, and facilitate Ubantu-themed workshops, countrywide.

Her decision to come home and settle in Eshowe was brought about by a nostalgic longing for the familiar, and a heartfelt appreciation for Eshowe's caring community.

II

Dr Donald Maxwell Clark was a Zululand veteran squash player, pilot and, for 48 years, had his own private medical practice in Eshowe, 25 years of which he was also the local medical officer of health.

In his youth, Donald was a champion middle- distance runner. In 1950 he ran the 440 yards in Springbok colours against a visiting American athletic team.

Donald's family has lived consistently in Eshowe since 1896 when his maternal great-grandfather, Colonel Thomas Maxwell arrived to join Charles Saunders as resident magistrate. Those magistrates had considerable powers in respect of the administration of justice, the collection of taxes, the registration of births and deaths, and the control of communicable diseases.

Prior to living in Eshowe, Colonel Thomas Maxwell served as King Lobengula's agent in Matabeleland (southern Zimbabwe).

In Eshowe, Colonel Thomas Maxwell brought up his family diagonally opposite the George Hotel next to

Tally's Corner. During that time, he was sent to command field forces at Melmoth. In fact, he was selected to sort out many problems, gaining the confidence and respect of a number of loyal chiefs while maintaining order in volatile districts. Historians have found his diaries at the Killie Campbell museum and various Zimbabwean museums as well as archives in Pietermaritzburg.

Colonel Thomas Maxwell's colleague in Eshowe, magistrate Sir Charles Saunders was born in 1857. He was a Zulu linguist and an authority on Zulu law and custom who, in 1876, became the administrator of native law. When Zululand was handed over to Natal in 1897, he became chief magistrate of the territory. He was knighted in 1907. The amaZulu called him 'uMashiquela' meaning 'The Autocrat'.

Colonel Thomas Maxwell's family and the Saunders family became well-acquainted with Earnest and Corrie Brunner and their home, 'Samarang'.

Earnest Brunner's parents, Reverend and Mrs Brunner were among the 80+ Hollanders to settle at New Guelderland, which is about a hundred kilometres from Pietermaritzburg. New Guelderland had been established by the Colenbrander family in 1859*.

In 1872 Earnest joined his sister, Jeanne, who had married into that Colenbrander family. He, himself, would marry Corrie who was Mr TC Colenbrander's daughter. Their family owned the first ever coach service to connect both Gingindlovu and Melmoth to Eshowe. In fact, Corrie was said to be the very first white woman to live in Eshowe. She was the sister of the handsome Johan Colenbrander (also known as the 'White Whirlwind'), who blazed his way through 'Samarang' and the pages of history, along with his adventurous wife, Mollie Mullins. Mollie was the daughter of an Irishman who settled in Zululand as a storekeeper. She was not only beautiful, but could outride and outshoot most men. She accompanied Johan everywhere including to the Matopos to a meeting with King Lobengula, the son of Mzilikazi who was King Shaka's general and the first king of Matabeleland. Johan, Mollie and Mollie's sister gained the confidence of Lobengula and accompanied Cecil John Rhodes to Matopos, to put an end to the Matabele rising that took place between 1896 and 1897.

Previously, in 1889, Johan accompanied King Lobengula's envoy and indunas (ambassadors and agents), Babayane and Mtshete, to an audience with Queen Victoria in London at Winsor Castle, with Frederick Selous after whom the infamous Selous Scouts were named. Johan's picture was in the London News.

On another occasion, Johan and Colonel Thomas Maxwell celebrated St Patrick's Day with King Lobengula. Johan explained to the king who St Patrick was, and King Lobengula thoroughly enjoyed the champagne. This account was written by John Cooper-Chadwick in his book 'Three Years with Lobengula': *'In between adventures Johan would visit his sister and brother-in-law at 'Samarang'. He, the White Whirlwind, was not only considered the most resolute frontiersman ever produced in South Africa, but also the most handsome brute by the ladies. Unfortunately, he drowned in 1918, attempting to save his leading lady whose horse*

---

* Among those parties of Hollanders were the Getkates, Vanderwagons, Wantinks and Webers, all of whom were to make their homes in Eshowe. Weber was a trader who established one of the very first stores in Main Street, between the railway bridge and the George Hotel. The house he built for himself is called 'Bishopshurst' and has, in the past, served as the official residence of the bishop of Zululand. It is now a bed and breakfast establishment.

stumbled in the strong current of a river while making a film about the Anglo-Zulu War. After the Anglo-Zulu War, during which Earnest Brunner partook in the battles fought at Nyezane and Gingindlovu, he was invited by Chief John Dunn to become his magistrate in the Eshowe area. It was during that time that Brunner's knowledge of the Zulu people flourished. His career as magistrate lasted until the arrival of resident commissioner Melmoth Osborn in 1883, who, with the support of the Nongqayi, made Brunner's position as magistrate redundant.'

III

Previously, in 1873, Brunner had established a store at Bond's Drift on the Natal side of the Thukela River, becoming butcher, baker and ferryman. Due to the inconvenience of his Zulu customers having to cross that often swollen river from the Zululand side, he sought an audience with King Cethswayo, at Ulundi, to ask permission to trade in Zululand. Incidentally, the name 'Thukela' means to 'get a fright' or to 'be startled'*. Earnest Brunner stayed with many missionaries on his journey to Ulundi: Norwegians Astrupp, Oftebro, Kyllingstadt, and Gundersen, a close friend of King Cethswayo's who accompanied Brunner to the king's kraal of over two thousand huts. Brunner also stayed with German missionaries: Frohling, Kugh, Schmidt and Brauel, and with the Anglican minister, Reverend Robinson of the very first Anglican Mission, KwaMagwaza. Reverend Robinson's wife was tragically killed when her overloaded wagon overturned just outside Eshowe, upsetting a millstone on top of her. Her grief-stricken husband, helped by Norwegian missionaries from KwaMondi nearby, constructed a

*When the amaZulu originally moved down from the north they were certainly startled by the size of that river – hence the name 'Thukela'.

coffin from timber doors he had been taking to KwaMagwaza. Mrs Robinson is buried at KwaMondi.

Brunner was delighted with Reverend Robinson's impressive library and garden, not to mention his talented Zulu organist and robed Zulu choristers who raised the rafters with their sung praises.

In 1906 Brunner left a fascinating account of the entire journey and his meeting with the dignified king, in the Lloyds of London Publication called '20th Century Impressions of Natal'. I quote: *'Following his magistracy, Earnest Brunner got permission to open a store in Eshowe. He set about building a trading business which became the largest in Zululand, covering three acres and carrying the largest stock comprising of everything to build and furnish a house, cultivate the soil, and feed the people. The business included a glass, oil and paint shop, a cabinet maker, a bakery, and fine stables to house six magnificent white horses to draw his carriage. Around 'Samarang' he cultivated five acres of oranges, lemons, pineapples and potatoes'.*

Apart from trading in his store, Brunner was the first auctioneer and valuer for the district. He was also the agent for Natal Breweries, the German East African Line of Steamers and the Alliance Fire Insurance Co.

Mr WT Brockwell (Hugh Lee's maternal grandfather) was the sole and very able manager of Brunner's concern, while Mr LP Johnson was the first baker who kindly gave Patricia Clark his bread recipe.

With his stores in able hands, in 1898, Brunner was willing to be elected the first member of parliament in Zululand, to serve on the Legislative Assembly for Eshowe, until the Active Union, in 1910, during which East Coast Fever ravaged oxen in the local district. Donkeys and mules were used as substitutes because Nagana (the disease carried from animal to animal chiefly by tsetse flies), had already destroyed the horses. Farmers had to walk everywhere. Brunner saved the situation by sending steam ploughs from Gingindlovu to Eshowe.

As member of parliament in Zululand in 1898, Earnest Brunner became actively involved in the mineral industry. He worked hard towards improving conditions of employment for prospectors and miners. A keen politician and a hard fighter in debate, over and above focusing on the Natal's mining legislation, he saw to the development of roads in the district. He also endorsed the feasibility of developing the harbour at Richards Bay. In fact, he turned down a position in the Legislative Counsel (Upper House) in order to serve his constituency in Zululand. Considered something of a financial wizard, as previously mentioned, he also served as treasurer in Sir Frederick Moor's cabinet. And he donated the land on which the Anglican Cathedral, St Michael & All Angels, was built in Main Street. There, he was very involved in the choir.

Brunner's grand-nephew's (chief magistrate of Zululand from 1963 to 1969), Coley Colenbrander's wife, the talented florist, Anne Colenbrander was as actively involved in the parish as was Brunner in earlier years. I got into huge trouble during my time serving as the parish secretary in 2009, when I took it upon myself, during a bored moment, to draw up the ladies' tea duty list. Anne, who commanded a certain degree of respect, stormed into the office and told me in no uncertain terms that the list had been one of her responsibilities for 'decades' and I was 'not to interfere'. I also got reprimanded when commenting on how much money her fund-raising Spring Ball had raised for the church (I unthinkingly referred to her Spring Ball as 'our little joll'). Despite my shortcomings Anne did buy one of my paintings, a still life of sea shells, that hung in her home in Kangela Street where she and Coley lived after his retirement from the bench. Their garden housed the largest collection of those magnificent orange clivias that are Eshowe's mascot flower.

It was fitting that Anne Colenbrander and her talented team, in more recent years, organised the floral display that was a beautiful tribute to Earnest Brunner who had come to Natal in 1872, working on a cotton and sugar plantation until he set up that first trading store on the Natal side of the Thukela River.

In 1883, with materials imported from Europe, Earnest and Corrie Brunner built the huge nine- roomed Victorian house, called 'Samarang', complete with a large veranda, on a prime location of eight acres in what was to be declared the 'Township of Eshowe' in 1891.

The township plan with names of streets was published in 1894. Walter Bosman was employed by the Natal government to oversee the maintenance of roads, drainage and pavements.

Little did the Brunners know, any more than Johan Colenbrander and Colonel Thomas Maxwell did, that 'Samarang' would be their link well over a century later when Dr Donald Clark (great-grandson of Colonel Thomas Maxwell) and Arnold Benjamin (Coley) Colenbrander (great-grand-nephew of Earnest Brunner) socialised together at 'Samarang' with their families.

IV

In 1929, three decades after the Boer War, Donald Clark was born in Johannesburg to Theodore Clark and Frances Clark (née Maxwell). Due to the market depression of those times, Theodore and Frances decided to raise Donald as an only child. Theodore owned a gentlemen's outfitters in Johannesburg. Frances' added income as a swimming coach allowed for Donald to attend private schools: Pridwin Preparatory School in

Johannesburg and Michaelhouse in the Natal Midlands.

While Donald was at Michaelhouse royalty visited from Britain. Scholars lined the streets where Queen Elizabeth asked Donald what he hoped to do after school. He told her that he planned to practice medicine (his maternal grandmother had in fact been a doctor in Scotland). The Queen responded: 'That is an honourable profession'. Donald went on to study medicine at Wits University in Johannesburg, qualifying in 1953. During the holidays he would hitch-hike up to Zambia (Northern Rhodesia at the time) and volunteer his services at hospitals and clinics. Thereafter he furthered his medical studies in England and the United States, obtaining a Diploma in Child Health.

Donald and Patricia (pictured overleaf) met while Donald was practicing in Johannesburg. Patricia was so beautiful and so polished and so charming. She was guaranteed the position of natural centre of attention wherever she went. They married and, in 1965, heard from Faith Stevenson (a radiologist at Eshowe Provincial Hospital, married to farmer James Stevenson who had attended Michaelhouse with Donald) that Dr Tom McHugh in Eshowe was in need of an assistant.

And so Donald took up private practice at Dr McHugh's consultation rooms situated in Sugar House where Jus Glass and Aluminium is today.

Patricia ensconced herself happily into the Eshowe community founding the History Club and the very first Book Club. She and Donald bought the house, 'Samarang', that was already a historical monument back then, situated at the junction of Main Street and John Ross Road – then called 'Gingindlovu Road'. They moved in with four of their five children: Jennifer, Susan, Andrew and Martin. Their fifth, Caroline, was born in

1970, seventy-four years after her great-great-grandfather, Colonel Thomas Maxwell was a guest at 'Samarang' while serving as Eshowe's resident magistrate. Steeped in Zululand's history, 'Samarang' has many historic names associated with it. Dr Donald Clark's oldest ever patient, Mrs Nellie Dunn, who turned 100, continued the association with 'Samarang' since Chief John Dunn visited Earnest Brunner there in 1872. John Dunn's daughter-in-law, granddaughter Pat and grandson Lawrence Dunn also visited 'Samarang'.

Patricia Clark researched 'Samarang' extensively and I am honoured to share her findings, but not before briefing you a bit more on the royal Zulu family, of whom King Dinuzulu played a large role in the history of 'Samarang'.

Chapter 14

King Shaka, who commanded fifty thousand warriors at the time of his death in 1828, when he was stabbed by his two half-brothers, Dingaan and Mahlangana, was succeeded by King Dingaan who, although a man who also ruled by fear, was friendly to the missionaries.

He gave them permission to establish missions throughout Zululand, promising to learn himself in order to set an example to his people. And he did indeed learn to read.

In 1840 King Dingaan's large military force was eventually wiped out by approximately two thousand Zulus, assisted by 335 Boers, under King Mpande (Dingaan's successor and half-brother).

Not a single Boer was killed. Instead, they captured some forty thousand cattle and became known as the 'Cattle Commando'.

King Mpande was succeeded by King Cethswayo in 1872.

On 4th July 1879, a force commanded by Lieutenant-General Lord Chelmsford invaded Zululand. That was the last major battle of the Anglo-Zulu War called 'The Battle of Ulundi'. Cethswayo's army resisted bravely, but King Cethswayo was seized and taken prisoner by the British.

He was deprived of his kingdom, and exiled to Cape Town's Castle together with his wives and his advisor, RC Samuelson of Norwegian ancestry.

The king was later moved to more comfortable surroundings at Oude Molen, a farm in Rosebank/Mowbray, Southern Cape Town.

There he was visited by Queen Victoria's two young grandsons, both naval cadets.

A painting by GF Angas of a Zulu warrior during Dingane's reign in 1840

An extremely homesick King Cethswayo implored them to please persuade their grandmother to return him to his own land. In fact, many influential people called on the king during that period and despite the fervent protests of Natal's legislature, he was formally granted permission to visit London in 1882.

In London, the king was installed in a house in Kensington and taken on tours of the city, drawing admiring crowds whenever he was recognised wearing tailored European fashion (but also his isicoco, the traditional head-ring worn by Zulu men). He was dubbed 'The Ladies' Man' and became the toast of London. Society hostesses vied with one another to entertain him. He also had a command of expression which appealed greatly to the British people. They became increasingly sympathetic to his cause. The king met with Queen Victoria who soon regarded him as a brave enemy and firm friend.

From prime minister, William Gladstone, the king plead for the restoration of his kingdom in Zululand. Despite the ferocity of Britain's humiliating defeat at the Battle of Isandlwana in January 1879, the newly elected Gladstone government in London, with added encouragement by Bishop John Colenso back in South

King Cethswayo in London 1882

Africa, approved Cethswayo's restoration. This was not accepted happily by the new white settlers in Zululand who feared possible ramifications. Accompanied with souvenirs from London and a pack of dogs of various breeds that got attached to him during his exile in the Cape, Cethswayo fully expected to resume as the restored king. When he arrived back in Cape Town he expected to immediately sail for Zululand, but much to his surprise, Sir Bulwer, governor of the Colony of Natal and special commissioner for Zulu affairs, now set new conditions in exchange for the king's freedom: the king had to give up almost a third of his land that was his best cattle grazing area (between the Thukela and uMhlatuze Rivers). He was told that if he did not sign the land over to the authorities he would be forced to stay always in the Cape.

So he signed under protest.

That area became a new government native reserve and the king was now barred from entering that area. Furthermore, if the king's followers wanted to cross the uMhlatuze River to see the king, they had to get permission from the Nongqayi Police.

On 7th December 1882, King Cethswayo was shown a new map indicating the 13 kinglets and the new chief of each appointed by the Natal government.

Although Cethswayo, and subsequently his son, Dinuzulu, administered one of those kinglets, the largest portions went to Chief Zibephu, Chief uHamu (Cethswayo's eldest brother) and, of course, John Dunn, former chief counselor to King Cethswayo, who was now appointed three magistrates to help him.

One magistrate was Earnest Brunner (of 'Samarang') whose area covered Eshowe and the surrounding district.

Chief Zibephu was an excellent military strategist described as Zululand's 'master of the ambush'. He had enjoyed a taste of glory during King Cethswayo's absence. While the king was in exile Zibephu had headed the house of the king's wives, his teenage son, Dinuzulu, and his cattle (that he had no intention of giving up easily). Hatred filled the heart of Cethswayo's young son, Dinuzulu, who had witnessed Zibephu's seizing of his father's wives and the plundering of the royal herds and, what's worse, the British authorities turning a blind eye.

A good-looking, athletic, intelligent young man who was a good shot and horseman, Dinuzulu had been overjoyed when his father, King Cethswayo returned from exile in 1883.

Then the British realised the futility of breaking up Zululand and restored Cethswayo as paramount leader of the territories. However, they left Cethswayo's relative, Zibephu, alone with his lands intact.

In July 1883, Zibephu attacked Cethswayo's new kraal in Ulundi, wounding the king and causing him to flee to Eshowe. There, although the medical officer gave his cause of death as 'fatty degeneration of the heart', he died on 8th February 1884, at the age of 52, of suspected poisoning by Zibephu's people.

His wives and supporters dramatically snatched his body from the 'Residency' and fled to Nkandla where he was buried just south of the forest.

And so, in 1884 Cethswayo died as a fugitive, in what is now William Chadwick Road in Eshowe, just over a mile from where he was born in 1826, at the royal homestead which was where Eshowe Provincial Hospital stands today.

His death brought no peace to the land and wars continued, with Zibephu still against Dinuzulu.

White families in Zululand, reading the papers, felt threatened as they absorbed the news in mounting horror: 'Last night everybody in Eshowe had to leave their homes and take refuge in Fort Curtis'.

I

On 21st May 1884 oil was poured over Prince Dinuzulu's head, anointing him as the king of the Zulus.

As the new king he inherited his father's enemies and a country which was in ruins: kraals were burnt, cattle and crops were destroyed.

The bitterness provoked by a civil war led to the final destruction of the Zulu Kingdom, as it had been before, because their wealth was destroyed and they were forced to seek out employment as paid labourers.

Dinuzulu had grown up witnessing the great military system of his uncle, Shaka, being revived. He had sat wide-eyed while watching men fight with savage bulls, bringing them down to their deaths. He saw the crowning of his father, Cethswayo by the secretary for native affairs Theophilus Shepstone*. But now intertribal warfare and conflict continued unabated. More deaths occurred than in the whole of the recent Anglo-Zulu War (which was basically a fight between blacks and whites for supremacy).

To contest Zibephu's succession, Dinuzulu appealed

*That event was captured in a painting by artist and explorer, Thomas Baines.

to the British but had no response, so he offered rewards of land to Boer farmers in the Vryheid and Utrecht districts, to come and fight on his side and restore the Zulu Kingdom. In return for their assistance, Dinuzulu allocated 271 thousand acres of Zulu land to the Boers for the formation of an independent republic with access to the sea. That short-lived 'Nieuwe Republiek' was recognised only by Germany and Portugal, with Lucas Meyer as its first and only president.

In 1886 the British government officially recognised the Boers as the legal owners of the farms in that allocated area around the town, Melmoth in Zululand, where gold was discovered. But that gold rush was short-lived and over by 1895.

Let's return to 1884: One hundred and twenty Boers, called 'Dinuzulu's volunteers' led by Louis Botha, and some Germans from the Luneburg area led by Adolph Schiel, joined some seven thousand Zulu warriors to face the power of Chief Zibephu.

After several clashes, Dinuzulu's volunteers finally defeated Zibephu at the Battle of Ghost Mountain, (also known as the 'Battle of Tshaneni') on 5th June 1884. The once mighty Zibephu and six thousand of his followers fled to Eshowe where they were given refuge by resident commissioner Melmoth Osborn, who had replaced magistrate Earnest Brunner of 'Samarang'.

II

In 1888 King Dinuzulu and his two uncles, Princes Ndabuko and Shingana, were sadly brought to trial at 'Samarang' in Eshowe, for leading that army to defeat Chief Zibephu who had, in fact, been granted refuge by the British.

The Eshowe courthouse was hopelessly inadequate

BRUNNER'S STORE, WHERE THE TRIAL OF DINUZULU TOOK PLACE

for a trial, but it so happened that Earnest Brunner had almost completed another business building on 'Samarang's grounds which was now requisitioned for the purpose of King Dinuzulu, Prince Ndabuko and Prince Shingana's trial. And it was adapted to give a suitably imposing judicial character.

The judge was clad in red robes while his two assessors wore black gowns, rudely referred to by Harriette Colenso (Bishop John Colenso's daughter) as their 'petticoats'.

Harriette Colenso, with her support group, camped close to 'Samarang'. She sat in on the proceedings for the whole six months to see that fair play took place. And she taught the royal prisoners to read and write while they awaited their sentences.

The leading Natal Judiciary included Harry Escombe (later prime minister of Natal in 1897), Sir Walter Wragg and other well-known figures. Attorneys Frank Dumat, and George Hulett (Sir Liege Hulett's son and Bryan Hulett's grandfather) who was to take up residence in Eshowe in 1905, acted for the defendants.

George Hulett left Eshowe in 1917, two years after

serving as chairman of Eshowe's local board and one year before becoming a senator in the Union Parliament. The royal Zulu prisoners spent their days in tents outside the gaol while the defense team stayed in tents at 'Samarang'. Frank Dumat, a member of the defense, built a hut for himself and his wife. Other supporters slept under Brunner's wagons. That camp was called 'the rebel camp' by disapproving authorities.

King Dinuzulu, Prince Ndabuko and Prince Shingana were found guilty of high treason and public violence. They were to serve more than several years' imprisonments on the island, St Helena.

Magema Fuze (a former student of Bishop Colenso) travelled to St Helena to serve as King Dinuzulu's personal secretary. Also, the king's tutor, Reverend Baker, who had also been trained by Bishop Colenso, was to teach the king to read, write, and play the piano and American organ, which he mastered.

King Dinuzulu's son, Prince Solomon was born on St Helena. Solomon's own son, King Bhekuzulu appointed Prince Mangosuthu Buthelezi, the South African politician and Zulu prince, to serve as the traditional prime minister to the Zulu royal family, from 1954 until his death in 2023.

When the accused were exiled to St Helena in 1889, the 21-year-old King Dinuzulu looked about him in bewilderment. He was accompanied by two males and two female attendants, his two uncles (Princes Ndabuko and Shingana), their wives and male attendants, Mr Saunders (their guardian and interpreter), Mr Anthony Daniels (the king's assistant) and their very own doctor. Later a midwife was sent there from Zululand. The king and his party were moved into a sizable house called 'Rosemary Hall' situated in large grounds with stables, just four miles from the seaport town and capital,

Jamestown. Much to their joy they were free to move around the island. Wearing English clothes, they attended concerts, picnics and cricket games at the governor's residence. Harriette Colenso and other appropriate guests visited King Dinuzulu there. In his regular correspondence with his mother, the king requested tobacco, snuff, medicine and money.

After his return to South Africa, on 5th January 1898, he was relegated by the British administration to the position of paramount chief of his Zulu clan. He requested a triumphal progression through Durban but was refused. Dr Donald Clark's great-grandfather, Colonel Thomas Maxwell had the huge responsibility of escorting the king and members of the Zulu royal party which included the king's young son, Prince Solomon (heir to the Zulu throne) and Harriette Colenso.

They trekked to Eshowe in many wagons, to a wood-and-iron house that had been especially requested by Queen Victoria. That house was last used by Cethswayo in 1907. In 1908 it was pulled down and re-erected in John Ross Road, near the gaol, to serve as a residence for one of the wardens.

King Cethswayo, having accumulated ton-loads of clothes, furniture, pictures, books, ornaments, animals and his beloved American organ, arrived in Eshowe on 10th January 1898, but soon after expressed his desire to move to Nongoma. This was agreed to on condition that he attend meetings in Eshowe. This arrangement did not last, however, due to the Boer War looming and six thousand war prisoners being sent to St Helena. Also the Bambatha Rebellion was not far off at Mome Gorge near Nkandla Forest, where Mahatma Gandhi and his people would play a crucial role, working tirelessly as stretcher bearers as they had done during the Boer War of 1899 to 1902.

During the 1906 Bambatha Rebellion, King Dinuzulu was accused of harboring Chief Bambatha and his wife. Not an unreasonable act as the father of his people, if you ask me. This resulted in charges of high treason and yet another court case in December 1907, this time in Greytown.

William Philip Schreiner was ably assisted by Eugene Renaud (farmer James Stevenson's grandfather), one of the best known criminal lawyers in Durban at the time. But in spite of that famous defense, Dinuzulu was sentenced to four years' imprisonment. 'My sole crime is that I am the son of Cethswayo,' he lamented.

Harriette Colenso, labelled 'fanatically prejudiced', was evicted from her own home and died in straitened circumstances.

In the meantime, Louis Botha (1862-1919), who had led 'Dinuzulu's volunteers' against Chief Zibephu back in 1884, became prime minister of South Africa in 1910. Years prior, he had started out as a sheep farmer taking his flock to Zululand where he and Dinuzulu met and became friends.

Botha believed that Dinuzulu was not responsible for the Bambatha Rebellion or the subsequent unrest. So Dinuzulu (to whom the Boers paid a pension until his death) with his wives and loyal friends were released to a farm, Uitkyk, in the Middleburg district. There, he settled down and lived quietly until he died at the age of 45, in 1913. He was buried with his fathers, the ancient kings of Zululand, in the eMakhosini Valley near Ulundi. A few months after King Dinuzulu's burial the institution of the Natives Land Act of 1913, by the Union of South Africa, saw the sanctioned dispossession of land from African people.

That land fell into the hands of white settlers and their British benefactors.

Chapter 15

The oldest house in Eshowe was built in 1883, by Earnest Brunner who first arrived in South Africa as an 18-year-old graduate from Leiden University. The Brunners named that nine-roomed house 'Samarang' after the birthplace of Earnest's wife, Corrie in Indonesia.

Built in the same year as the Nongqayi Fort, 'Samarang' is one of the most historic buildings, not only in Eshowe, but in the whole of Zululand.

Author and magistrate Hjalmer Braatvedt described a visit to Brunner who was known as 'Mashyinyioni', meaning one who accurately captures birds, because of his fine aviary. Also, peacocks wandered freely about the grounds and white doves perched, among rare trees, shrubs and flowering plants, in a garden tended by Indonesian staff who were brought to Eshowe by the Colenbrander family.

The house continues to stand graciously in its two-acre garden. Opposite is a painting of it by artist Rowena Bush.

Earnest and Corrie Brunner, successful traders of farming implements, groceries and hardware, entertained well at 'Samarang'. An invitation card to a formal ball, held on 27th March 1903, was framed in their library. It is a treasured relic of a graceful era, and the emotional relief felt after the 2nd Boer War ended. Another charming dance programme is a reminder of a ball held at Samarang in March 1908.

In 1915 the first local board of Eshowe was elected*. In 1917 Brunner was elected as the second chairman of

---

*Councillors included C Wynne, GH Hulett, CF Adams, TH Parkins, JY Hunter, Mrs Agnes Vanderplank and EA Brunner.

that town board in which capacity he welcomed the very first train into Eshowe.

That same year Corrie died. Among the mourners were: Dr Balfe (the first medical officer of health in 1890 who lived in what is now actress Ida Gartrell's house; Marshall Campbell (who together with Edward Saunders was responsible for introducing the first rickshaw to Durban); Mrs Randle (a member of Anne Cadman's family who date back to the 1830s); Colonel and Mrs Addison (members of Janey Chennells' family); the Clifford Wynnes, the Brockwells and James Rorke of Rorke's Drift.

Although known as the 'Father of Eshowe', Earnest Brunner died in Holland in 1920, at the age 67.

In 1927 the local board was elevated to the dignity of a town board.

In 1954 the 'Borough of Eshowe' was proclaimed*. A week later, councillor HF Johnson became Eshowe's first mayor. He was re-elected in 1955 and succeeded, in 1956, by councillor Guy Taylor.

I

'Samarang' was bought from Earnest Brunner by Robert Hall, one-time cavalry officer and wealthy Ladysmith farmer. Robert had no use for Brunner's successful business, and so, 30 years after the business had been established by Brunner, it was sold to Charlie Adams whose father, Alfred, as you know, was the founder of A Adams Camp Store in Eshowe.

Charlie moved the Brunner's business premises to diagonally opposite 'Samarang', where his own butchery was situated. He called the new enterprise 'Adams & Co'.

It is extraordinary that Brunner, who devoted himself to the upliftment of his adopted country, serving it to the absolute best of his ability, was not recognised in Eshowe. At the Clarks' request he had an area named after him. 'Brunner Place' is situated next to Laing's Building, previous home of C & H accounting firm, in Osborn Road.

Indeed, 'Brunner Place' is a tribute to a public-spirited man who served Zululand faithfully and sat on so many committees, for almost half a century.

Subsequent to Brunner, Robert Hall owned 'Samarang' for 24 years, during which time Madge Pennefather, the finest horse-woman in Eshowe, cared for his horses during his many absences.

His three daughters, who lived in England, caused quite a stir among the young men of Eshowe when they visited 'Samarang', their country holiday home. They played tennis matches against resident Eshowe-ites and entertained often, making good use of the wine cellar below the main bedroom. One of them stayed behind to

*Members were R B Lagerwall, A V Myburgh, W Kerr; J W Reid (yet to be mayor from 1958 to 1959), HJ Streek, HF Johnson, J R White, N Atkinson and G Taylor.

The very first Standard Bank building in Eshowe. In 1935 it moved to premises in Osborn Road. Then it once again shifted to where the Old Mutual building is now. The Fort museum houses a large pair of scales presented to them by the Standard Bank. They were used for the weighing of gold nuggets in the early years of prospecting.

marry Trevor Becker who arrived in 1919. Trevor was the manager to establish the very first Standard Bank in Eshowe. Their son, Fleetwood was born at 'Samarang'.

II

In 1944 Mr and Mrs Alan and Dora Vanderplank of St Kitts Estate bought 'Samarang' from Robert Hall. Alan's own ancestors had arrived in their own schooner from Tasmania in 1839.

Dora Vanderplank was admired for her gracious hostessing skills. Her father, Sir Charles Gubbins came to Natal as a surgeon with the troops in the Anglo-Zulu War of 1879. In 1880 he married Maud Bradstreet (née Scoble). He became minister of education and a senator of the Union of South Africa under General Louis Botha. An astute politician, he deputised for Sir Frederick Moor as prime minister and minister of native affairs while the latter attended the national convention, which Sir Charles Gubbins, himself, attended as a delegate for Natal in 1910. He was knighted in the same year.

Alan Vanderplank's sister-in-law, Mrs Walter Vanderplank, a trained nursing sister, was the first woman in South Africa to be elected to a town board – that was in Eshowe. It was she and her husband, lawyer Walter Vanderplank who entertained Mahatma Gandhi when he visited Eshowe. Walter's legal firm was later to become the firm we know today as Wynne & Wynne. He was also 'Major' Walter Vanderplank who commanded Eshowe's first regiment ZMR*. The regimental flag, presented by the ladies of Eshowe is now on view at the museum.

A keen gardener, Walter's brother, Alan held many musical evenings at 'Samarang'. In 1947 his wife, Dora was approached by a specially formed committee for the use of 'Samarang' for the visit of the royal family to Eshowe. However, due to the poor economy at that time, and much to Dora Vanderplank's dreadful disappointment, it was decided that the royal family would be accommodated on the luxurious White Train while refreshing themselves at the provincially owned 'Residency'. There, the bell-indicator hanging in a passage still carries markers 'Queen's Room' and 'Princess Elizabeth's Room'.

After Dora Vanderplank's death she left 'Samarang' to

---

*Walter Vanderplank's officers were VGM Robinson, Captain and Adjutant, Captain RC Flindt, Lieutenants HJ James, JA Cooper, JS Hedges, DJC Hulley and EB Walton, Lieutenant and Quartermaster Charlie Adams. Captain GK Moberly of the Natal Medical Corps acted as medical officer to the regiment. Finally, there was Regimental Sergeant-Major Smith, ex-Natal Police.

The Residency was built in 1894 by the Public Works Department of Natal. It was carried out by JW Ogden and Mr Schmidtmann together with Charlie Fraser, who arrived in Eshowe in 1901 and was to also construct the early golf course. The three built many of the older houses in the town.

her daughter, Felicity Briscoe who was unfortunately unable to maintain the large property. The building on the premises, in which King Dinuzulu's trial took place 69 years before, was dismantled and re-erected on her farm.

III

In 1958 pharmacist Ralph Edwards* bought 'Samarang' together with his wife Phyllis. Their son, Chris Edwards was the well-known Natal rugby administrator. Ralph Edwards did not enjoy good health and died a few years later. Mrs Edwards married Levison-Gowerand and they moved to Johannesburg.

As I've mentioned, James Stevenson of 'Fairfield

---

*There were to be two branches of Edwards Pharmacy in Eshowe: the one that remains in the same place today, in Osborn Road since before the 1st World War, and one that was on the corner of the Adams establishment where Kwikspar is today.

Farm' and his wife, Faith introduced Dr Donald and Patricia Clark to 'Samarang' in 1965. James was the grandson of Eugene Renaud who defended Dinuzulu at his 2nd trial in Greytown, after the Bambatha Rebellion.

Eshowe was actually no stranger to Dr Donald Clark who visited 'Fairfield Farm' from the age of two, together with his mother, violin teacher Frances Clark. 'Fairfield Farm' belonged to Frances' aunt, Ida Harke.

Eugene Renaud's daughter and son-in-law, Colin Stevenson (James Stevenson's parents) purchased 'Fairfield Farm', from Ida Harke.

Frances' cousin, Yvonne Butcher (née Barry) along with her husband, Cyril Butcher farmed across the way at Netherley Farm (later to become the property of Norman and Cheryl Steenberg).

IV

Since the Clarks bought 'Samarang' in 1965, they have seen many changes in Eshowe. They met Coley and Anne Colenbrander at the 'Residency' where the Coleys' had entertained the prime minister to a braai when he came to Eshowe to open the Zululand Agricultural Show.

Coley was the principal magistrate of the Eshowe district like his great-uncle, Earnest Brunner of 'Samarang', who, we have already learned, had been appointed as magistrate by John Dunn in the previous century.

As I've also told you, Dr Clark's grandfather, Colonel Thomas Maxwell, a long time ago, in 1896 and 1897, was appointed custodian of King Dinuzulu and his large royal retinue, to return them to Eshowe and ultimately to Nongoma, together with Harriette Colenso.

V

Back to Brunner's grand-nephew: Coley Colenbrander who was called 'Mashanela' by the amaZulu meaning 'he who sweeps until the floor is clean'. He inherited the spirit of his colourful grand-uncle, the White Whirlwind, Johan Colenbrander – Both were men of much adventure.

Coley compiled his memoirs in a book called 'Coley's Odyssey' that was published in 1993. Coley and Anne Colenbrander were charming hosts. Through them, Dr Donald and Patricia Clark met many of the judges of the circuit court. Many became firm friends.

The Clarks also befriended the Cadman family who moved to 'Parkside' in Eshowe in 1970. Radclyffe Macbeth Cadman (1924-2011) was married to Anne Cadman (née Randles) whose family were associated with James Rorke, after whom Rorke's Drift was named. Radclyffe Cadman was a lawyer who served on the National Wildlife Board and helped sponsor a number of books on environmental subjects. His home, 'Parkside' was built by the Shepstone family who played such a prominent part in Natal history. At 'Parkside' the Clarks were fortunate to share many events with the Cadmans during Radclyffe Cadman's appointment as administrator of Natal.

'Parkside' later became the official home of Dr Frank Mdlalose (1931-2021), the first Premier of the renamed KwaZulu-Natal province. The Clarks also met British ambassador, Patrick Moberly and his wife at 'Parkside'. On their way to Ulundi, the following day, the Moberlys stopped at 'Samarang' with the British Consul.

'Samarang' has entertained many old friends and acquaintances, judges, artists, musicians, actors and naturalists. Dora Vanderplank's grand-daughter, Mrs Clark (no relation), her husband and her children, and Fleetwood Becker with one of his two beautiful English aunts (Miss Kathleen Hall), have visited Samarang' to recall past memories.

The Clark's 55 years spent there were made up of

many memories with the endless activities of their five children. Their grandchildren have their names engraved on stepping stones in the garden where there are also the very same stepping stones that Zulu King Dinuzulu stepped on during his first trial. One can also see the concrete slab that was the veranda of Brunner's Store that he built in 1888.

Many events and personalities, who shaped South Africa's destiny, are inextricably linked with 'Samarang'. For example, the Clarks' grandchildren: Christopher, Caroline and James (children of Craig Theunissen and Patricia's daughter, Susan who grew up at 'Samarang'), are the great-great-great grandchildren of Daniel and Caroline Neilsen – the Norwegian couple with missionary zeal who arrived in 1860, during the reign of King Mpande, to join Bishop Schreuder. Together they built churches and school rooms, not only at Entumeni and Empangeni, but also at KwaMondi where the British were held siege by the amaZulu in 1879.

Historian Ian knight, his wife, Carolyn and son, Alexander stayed at 'Samarang'. They kindly produced the publication of Donald Clark's great-uncle, John Maxwell's, (Colonel Thomas Maxwell's brother's) diary called 'Reminiscences of the Zulu War'. That book described the horror at Isandlwana and then at Rorke's Drift on their return. After the war, John Maxwell lived in Eshowe until he died in 1905, at the age of 68.

Once upon a time, 'Samarang's rooms were filled with screens, porcelain, and lacquered furniture from the East. Later, the Clarks lined their passages with photographs that captured Samarang's rich history. These included pictures of members of the royal families – British and Zulu – who were photographed with Dr Donald Clark and members of his family.

It has been suggested that 'Samarang' be utilised for

tourists as a museum where they could enjoy the grounds and replenish on its wrap-around veranda which seats one hundred. Then be free to wander through the gates to experience the vibrancy of its people and help benefit the economy by boosting local traders.

Around 'Samarang', progress has enveloped the playground of Kings Zenzekona, Shaka (1787-1828), Dingaan (1795-1840) Mpande (1798-1872) Cethswayo (1834-1884) Dinuzulu (1862-1913), Solomon (1891-1933), Cyprian (1924-1968) and Goodwill Zwelithini (1948-2021) who have all left their footsteps on the pavements where the children and grandchildren of King Cethswayo and Queen Victoria met and, where long ago, the Brunners looked out for empty miles.

The story of Brunner and 'Samarang' have appeared in 'Garden and Home', the 'Zululand Observer', and a Dutch publication: 'Zuid Africa in Amsterdam'. The house has also been used as a film set.

'Samarang's visitors' book and photos are testimony to a more recent history where personalities from afar and near, many of whom have contributed to the development of this province, have graced the house.

David Rattray of Fugitives' Drift Lodge at Rorke's Drift fame also spun his magic there when he and his wife, Nicky visited at a large gathering.

A charming visitor to 'Samarang' was Chief Mbatha, a grandson of King Dinuzulu and loyal patient of Dr Clark's, who visited 'Samarang' to hear the story of his grandfather.

He presented Donald with a handsome walking-stick when he bade farewell. Other guests at 'Samarang' included Fynney, a brilliant Zulu linguist, who interpreted for King Cethswayo when the king visited England in 1882.

Let's not forget members of our Dunn family. On

Donald's 60th birthday in 1989, 'Samarang' hosted many friends from all around the country. Donald's faithful nurse, Sister Florette, unbeknown to him, organised Zulu dancers in their full regalia to perform on the front lawn. Donald and Patricia were deeply touched by that gesture.

VI

Since 1971 at the age of 42, Dr Donald Clark rented, from the Jenkinson family, the little wood-and-iron house opposite the hospital in Kangela Street.

Lorraine Jenkinson was a cousin of Donald Clark's. She was married to Viv Jenkinson who had inherited all the courage and enthusiasm of his forebears, the Braatvedts.

There, in that house, Donald Clark set up his own private practice where, for 48 years, he treated the people of Eshowe.

During this time, he was fortunate to employ the super-efficient Colleen Swan who was previously secretary to the town clerk. Colleen aptly ran the front desk at the rooms while Donald visited rural clinics in the afternoons and worked part-time for Eshowe Provincial Hospital. For over 40 years he was on constant call-out for two nights a week and every second weekend. For some years he ran the male ward, and then the female ward for a short while. He also worked in outpatients on the odd morning, and at the Eshowe Borough Clinic, with Caryle Kippen, once a week.

Every Christmas Dr Donald Clark received a generous gift from Mrs Shembe and her family who were loyal patients of his. King Dinuzulu's son, King Solomon married Zondi Shembe, daughter of the prophet Isiah Shembe (1867- 1935), the Zulu religious leader of the

Mangosuthu Buthelezi in tribal dress

amaNazarites, the largest independent religious movement among the amaZulu today. Over thirty thousand followers, draped in white robes, gather each year in Judea outside Eshowe. Of royal blood from the bloodline of King Shaka, Constance Magogo (1900-1984) was the daughter of King Dinuzulu, and the sister of the late King Solomon. A composer as well as a poet, she brought fame to KwaZulu-Natal in 2002, with her world acclaimed Zulu-inspired full-length opera called 'Princess Magogo Dinuzulu'. It was broadcast on Belgium Radio and heard by 40 delegates attending the prestigious Liege International Trade Fair.

Many academics consulted Princess Constance Magogo on Zulu folklore. Her son, Shenge Buthelezi refers to his mother as 'a woman of compassion' who sold her own cattle to pay for his tertiary education when his father refused to do so. It is the descendants of the Zulus, the Shembes and Buthelezis, who have a close association with 'Samarang'.

Donald's deep love for the people of Zululand is evident in his poetry, many of which were compiled into a delightful collection called 'Poems from Samarang'. My favourite of Don's poems is titled 'An old Zulu's hospital visit'. It won 1st t prize in a 2002 newspaper competition and was printed in 'The Golden Thread: An Anthology of African Verse':

*'In the ward so clinical and bright,
A grey bent man came shuffling out the night,
Smelling of beer and bush smoke, dazed and sad,
Seeking his mate, knowing the news was bad. He found her in a cage-like white cot bed,
Haemorrhage ploughing turmoil in her head, Snuffing out all vestiges of life
From this poor ravaged creature, once his wife. He gazed through smokey cataracts of age, His book of life turned back a page by page, His wedding day, his beaded laughing bride, He met the envious glances with such pride.
She bore him babies every other year,
And ground his corn and cooked and brewed his beer.
In drunken states, he'd beat her without cause, But she, in blind acceptance of the laws, Endured this loss of dignity and shame,
And always proud to take her warrior's name.
And now an empty hut, a silent kraal, And only beer and dagga's friendly call May give him will to live a few more years
And dry those blinding sad remorseful tears.'*

Chapter 16

Subsequent to the Clarks, since 2013, 'Samarang' belongs to Fred Volbrecht Jnr, son of Eshowe's quantity surveyor, Fred Volbrecht Snr.

In 1987 both Freds embarked on a spearfishing adventure with local dentist, Dr John Bernard Andrews (fondly known as 'Droes Andrews').

Other members of the group were citrus farmer Kobus de Kock, Rory Ferguson (Stan and Wendy's son) and Ters Malherbe who was Droes' main and oldest spearfishing friend.

Droes Andrews' other outdoor interests included microlighting, paragliding and paramotoring. He had, in fact, served in the parachute battalion in the army. In his youth he also did off-road scrambling, wrestling, weight-training and long distance running. He ran the Comrades Marathon in 1980 and paddled the Berg River Canoe Marathon.

Part of a seven-man crew in 1987, Droes headed out to sea in a hired trawler called the 'Gilbert Guy'. It had a rusted hull and rotten floorboards. There was also no auto-pilot steering so everyone had to take turns at the wheel. They felt quite important as helmsmen en route to spearfish at Bassas da India. After, they would visit Europa Island, one of the world's most important nesting sites for the endangered green turtles. Between eight and fifteen thousand female turtles nest on the island every year. Up to 2.4 million juveniles hatch. Europa Island is also used as a stopover for birds migrating between Africa and Madagascar.

Dr Droes Andrews was the undisputed leader among that particular party. He had a wonderful way of sharing his knowledge – that was absolutely everything there is to know – about spearfishing. He knew where the best reefs were and how to spear different types of fish.

An old sea dog without pretention Droes could share a bottle of cane with a strange fisherman on the beach, or ask a straight upper-lipped person how the stock market was performing. His favourite saying when something took his fancy was 'Mamba!'

Born in Middleburg in the Transvaal, Droes attended Middleburg Hoërskool. It so happens that my first husband, Ray van Schalkwyk attended boarding there with Droes. When Ray came to visit Lara and Keri in Eshowe, Droes recognised him immediately, some 30 years after Ray was caned at that school for bouncing a ball on a Sunday.

Droes wanted to be a vet, but despite six 'A's on his matric certificate, he was not accepted to do the course. So he studied dentistry instead, at the University of Pretoria.

After qualifying he worked in England for a year, but he longed for the South African sea, sunshine and boerewors. Returning to South Africa, he looked for a practice on the south coast, but the closest he got was Eshowe where he bought a dental practice from his relation, Thys Matthe. Ironically, Thys was wanting to go back to England.

A condition of the deal was that whomever bought his practice would buy it with Nurse Ileen Counter as part of the package. Ileen worked for Dr Thys Matthe who travelled from Empangeni to Eshowe twice a week. Ileen's sister, Jenny, is married to Dr Eric Brits' brother.

Ileen and Jenny have another sister, Fiona. The three Counter sisters are cousins of artist Marian Mattinson and farmer Louis Gunter (their mother was Lionel Gunter's sister, Naomi who owned a trading store in the rural area called 'Oliver's Mount'). The girls' father, Ernest Counter came from the Karoo to work on Shane Pett's father's farm. From there he went on to manage at Entumeni Wattle & Sugar Estate. (Before sugar cane farmers in Entumeni farmed wattle and cattle.) The three sisters had a fabulous life growing up on a farm and attending boarding school at Eshowe Junior and Eshowe High School.

And so it was that Droes bought the practice in Eshowe in 1979. Ileen worked for him for almost three years during which time she says they just 'clicked'. In December 1981, Droes bought the double-story house in Bulwer Avenue, which adjoins the back of Mike's and my property. He married Ileen a month later. The dental practice was set up on the ground floor and they lived upstairs. When they were expecting Stanley, they moved the practice to next to the Hospital Tea Room, but the constant litter on that busy street bothered Droes. So, together with Dr Mike Damp, he bought the property at 49 Kangela Street which is called the 'Healthmed Dental & Medical Centre'. Pat Brenchley had his 'sugar office' there, and Dr Craig Pryke, the vet, opened his practice next door. Vanessa Cadman practiced physiotherapy at Dr Mike Damp's rooms, and to this day Moffatts Optometry have their rooms there. Droes' rooms are occupied by other dentists.

After her aerobics teacher left Eshowe, Ileen did the necessary training and has been an aerobics instructor since. She shared Droes' love for the outdoors and has even climbed Mount Kilimanjaro.

Droes and Ileen had two sons, Stanley and Ernest, who went to Eshowe Junior School followed by Landbou Hoërskool in Vryheld. After school Stanley spent some time in Texas driving 14-wheeler lorries used to transport animal feed. He returned to Eshowe and started a garden service. A few years later he was sourced by Guy Emberton to be his farm manager and still works for him today. He married Derek and Wendy Coley's daughter, Teri, and together they have two sons.

Droes and Ileen's second son, Ernest loved to dive and spearfish with his father. He also enjoyed paragliding and paramotoring. Hooked on helicopter flying, he qualified as a four-seater commercial helicopter pilot. He then entered the lucrative coffee industry as a barista, at only 20-years-old. He remains involved in the world of coffee across different roles including quality controller and roaster.

Back to spearfishing at Bassas da India in 1987. That group of seven considered themselves 'Men of the Sea' with saltwater pumping in their veins. Departing from Durban docks they felt like Hemingway in the early days of safari, facing the dangerously unknown – They were setting out to explore and hunt in one of the last truly wild frontiers of the world.

Kobus de Kock recorded their experiences in a most enjoyable read called 'Bassas: A Spearfishing Adventure' from which I glean the following information: Bassas da India is an uninhabited island with a coral atoll in the southern Mozambique channel. It is about four hundred kilometres west of Madagascar and five hundred kilometres east of Africa. The island was formed by the rim of an extinct volcano, the highest point being only two-and-a-half metres above the surf. The coral atoll is almost perfectly round with a diametre of 11 kilometres and a coastline of 35.2 kilometres. Tropical waters are so warm that donning a wetsuit is purely for the protection against the coral. Spearfishing at Bassas is simply bliss. Although they had two small ski boats, those Eshowe-ite fishermen often chose to dive around the anchored Gilbert Guy. Under the water is a mangled wonderland of coral, gullies, caves and potholes rolling out on all sides for as far as the eye can see. Colours and varieties are mind-blowing. Something new and fascinating lurks around every corner.

Spearfishing is not a sport without its hazards. Kobus remembers, at Cape Vidal, a poorly speared Sea Pike bit right through the nose tweaker of a diver's mask and cut into his upper lip. The most common cause of death among spear fishermen is actually black-outs caused by holding their breath for too long. Not long after that expedition to Bassas, Stan and Wendy Ferguson's son, Rory tragically drowned at Cape Vidal during a spearfishing excursion.

On board the 'Gilbert Guy' in 1987, playing Trivial Pursuit for hours on end, everyone was impressed by Droes' general knowledge. For instance, he knew that the Czech long-distance runner was Emile Zatopec, and the apes of Gibraltar are called 'Barbary Macaques'. Kobus didn't take Droes for a great reader but Droes certainly made it his business to know everything worth knowing when off on one of his great expeditions.

Fred Volbrecht, the quantity surveyor, was jokingly accused of dedicating most of his time to the depletion of the 'Gilbert Guy's' stock of beer. Although, admittedly, keeping up with the French skipper, Roger was well beyond his ability. Apart from what they drank, Fred remembered that they ate rabbit and duck le orange, typical French cuisine, but served in such limited portions that it had to be shared out very carefully. Sleeping quarters were full of cockroaches and other creepy crawlies, but this was a small price to pay in their efforts to shoot the 'big one' that, in your imagination, will grow heavier and heavier and take longer to fight and bring to the surface. The one that will almost drown you when it suddenly takes off again with your float-line. The big monster whose photo or taxidermy will grace your walls, reminding you of the exact experience.

Expected at Bassa da India were huge sea pike, barracuda, dog-toothed tuna and giant king fish weighing over 50 kilograms. The crew mostly wanted those giant king fish (also known as 'trevally'). Kobus de Kock dreamt of breaking his personal 40-pound barrier, but his big fish came years later when he speared a 72-pound wahoo in Sodwana on yet another trip with Droes.

Spearfishing is hunting in its most primitive form, hopefully with decent visibility because it's no fun diving in pea soup conditions. Spearfishing is also quick, almost instinctive shooting like handling a shot gun. You can't afford to dilly-dally.

Kubus continues to tell us that Droes' philosophy was 'sharks are nothing, surf is everything.' Before he got a ski boat he used to swim out into the ocean to spearfish – no small feat when laden with equipment including belt-weights to maintain neutral buoyancy.

Over the years, Kobus de Kock, as regular crew member, helped to destroy two of Droes' boats: the 'Voyager' and the 'Calemba'. On the one occasion he and Droes pushed the 'Voyager' through some challenging surf when the engine stopped as it was going through a huge swell. Droes was flung forward, breaking the Voyager's steering wheel with his head. Bleeding profusely from a cut above his eyebrow, he surveyed the damage: the windscreen was completely ripped off taking the huge old-fashioned echo-sounder with it. Droes was in need of urgent medical attention, but he was the skipper and had to steer, so Kobus tied Droes' blood-soaked cotton glove in place with a fish-slime and oil-stained t-shirt and they headed to shore.

Following their spearfishing at Bassas, the 'Gilbert Guy' moved on to Europa Island where the crew watched baby turtles hatching in their hundreds. They literally bubbled out of the sand and, without hesitation, scrambled to the surf as fast as their tiny little flippers would allow. They swam past the moored 'Gilbert Guy' until late that night.

The whole three-week trip stripped the crew's existence down to the very basics: clothing to prevent being burned and eating what little the skipper fed them. Work on deck and diving was better than a workout at the gym, and they only washed their hair when they could no longer stand the slimy diesel gel. Drinking beer was simply to quench their thirst while they swapped fish for fuel with other ships at sea. In its simplicity life was wonderful.

Droes with his 65-kilogram catch

Then there was the storm. Bobbing in the middle of the ocean at the full mercy of a howling south-westerly it was bloody scary on the trawler, except for Quantity Surveyor Fred. He remained cool and calm and collected, with Dutch courage coursing through his veins, while the others entertained images of nails popping out of the rotten planking of the hull.

When they arrived at the filthy Richards Bay Pier, Kobus kissed the concrete and said, 'Never again!' (until next time).

I

Eight years later, in December 1995, after many other excursions, Dr Droes Andrews, his adoring wife, Ileen and their two young sons, Stanley and Ernest accompanied a few old friends on a two-month long camping, snorkelling and spearfishing trip across Africa. This was just before Pat Brenchley and I arrived in Eshowe in 1996, only to hear all about their wonderful adventures. I am honoured to draw from Ileen's delightful scrapbook – Such lovely memories.

Ileen, of course, saw to all the practicalities of the trip. She got the roof-rack put onto their bakkie, new ropes fitted onto the sails and had a hole in the tarpaulin patched (They did, however, indulge in a brand new five-man nomad tent). Ileen got the family vaccinated against Yellow Fever, Cholera and Tetanus. She packed a first aid kit containing bandages, drips, stitches, antibiotics and painkillers. She had her hair cut very short and shaved the boys' heads bare. Her skills were yet to include the digging of a long-drop toilet.

They set off, fully packed including Droes' 24 cases of beer. Departing from a cold wet Eshowe, they headed to Zimbabwe where they couldn't get enough of the beautiful open spaces and the friendliness of the people. Some tried to sell them gold at the petrol station.

There were, of course, the odd inconveniences along the way that included blown exhausts, slow punctures and some roads so bad that car batteries were almost lost. Plus, the spring packed up on the trailer. Then they peeled the plastic off their extension cord so they could use the wire to hold the exhaust together.

Due to poor signage, they had to stop regularly to ask directions to Cabora Bassa, the huge dam and hydro-electric facility on the Zambezi River in western Mozambique. There they suffered temperatures of 42 degrees while Droes speared tiger fish for their meals.

They left Mozambique for Malawi, absolutely loving the beautiful Samora Machel Bridge built across the Zambezi River. They set up camp at the Limbe Country Club in Limbe, Blantyre where, despite pestering baboons, they enjoyed the golden sands and the water that was so clean and so blue. The rocks and the water at Otto Pioing were the most beautiful on their entire trip.

Then they set off for Nampula in Mozambique, passing the rocky mountain range that Ileen thought too magnificent for words.

During the trip Ileen did not neglect her personal fitness routine. She practiced aerobics, did her weight-training and power-walked or ran on the open beaches. She remained positive through mishaps like the gas pipe exploding on her when she was cooking, and her Droes' beloved beers getting stolen off the back of their bakkie. She even kept her head when she returned to camp to find Ernest sitting on the roof of the bakkie, because a Boomslang was curled up on the earth underneath.

Then poor Ernest got malaria. Running a temperature, he felt miserable. He also got a runny tummy despite Ileen treating their water with Milton Steriliser. Stanley did what he could to cheer Ernest up.

Surrounded by coconut plantations, the group set up camp for three weeks at Pandane Beach. Localites there built their homes with plaited coconut leaves. Their homes and villages were spotless. While there, Droes too came down with malaria. Ileen remained strong, playing the guitar for everyone to sing 'Love is all Around'.

Droes was soon back to spearfishing in the clean blue water, smoking his catches for their supper. They drove home to Eshowe via Badplaas so Droes could do some flying there. He and the boys did some trout fishing too.

In the year 2000, Droes hired the large plot of municipal land that borders our respective properties in Eshowe. He covered the area with tunnels and, until 2008, supplied farmer Warren Hulett with the juiciest, tastiest tomatoes.

Sadly, in 2008 Dr Droes Andrews was shot dead during a burglary gone wrong in his home. Ileen Andrews continues to live in the house. She is the most accommodating next door neighbour ever. Her extensive garden includes a coconut tree brought back from Pandane Beach in 1996.

II

I have been asked to include a bit about my own history since I now qualify as a tried and tested Eshowe-ite – and proudly so. I have written my childhood memoirs in a book: 'Wars of the Weavers' that is based mostly in Bulawayo where I was born, and told against the backdrop of the Zimbabwe/Rhodesian bush war during the 1970s. But going back further to the 1800s, my father's grandfather, Robert William Hunt and his brother, as young teenagers, fled an abusive father in England. They stowed away on a ship to Australia, but weren't there long when they boarded a ship to Cape Town. My great-uncle remained in Cape Town where he became a successful businessman.

Robert William Hunt headed north and became a mounted captain on the mines. Correspondence ceased between the two brothers when my great uncle wrote

Robert William Hunt

from Cape Town, to Great-grandfather Robert Hunt, that he was appalled at the way black people were treated in this country.

Great-grandfather Robert married and produced sons: Robert Jnr and my grandfather, Lionel Joseph Hunt who met and married my Granny Constance. They relocated from the Union to what was then Southern Rhodesia where my father, Errol Clifford Hunt was one of five children born to them. After school my father served an apprenticeship, as a boiler-maker, with the Rhodesian Railways. He joined his brother, Lionel in welding together the joints of railway tracks from morning 'til night for months on end in the full blaring heat of the African sun.

It so happened that my father's family were firm friends with my mother's paternal aunt who suggested to my father that he meet her niece, Audrey Buckle who was in training as a preschool teacher. Although my parent's marriage ended in a bitter divorce, my father never forgot the vision of my mother sitting on the stoep in Bulawayo where he was yet to play the guitar and serenade her, until they married in 1964.

My mother was of Afrikaans descent. Her father's father, Petrus Johannes Buckle (1892 -1963) was a cattle and crop farmer married to Anna Margarita Buckle (née Erasmus). A deeply religious man, who said a prayer and sang a hymn every morning and night, Oupa Petrus Buckle was largely instrumental in establishing the Dutch Reformed Church in Bulawayo. My mother's mother was the last of nine children born to cattle and

crop farmer, Helgard Rademeyer (1880 - 1959) and Adriana Maria Rademeyer (née vanZyl). The Buckle and Rademeyer families were both pioneer families farming on the Khami Road outside of Bulawayo, which is how it came about that my mother's parents, Peter Buckle and Marie Rademeyer met.

In this photograph of the Rademeyer family, my much-loved oupa-grootjie Helgard is in the centre. When my mother showed me the carriage of the Zeederberg Coach Company on display in Bulawayo's Natural Museum, that brought her grandparents to Matabeleland, I took it to mean that my great-grandparents had personally sat on that very carriage. I ran my hand over the seat and felt adventure for the first time. As a seven-year-old, my love for history was thus begun. Growing up, I constantly listened to fond tales about my oupa-grootjie Rademeyer. My mother remembered how he would round up his grandchildren and hold them spellbound with stories like that of Die Hoene en die Jakkals (The Chicken and the Jackal). He had a bump on his forehead that the children were lead to believe were excess brains trying to escape. The Rademeyers were, in fact, said to be an 'educated family' which probably means they completed high school. When they were children in South Africa during the early 1900s, the high Dutch their parents had spoken was spiced with words from other languages such as German, and those of various slaves. This new tune was called 'Afrikaans'. After the defeat of the Boers by the British, in 1902, when the republics of the Transvaal and

Orange Free State were made part of the great British Empire, Milner made it law that all teaching in the country's government schools be in English, except for a few hours a week in Dutch for religious instruction. In fact, English had been the only language of the courts and schools in the 'Cape' since 1822, even though Dutch settlers outnumbered the British by eight to one. Many Dutch parents kept their children away from school because they could not understand the subjects taught to them in a strange language, and the history taught was of England (starting in 1066).

Then, in 1875 a group of young Capetonians founded what translated in English to the 'Society of True Afrikaners'. It was their intention to elevate their language into literary form. They composed an Afrikaans anthem and produced their very own newspaper. Actually, Afrikaans spellings only really steadied itself apart from Dutch in 1881.

In 1902 the Dutch Church organised their own private schools, and by 1906 there were at least two hundred of them taught by their own community.

III

Up until the mid-1990s, Eshowe High School allowed for Afrikaans-medium tuition. Then it became fashionable for parents to send their children to boarding school in Vryheid. Eshowe Junior School, for decades, accommodated Afrikaans learners. After living in Eshowe for so long, I'm still astounded at the closeness of our community – Black, white, mixed-race, Indian – isiZulu, English and Afrikaans. There are not enough pages in one book to cover our history. I look forward to compiling for you, my valued reader, a continuation in Volume 2 of this same title.

My girls: Lara, Keri and Jodie in 1997. While I only had three children I had the time to stitch up their matching outfits especially for this studio photograph

My brood: Colin, Jodie, Lara, Keri, Dale and little doggie, Flower in 2009

Bibliography and Recommended Reading

Bassas: A Spearfishing Adventure by Kobus de Kock
City Set on a Hill by Selwyn Moberly
Coley's Oddesey by AB Colenbrander
Diamond Bozas Life and Work
Discovering Southern Africa by TV Bulpin
Images From The Past by Sidney Mears Miller
John Dunn Cetywayo and the Three Generals by John Dunn
KwaBaka by Dr Jon Larsen
Once Dark Country by Albert Lee
River of Life by Hugh Lee
Roaming Zululand with a Native commissioner by HP Braatvedt
The Adams' Story by Margaret Mikula
The Eshowe Concentration and Surrendered Bhergers Camp during the Anglo-Boer War by Dr Johan Wassermann
The uBantu Girl by Sonja Kruse
This is my Story by Anthony Balmer
Three Years with Lobengula by J Cooper-Chadwick
Zululand True Stories 1780 to 1978 by JC van der Walt
Zulu Knight by Albert Lee

By the Same Author

One Green Bottle
Wars of the Weavers

www.ingramcontent.com/pod-product-compliance
Lightning Source LLC
Chambersburg PA
CBHW050851160426
43194CB00011B/2113